Dewey's New Logic

———————

DEWEY'S NEW LOGIC
A Reply to Russell

Tom Burke

THE UNIVERSITY OF

CHICAGO PRESS

CHICAGO AND LONDON

The University of Chicago Press, Chicago 60637
The University of Chicago Press, Ltd., London
© 1994 by The University of Chicago
All rights reserved. Published 1994
Paperback edition 1998
Printed in the United States of America

03 02 01 00 99 98   2 3 4 5

ISBN: 0-226-08069-2 (cloth)
ISBN: 0-226-08070-6 (paperback)

Library of Congress Cataloging-in-Publication Data

Burke, Tom (Thomas)
    Dewey's new logic: a reply to Russell / Tom Burke.
        p. cm.
    Includes bibliographical references and index.
    1. Dewey, John, 1859–1952—Contributions in logic. 2. Russell,
Bertrand, 1872–1970—Contributions in logic. 3. Logic, modern—20th
century. 4. Language and logic. I. Title.
    B945.D44B87 1994
    160'.92—dc20   94-1618
                                                            CIP

To my daughter Sera

Contents

Preface

This book addresses a number of issues which arose in the debate between John Dewey and Bertrand Russell following the appearance of Dewey's *Logic: The Theory of Inquiry* in 1938. Russell's part in this debate appeared in three works. He initiated the debate with his contribution (1939) to the *Library of Living Philosophers* volume devoted to Dewey. Later he included a chapter on warranted assertibility in his *An Inquiry into Meaning and Truth* (1940), and then his chapter on Dewey in *A History of Western Philosophy* (1945). Dewey's responses to Russell appeared in two works: as part of his general reply to the contributors to the *Library of Living Philosophers* volume (1939a), and later in a *Journal of Philosophy* article (1941) written in reply to Russell's *An Inquiry into Meaning and Truth*.

My analysis of this debate focuses on several issues which were misrepresented or ignored by Russell, and which need to be satisfactorily squared away before attempting to address many of the larger topics around which the debate was centered. It will be argued that from the outset Russell misunderstood several concepts and distinctions which are fundamental to Dewey's views, in which case it follows that he was not in a good position to appraise Dewey's logical theory.

A major target here will be to explain Dewey's distinction between propositions and judgments. One cannot understand his logical theory as a whole without understanding this distinction.

And one must understand his conceptions of inquiry, situations, and other basic notions in order to understand this distinction.

So, following an introductory chapter which includes some biographical and historical notes, Chapters 2–4 address some of these more basic issues, before we focus on propositions and judgments in Chapter 5. In each of these chapters, several of Russell's arguments are analyzed in detail, to show how his misconceptions of these notions skew his picture of Dewey's logical theory.

The final chapter addresses Dewey's conceptions of warranted assertibility and truth, his theory of knowledge, and the theory of intentionality and intelligence which these conceptions support. Contributions of Dewey's logical theory to current developments in formal semantics and the philosophy of language are discussed. As a result of unsympathetic reviews such as Russell's, and otherwise because of the untimely nature of Dewey's views in the 1930s and 1940s, Dewey's logical theory has been thought to be obscure, naive, and irrelevant, when in fact it is complex, subtle, and increasingly relevant to current investigations of language, information, and intelligence.

The title of this work warrants a brief explanation. The article by Russell which initiated the debate addressed in this book was entitled "Dewey's New *Logic.*" In 1939, when this article first appeared, Dewey's book *Logic: The Theory of Inquiry* was in fact new. And of course, it is no longer new. But many of the ideas that Dewey developed in this book are surprisingly relevant to current developments in logic and the cognitive sciences. Though published in the early part of the twentieth century, the ideas which Dewey explored are only now starting to be sufficiently appreciated. In that sense, his ideas are still new to most of us, even if that particular book has been around for over fifty years. In the title of the present work, the italics font in Russell's title has been dropped. The reference is not to the book but to the ideas themselves as still new.

It is not that Dewey presented an alternative view of logic so much as a broader and more complex view which the modern logical community is starting to discover for itself, though with mathematical tools which Dewey did not have at his disposal in the 1920s and 1930s. Frege was only just then doing his work around the turn of the century when Dewey was formulating most of his own ideas on the subject. As a rich source of intuitions independent of a Fregean ideology, Dewey's work has the potential to affect future developments in modern logic at a crucial point in its history. Dewey's work belongs at the cutting edge of current research. It is ripe for further development. It is not just a historical oddity. Logic is in fact progressing beyond the narrow limits which Russell was defending, becoming more and more Deweyan in character despite the pervasive ignorance of Dewey's work. In contrast, the view of logic which Russell helped develop and was defending in his debates with Dewey is now *old*. Dewey's views are very much more timely these days than ever before, whereas Russell's way of thinking about logic is now passé.

Acknowledgments

I would like to thank Denis Phillips, John Perry, John Etchemendy, and Jon Barwise for reading earlier versions of this material and for their comments and suggestions during the early stages of the writing. I would also like to acknowledge the support I received from the Department of Philosophy and the Center for the Study of Language and Information at Stanford University while completing this work. And I would like to express my gratitude to the anonymous reviewers for many good suggestions, most of which I have gladly heeded. Finally I would like to thank everyone at the University of Chicago Press who had anything to do with the publication of this book. Their editorial and production efforts have greatly improved it in ways I never would have expected. I have to confess, unfortunately, to a certain degree of mulish obstinacy about certain things, which makes me wholly responsible for any aspect of this writing that is misguided or of poor quality otherwise.

Parts of this book are revised versions of works that have appeared elsewhere and are reprinted here with permission of the publisher. Passages in Chapter 4 are taken from "Dewey on Defeasibility," in *Situation Theory and Its Applications*, ed. Robin Cooper, Kuniaki Mukai, and John Perry (Stanford: CSLI Publications, 1990, Vol. 1, 233–268). Much of Section 3.3 appeared in *Ecological Psychology and Dewey's Theory of Perception*, Report No. CSLI-91-151 (Stanford: CSLI Publications, 1991).

1

Introduction

John Dewey is remembered largely for his work in the philosophy of education and, more generally, for his role in the development of American pragmatism. He is not remembered specifically for his ideas about logic. Yet, beginning in the 1890s and continuing well into the 1940s, he wrote several books and articles on matters pertaining to logic and what would now be called the philosophy of language. His most fully developed book on the subject, *Logic: The Theory of Inquiry*, appeared in 1938.

At the time this book appeared, Dewey's views were already considered by many to be unorthodox if not rather obscure. By 1938, the new "formal logic" of Tarski, Gödel, Church, et al., was beginning to achieve a full head of steam as a research paradigm, and Dewey's logical theory surely seemed irrelevant to these developments. Some highly negative criticisms at the time, particularly those of Bertrand Russell, did not add to Dewey's credibility. The net result has been that logicians in the last half-century have completely ignored Dewey's logic—many logicians these days have probably not even heard of Dewey, let alone forgotten him.

But to explain why his philosophy of logic so thoroughly slipped into oblivion, one could just as well argue that Dewey was working several decades ahead of his time. He refused to ignore some rather difficult issues and problems which logicians today are taking quite seriously—indexicality and context-sensitivity in formal semantics, for instance; or defeasibility, nonmonotonicity, and other

1

matters now salient in computer science. With the (re-)emergence of interest in information in philosophy as a result of its importance in the cognitive sciences, we are finally beginning to develop concepts useful to understanding Dewey's position. Dewey's characterization of propositions as *means* to furthering and completing some given inquiry is essentially part of a general theory of how information accrues and is used in problem-solving contexts.

In defense of Dewey's philosophy of logic, I aim to do two things in this book. On one hand, I want to reply to portions of Russell's critical 1939 review of Dewey's *Logic*. But more generally, I want to explain and justify Dewey's naturalistic and ecological conception of logic in Dewey's own terms.

In the opening remarks of Chapter 2, "Logic and Information," in *The Situation in Logic* (1989), Jon Barwise writes:

> This chapter argues for a broader conception of what logic is all about than prevails among logicians. In particular, it claims that ordinary usage of the words *logic*, *inference*, *information*, and *meaning* defines a natural subject matter that is broader than logic as presently studied. More specifically, I argue that logic should seek to understand meaning and inference within a general theory of information, one that takes us outside the realm of sentences and relations between sentences of any language, natural or formal.

Similar remarks occur in a short article by Gian-Carlo Rota (1985) relating a brief conversation with Stanislaw Ulam about how we need to "enrich formal logic" if we are to make any headway in solving the problems of AI. I want to try in this book to give some idea of what Dewey's "broader conception" of logic was, and to show how, early in the twentieth century, he was already anticipating such remarks as these.

Dewey's earliest works on logic were published ten or so years after Frege's *Begriffsschrift* first appeared. Dewey and Frege were in fact contemporaries, Dewey being just eleven years younger than Frege. On the other hand, Dewey's last volume on logic appeared seven or eight years after Gödel's papers on completeness and consistency. The modern revolution in logic was very much something of Dewey's own time. And he seems to have been largely unswayed by it.

It is not surprising that Dewey seems to have been unfamiliar with what Frege was doing, given (1) the geographical, cultural, and professional distance between them; and (2) the fact that general appreciation of Frege's work was a bit slow to catch on anyway, even among those who would have found his work appealing but who had to wait until his writings became more widely available. Dewey was familiar with nineteenth-century German philosophy, but it is doubtful that he read Frege's work. It was not until the 1950s and 1960s—after Dewey's death—that English translations of Frege's work were becoming available to American philosophers. Meanwhile, there is evidence in Dewey's correspondence with Arthur Bentley (Ratner et al. 1964, pp. 251, 587–8) that, along with the American philosophical community at large, Dewey became aware of Tarski's work only relatively late in the 1940s. But Dewey was *not* unacquainted with Russell, given their ongoing confrontations over a period of several decades. So Dewey was not working in a vacuum so far as developments in early twentieth-century logic were concerned. He nevertheless gave no sign, even throughout the 1940s, of accepting the general tenets of what has come to be known as formal logic.

Dewey's logical theory will therefore appear to be relatively unusual by current standards. One might want to say that he was doing something else besides "logic," perhaps developing instead a generalized theory of scientific method. But fusing logic and problem-solving methodology is characteristic of American pragmatism, beginning with C. S. Peirce. Dewey's logical theory is quite in line with this general orientation, meaning that in his view we should think again about what we think logic is.

It is not insignificant that Frege, the founding father of twentieth-century logic, was a mathematician. His interest in logic was primarily motivated by an interest in analyzing fundamental mathematical concepts. In much the same way that Newton devised a formal calculus from scratch in order to be able to properly talk about certain aspects of the physical world, Frege designed his own "formula language" just to be able to properly talk about mathematical concepts (van Heijenoort 1967, pp. 1–3). Mathematics has subsequently done well by Frege. And his program has largely set the tone for the field of logic over the course of the twentieth century. But it is important to keep in mind Frege's original motivations as a mathematician when one reads his material bearing more directly on natural-language semantics, e.g., in "On Sense and Meaning" (1892) or later in "The Thought: A Logical Inquiry" (1918).

Dewey on the other hand was concerned (not as a mathematician but as a philosopher of logic nonetheless) with a wider range of concerns, including psychology, biology, social philosophy, education, ethics, and æsthetics. Psychology around the turn of the century was not yet an independent discipline separate from philosophy. And Dewey was interested in "pedagogy" insofar as the latter could supply an empirical framework in terms of which psychological theory could be applied and tested (Jane Dewey 1939, p. 27). One need not conclude from this that Dewey's logical theory was psychologistic or subjectivistic, a point discussed at length in Section 3.4 below. But he did develop his conception of logic in the context of trying to understand the reciprocal relationships between learning and experience, knowledge and action, and other disparate features of human nature which are ordinarily not considered to be part of the subject matter of logic.

Dewey's interest in logic was primed by his association with George S. Morris, a Hegelian scholar at Johns Hopkins University at the time Dewey was a graduate student there.

> The influence of Professor Morris was undoubtedly one source of Dewey's later interest in logical theory. Morris was given to contrasting what he called "real" logic, [which he] associated with Aristotle and Hegel, with formal logic of which he had a low opinion. Dewey ... developed the idea that there was an intermediate kind of logic that was neither merely formal nor a logic of inherent "truth" of the constitution of things; a logic of the processes by which knowledge is

reached. Mill's logic seemed to him an effort in this direction, but an effort that was disastrously blocked and deflected by Mill's uncritical acceptance of a sensationalistic and particularistic psychology. (Jane Dewey 1939, p. 18)

As late as the turn of the century and before he had quite worked out this "instrumentalist" conception of logic, Dewey was giving seminars at the University of Chicago focusing on the logical writings of Bradley, Bosanquet, and Lotze, as well as those of Mill, Venn, and Jevons. His analysis (1903b) of Lotze's idealistic logical theory during this period "marks a final and complete break with his early Hegelian idealism and launches his instrumental theory of reflective thought" (Jane Dewey 1939, pp. 32–3).

Over the next decade at Columbia University, Dewey was fully engaged with the realistic movement predominant at the time. His associations there, especially with F. J. E. Woodbridge, a proponent of Aristotelean naturalism, apparently had a strong impact on his thinking. These times constituted a period of transition in his thought which laid the foundation for his work in the 1920s and 1930s (Jane Dewey 1939, pp. 35–6). His logical theory began to take shape in *How We Think* (1911/1933) and in *Essays in Experimental Logic* (1916b), though these writings were as much a reflection of his time at Chicago. Many of the same topics and concerns were reworked and further developed in *Experience and Nature* (1926) and *The Quest for Certainty* (1929). And there were innumerable pieces submitted to periodicals, many of those collected in Morgenbesser 1977. His logical theory was later most fully developed in *Logic* (1938), a book which took Dewey at least thirteen years to write and which appeared nine years after his retirement.[1]

There is of course a great deal which remains intact over the course of these writings, the sequence being more one of progressive development than of revision. Some basic tenets of his later logical theory can be clearly traced even to early papers written in the 1890s, such as "Is Logic a Dualistic Science?" (1890), "The Present Po-

---

[1] See Poulus 1986 (pp. 533–49) for details concerning the production of *Logic*.

sition of Logical Theory" (1891), "The Superstition of Necessity" (1893), and "The Reflex Arc Concept in Psychology" (1896).

If the views developed in these books and articles are viable and appropriate to the subject matter of logic, then the question arises as to why these views have been ignored by the logic establishment in the many decades since *Logic* was published. Dewey's early *Studies in Logical Theory* (1903b) might hardly have been noticed if not for the laudatory review given it by James; and even then the recognition it got from the philosophical community was largely negative (Jane Dewey 1939, p. 33). His later writings on logic were not any more successful in this regard. The apparent incompatibility of Dewey's views with dominant developments in logical theory initiated by Frege and Russell appears to have been enough to substantially divert attention away from Dewey.

But Dewey took on a more ambitious project than Frege did. His theory is decidedly broader in scope than what Frege had initially set out to deal with. Frege was careful to exorcize anything (such as "ideas" or "experience" or "judgment"—see Frege 1892, 1918 particularly) which did not accommodate an analysis of mathematical concepts, whereas such things were a major focus of Dewey's logic. Measured against Frege's work, Dewey's logic seemed too broad in scope, if not hopelessly incoherent because of this.

One has to respect Frege's genius for knowing what to address and what to ignore in developing a formal language designed for clear and concise exposition of mathematical concepts. But we should also appreciate the different kind of genius exhibited by Dewey, who was insistent upon holding onto the larger view of things while pursuing more general goals bearing not only on mathematics but on our natural cognitive abilities at large. Because of this broad scope, Dewey's theory did not appear to lend itself to symbolic formulation along the lines of Frege's "formula language." In the absence of a principled justification for using it and in order not to bias the subject matter of logic toward purely syntactic aspects of language, Dewey consciously avoided any such symbolization (1938, pp. iv, 19–20, 192, 198; Ratner et al. 1964, pp. 562–4). This rationale seems to have only lessened regard for his project. Without this focus on syntax, his logical theory will easily have seemed naive and misguided if not confused and intractable.

If this was not enough, Dewey's debate with Russell shortly after the appearance of *Logic* was surely devastating to Dewey's chances for serious consideration by philosophers and logicians. This is not to say that Russell was right and Dewey was wrong. Russell's criticisms were forcefully presented with characteristic wit, but he simply failed to comprehend Dewey's views. Nevertheless, as a popular and formidable influence in analytical philosophy at the time, his opinions alone greatly undermined the chances of Dewey's views being taken seriously.

Dewey's replies to Russell apparently did not substantially help matters. To a reader untutored in Dewey's thought and perhaps unfamiliar with Russell's reputed propensity rather to "make a wisecrack than a correct observation" (Lamont 1959, p. 35), it will seem that Dewey was able to pinpoint instances where Russell had misread him or where their opinions differed, but not to convincingly explain, outside of what took several hundred pages in *Logic* itself, why his opinions in these instances were what they were and why they were superior to Russell's. To someone familiar with Dewey's work, his replies carry more force. The basic design of the present work is to explain some key ideas in Dewey's conception of logic in the context of addressing Russell's criticisms and thereby to show that, if Dewey's replies to Russell seem to lack force, it is because Russell's criticisms lack significant bearing on Dewey's actual views.

The debate between Dewey and Russell on matters of logic and epistemology actually stretched over several decades. In particular, Russell in 1909 reviewed Dewey's *Studies in Logical Theory* (1903b), and in 1919, Dewey's *Essays in Experimental Logic* (1916b). The latter of Dewey's books contained a chapter critical of Russell's *Our Knowledge of the External World* (1914). Otherwise, remarks on various aspects of Russell's work were sprinkled throughout Dewey's writings in the 1920s and 1930s.

An account of early exchanges between Dewey and Russell in the first couple of decades of this century can be found in Hook 1979, Chapter 4 of Sleeper 1986, and Chapter 1 of Tiles 1988. I am focusing here on the later debate, between 1938 and 1945, centered on Dewey's *Logic*.

Several articles dealing with Dewey's logical theory appeared soon after the publication of *Logic*; for instance, Cohen 1940, Cunningham 1939, Hocking 1940, Kaufmann 1940, Lewis 1939, Mackay 1942, McGilvary 1939, Murphy 1939, Nagel 1939, 1940, and Piatt 1939.[2] Russell wrote two such pieces. The first, "Dewey's New *Logic*," appeared in 1939 in the *Library of Living Philosophers* volume devoted to Dewey (the first in the well-known series edited by P. A. Schilpp). Dewey's response (1939a) is also included in that volume (particularly pages 520–9, 544–9, 568–74). Russell's second piece, a reply to Dewey's rejoinder in the Schilpp volume, appeared as a chapter, "Warranted Assertibility," in his book *An Inquiry into Meaning and Truth* (1940). Dewey replied to the latter in a *Journal of Philosophy* article, "Propositions, Warranted Assertibility, and Truth" (1941); and Russell continued the discussion in a chapter on Dewey in *A History of Western Philosophy* (1945), to which Dewey gave no reply.

One might bear in mind that, as is customary in the volumes in the Schilpp series, Dewey's initial reply to Russell was in response to just one of a crowd of commentators on his philosophy at large. Dewey was apparently hampered by time constraints, and his reply to Russell is merely part of a larger defense on several fronts. It may be expected to "show little of the freshness of thought and acuteness of perception" which would otherwise have been the case (Sleeper 1988, p. xi). His response to Russell's chapter on warranted assertibility, on the other hand, was addressed not only to a single critic but with regard to a more limited range of issues particularly relevant to his notion of warranted assertibility.

---

[2]Dewey's responses to these articles can be found in Morgenbesser 1977 and in Dewey 1946. Some of these articles are discussed in Sleeper 1986, pp. 162ff.

It is not inappropriate to view this exchange as an example-in-miniature of a collision between two "world views" or "paradigms," where one expects a good deal of miscommunication due to the incommensurability of two unreconcilable ways of viewing the world. Though this debate was indeed hampered by a significant amount of miscommunication, I intend to show, at least with respect to the issues I discuss here, that Dewey's replies to Russell were technically (if not rhetorically) sufficient to parry Russell's various criticisms, to whatever extent these had any bearing on Dewey's actual views.[3] Still, even with regard to the limited number of issues touched on here, Russell raised several questions which Dewey may seem to have left unanswered. I will show that Dewey's discussion of more general matters raised by Russell often handles these points in a wholesale if indirect way—though it will be more convincing, in defense of Dewey, to actually draw out his replies and show how they handle the specific questions Russell raised.

There are in fact several more or less traditional attitudes about American pragmatism that we will want to dispose of in the course of discussing this exchange between Dewey and Russell. For one, Dewey was writing about the "instrumental" character of scientific theories as early as the first decade of the century, and he continued to do so for the next forty years. So is he a *mere instrumentalist*, in the pejorative sense that he is alleged to hold that theories say, and are expected to say, little or nothing about *the truth* or the way things really are, but are evaluated only in terms of their effectiveness and usefulness in predicting experimental results? Certainly, empirical adequacy is an important part of evaluating scientific theories, but that hardly does justice to Dewey's view of the instrumental role of theorizing in scientific inquiry. In particular, we will claim that Dewey's original brand of instrumentalism, as a view concerning

---

[3] A more ambitious defense of Dewey would proceed to show that Dewey actually understood Russell's position quite well whereas the miscommunication was entirely Russell's problem. This is not the line pursued here, though I am mainly concerned with countering Russell's misreadings of Dewey, since it is Dewey's philosophy of logic, not Russell's, which is of interest here.

Peirce as precursor of Information theory

the role of propositions (and hence theories) in inquiry, was a precursor of the broader view of logic as, or as part of, a general theory of information—that propositions are best viewed as pieces of information used in specific ways to further some inquiry. Today, if we must, we might call this view informationism, or informationalism. It should be clear that this has little or nothing to do with the simplistic, watered-down view we have subsequently come to associate with the term 'instrumentalism'.

Likewise, pragmatism is sometimes seen as a peculiar brand of empiricism, but only half-baked and ultimately rather insipid without the logical expertise exhibited by hard-nosed empiricists like Carnap (1954) or Hempel (1952). Is Peirce's pragmatic maxim nothing more than a sketch of an empiricist theory of meaning? Well, it is in part a sketch of an empiricist theory of meaning; but there are at least two reasons why we have to think of it as more than *merely* that. The maxim itself was formulated by Peirce in various ways, but here is the earliest and as good a statement of it as any:

> I only desire to point out how impossible it is that we should have an idea in our minds which relates to anything but conceived sensible effects of things. Our idea of anything *is* our idea of its sensible effects; and if we fancy that we have any other we deceive ourselves, and mistake a mere sensation accompanying the thought for a part of the thought itself. It is absurd to say that thought has any meaning unrelated to its only function.... It appears, then, that the rule for attaining the third grade of clearness of apprehension is as follows: Consider what effects, that might conceivably have practical bearings, we conceive the object of our conception to have. Then, our conception of these effects is the whole of our conception of the object. (1878, *CP* 5.401–2)[4]

---

[4]This citation refers to volume 5, paragraphs 401–2, in the *Collected Papers of Charles Sanders Peirce* (1931–1958). Some other statements of the same principle go as follows:

> If you look into a textbook of chemistry for a definition of *lithium*, you may be told it is that element whose atomic weight is 7 very nearly. But if the author has a more logical mind he will tell you that if you search among

First, the view expressed by Peirce does not entail the passive sort of empiricism one finds in Mill or Locke, but rather it is an active, operation-based experimentalism. Data are gotten as results of actions, not passively registered through merely receptive sensory channels. A Peircean theory of meaning paints a picture of perception and knowledge as dynamic, active, progressive, experimental—which puts a different twist on how we think about human mentality, in contrast to a standard representationalist view. (These points are

---

minerals that are vitreous, translucent, grey or white, very hard, brittle, and unsoluble, [and then Peirce describes some expected results of half a dozen experimental procedures] . . . *that* is a specimen of lithium. The peculiarity of this definition—or rather this precept that is more serviceable than a definition—is that it tells you what the word lithium denotes by prescribing what you are to *do* in order to gain a perceptual acquaintance with the object of the word. (c. 1902, *CP* 2.330)

[A]ll reasonings turn upon the idea that if one exerts certain kinds of volition, one will undergo in return certain compulsory perceptions. Now this sort of consideration, namely, that certain lines of conduct will entail certain kinds of inevitable experiences is what is called a "practical consideration." Hence is justified the maxim, belief in which constitutes pragmatism; namely, *In order to ascertain the meaning of an intellectual conception one should consider what practical consequences might conceivably result by necessity from the truth of that conception; and the sum of these consequences will constitute the entire meaning of the conception.* (c. 1905, *CP* 5.9)

Endeavoring, as a [laboratory man] naturally would, to formulate what he so approved [concerning methods of thinking, I] framed the theory that a *conception*, that is, the rational purport of a word or other expression, lies exclusively in its conceivable bearing upon the conduct of life; so that, since obviously nothing that might not result from experiment can have any direct bearing upon conduct, if one can define accurately all the conceivable experimental phenomena which the affirmation or denial of a concept could imply, one will have therein a complete definition of the concept, and *there is absolutely nothing more in it.* For this doctrine [I] invented the name *pragmatism.* (1905, *CP* 5.412)

Suffice it to say once more that pragmatism is, in itself, no doctrine of metaphysics, no attempt to determine any truth of things. It is merely a method of ascertaining the meanings of hard words and of abstract concepts. All pragmatists of whatever stripe will cordially assent to that statement. . . . All pragmatists will further agree that their method of ascertaining the meanings of words and concepts is no other than that experimental method by which all

examined in Chapters 2–4.) Second, if we really take this operation-based theory of meaning seriously, we will have to rethink the very nature of semantics and hence the nature of the logic taken for granted by "hard-nosed" empiricists like Carnap, Hempel, or Quine (1951) for that matter. Whatever kind of technical expertise they were exhibiting in their exposition of empiricism, it is not characteristic of a pragmatist theory of logic.

These last remarks apply as well to the claim that pragmatism is just a peculiar brand of operationalism. Dewey (1929, pp. 110–12) does not exactly endorse the views of Bridgman (1927) and Eddington (1928), but with a certain amount of goodwill he compares their views with Peirce's, and notes similarities with James's views as well as his own instrumentalism. Back in 1929, one could be so hopeful. Since then, operationalism, like most isms, has not enjoyed a great deal of popularity, though this is largely because of the way Bridgman and others presented it. Operationalism as it is now understood is basically an oversimplification and misuse of otherwise valid intuitions expressed in the pragmatic maxim. Dewey would not want to wield the pragmatic maxim like an axe, hacking away at anything conceptual that could not be given an "operational definition." As we have already said, he wished to espouse rather an *experimental* empiricism (those are his very words), in contrast to the passive empiricism of Mill; and he found support for this in the then current views of Bridgman and Eddington. He also wished to generalize this insight to concepts in general and to a general study of logic and epistemology, rather than address only scientific concepts and scientific methodology.

> From the standpoint of the operational definition and tests of ideas, ideas have an empirical origin and status. But it is that of *acts* performed, acts in the literal and existential sense of the word, deeds

---

the successful sciences (in which number nobody in his senses would include metaphysics) have reached the degrees of certainty that are severally proper to them today; this experimental method being itself nothing but a particular application of an older logical rule, "By their fruits ye shall know them." (c. 1906, *CP* 5.464–5)

done, not reception of sensations forced on us from without. Sensory qualities are important. But they are intellectually significant only as consequences of acts intentionally performed. (Dewey 1929, p. 112)

This is not an admonition to scientists or would-be scientists to operationalize everything they were thinking and doing, but rather Dewey's point was only to identify "action" as a foundational notion in logic and epistemology. This is a strong claim with important theoretical consequences, but it is not what Bridgman was saying. One could be an empiricist and/or operationalist in Bridgman's sense, and still adhere to the view of logic employed by Carnap, Hempel, and even Popper. For this reason I prefer to label Dewey's view of concepts and meaning(fulness) as operation-based, rather than operationalistic. We will explore this view further throughout the rest of the book.

Then there is the matter of a pragmatist theory of truth. This whole matter is tangled up with the idea that instrumentalism entails the view that truth is measured by verification or mere usefulness, rather than by correspondence with reality. In 1907, G. E. Moore expressed many of the same criticisms of William James's "pragmatist conception of truth" (James 1907) which Russell (1909, 1919) leveled against James and Dewey. Though Moore's and Russell's criticisms of James have been generally regarded to be a serious indictment of some basic principles of American pragmatism, one could argue along with Hertz 1971 and Phillips 1984 that Moore shot holes not in James's pragmatist conception of truth but rather in an unsympathetic and fabricated misrepresentation of James's actual views. James (1909) pressed this point in his own defense against Russell, though Moore and Russell seem to have subsequently won the day.

Russell wrote later (1959, p. 181) that his criticisms of Dewey's *Logic* were not basically different from his earlier criticisms of James, meaning to say most likely that Dewey's views had not progressed beyond James's. Russell perhaps did not see the progress, and in 1939 he was essentially re-issuing criticisms he made of

James in 1910. If this is so, then it helps to explain why much of what he had to say about Dewey's *Logic* missed the mark. Building on the works of both Peirce and James, Dewey was able to develop similar ideas with greater care and with a bit of hindsight that these earlier pioneers of pragmatist thought did not have. Dewey's writings were on the whole more organized, if not more systematic, than Peirce's, though the emphasis on inquiry and the adoption of an operation-based theory of meaning is traceable to Peirce, perhaps via James. Although he was strongly influenced by James, particularly *The Principles of Psychology* (1890), Dewey was able to avoid some of the terminological pitfalls which left James vulnerable in a changing philosophical climate which favored the techniques of stricter linguistic analysis. For instance, where James spoke only of "truth," Dewey spoke of several things: warranted assertibility, verifiability, truth, etc. Russell missed this point, but this finer kind of analysis in fact served to salvage the epistemological intuitions underlying James's theory of "truth."

I will not be concerned here with Russell's and Moore's arguments against James. Many of the replies to Moore made by Hertz and Phillips in defense of James, and by James in his own defense against Russell, nevertheless carry over to a defense of Dewey. That is, time and again the crux of the reply to this or that criticism is simply that Russell misread Dewey in a way which made Dewey's views *seem* absurd. The main task in each of these instances is to explain what Dewey *did* and *did not* actually say, not what Russell apparently thought he did or did not say.

But there is more involved here than rectifying a misreading of Dewey. Russell, whether or not he was reading him correctly, had good reason to attack Dewey's logical theory, for Dewey was proposing a conception of logic which does undermine much which is central to logic as Russell conceived of it. What is at issue here is not just how to think about some key notions of interest to logicians but more generally how to conceive of the very subject matter of logic. Russell's and Dewey's debate over the proper conception of particular logical concepts is ultimately a debate about what logic is.

In the first of three pieces dealing with Dewey's *Logic*, Russell presented an array of criticisms under two broad headings. The first set of criticisms deal with Dewey's supposed holism (Russell 1939, pp. 138–42), and the second, with Dewey's instrumentalism (pp. 143–56). In the first case, Russell took issue with Dewey's concept of situations, arguing that Dewey's definition and use of this concept entail holistic consequences which Dewey would not want to endorse. In the second case, the central issue was Dewey's notion of warranted assertibility, which Russell found unacceptable as a theory of truth.

Both Russell's and Dewey's views remained virtually unchanged over the course of their debate in the early 1940s, though Russell focused almost entirely on Dewey's notion of warranted assertibility in his later two articles, essentially dropping the discussion of Dewey's concept of situations. Russell's misunderstanding of this latter concept nevertheless bears directly on his unwillingness to accept what he thinks is Dewey's notion of warranted assertibility. Without a proper understanding of the role of situations in Dewey's logical theory, one cannot hope to understand his concepts of inquiry, propositions, judgment, existence, reality, truth, warranted assertibility, or any other notion which has a distinctive part to play in a Deweyan view of logic.

As already indicated, I will not systematically discuss the entire Dewey/Russell debate here. I will focus instead on several preliminary matters which have to be squared away before one can adequately assess Dewey's notion of warranted assertibility, specifically, and his theory of knowledge more generally. My general aim will be to clarify some ideas which are often only hastily treated or ignored but which are fundamental to a discussion of Dewey's views.

In particular, Russell gave no evidence of understanding Dewey's distinction between propositions and judgments, hence his criticisms aimed at the notion of warranted assertibility show every sign of falling wide of their mark. These latter criticisms are of course worth looking into in some depth, as a foil for discussing Dewey's notion of warranted assertibility. But there is no point in attempting that project without first laying the appropriate groundwork.

My main target then will be to explain Dewey's distinction between propositions and judgments, which requires that one first understand his conceptions of inquiry, situations, and other notions peculiar to his approach to logic. The next three chapters deal with some of these preliminary issues, before we focus on propositions and judgments in Chapter 5. Chapters 2 and 3 address what Dewey means by a *situation* and, in particular, the bearing this has on his distinction between *existence* relative to a situation and *reality* in a nonrelative sense. Failure to comprehend this distinction alone is enough to make much of what Dewey wrote seem absurd. This distinction is particularly important to explaining how Dewey uses the term 'fact' and, for instance, why he questions Russell's commitment to "atomic propositions." These chapters also include a discussion of the charge that Dewey's logic is subjectivistic.

Chapter 4 addresses Dewey's notion of *inquiry*. A number of Russell's remarks which bear directly or indirectly on this notion are examined, with the aim of dispelling various claims and charges which misrepresent Dewey's views. The concept of inquiry is obviously a key notion in Deweyan logic, as the title of his book indicates, and Russell persistently failed to render it properly in his reviews and critiques before addressing alleged shortcomings in the view of logic as the theory of inquiry. The notion of inquiry is especially important to understanding what Dewey means by *judgment*.

Chapter 5, then, addresses Dewey's conception of *propositions* as distinguished from judgments. Dewey's treatment of propositions, particularly as summarized in Part 3 of *Logic*, is one of the more important and yet one of the more enigmatic aspects of his logical theory. Chapter 5 attempts to shed some light on this topic, though many questions as to the details of Dewey's thinking along these lines will remain unaddressed. A major goal here is to show that Russell was far from appreciating the subtlety and depth of Dewey's views as to the nature of propositions. Rather than the timeless entities we find in Fregean logic, propositions in Deweyan logic are treated as formulations of *information* relative to concrete situations in particular inquiries. I want to suggest that Dewey's "instrumentalist" conception of propositions, when translated into more current jargon, serves as the basis for an information-theoretic view of logic.

So far as this book goes, the discussion of propositions and judgments in Chapter 5 will be the final part of any systematic treatment of the Dewey/Russell debate. As an outline of points to be addressed if this exchange were to be investigated further, Chapter 6 summarizes some key topics discussed at length in the debate but not treated in sufficient detail here. These include the finer details of Dewey's conceptions of warranted assertibility and truth, his theory of knowledge, and the theory of intelligence and intentionality which these conceptions support. I will also briefly discuss prospects for bridging Dewey's approach to logic with more recent developments in formal semantics and the philosophy of language. Besides deflecting Russell's criticisms, a convincing defense of Dewey's logical theory will eventually have to include some kind of formal development and application of the theoretical perspective he was recommending. In the long run, a solid vindication of Dewey's conception of logic will require that it assimilate what has been accomplished in mathematical logic over the last several decades.

2

Dewey's Alleged Holism

Following a brief discussion of Hegel's influence on Dewey's thinking, two related issues are discussed in the next two chapters. First, it is important that we clarify Dewey's notion of *situations*, a concept which is central to Dewey's entire logical theory and which Russell seriously questioned. Secondly, it is important to understand Dewey's distinction between the *existential* and the *real*—a distinction which is based on Dewey's theory of situations and which bears directly on answering Russell's criticisms of Dewey's "instrumentalist" characterization of propositions.

2.1 Dewey's Hegelian Roots

Russell begins his analysis of Dewey's notion of situations by noting that Dewey was strongly influenced early in his career by Hegel (Russell 1939, pp. 138, 143, 154). We should address these opening remarks by Russell concerning Dewey's alleged Hegelianism, since they set the tone for the rest of Russell's review. Russell wants to associate Dewey with Continental "synthetic" philosophy, in contrast with his own British "analytic" bias, which he then cites repeatedly as a major source of their differences.

Dewey was hardly hesitant to acknowledge Hegel's influence on his early thinking, though he had fully rejected Hegelian idealism by the end of the 1890s. Russell quotes part of a paragraph in which Dewey admits "that acquaintance with Hegel has left a permanent deposit in my thinking." Russell's remarks about this influence are such as to insinuate that Dewey's views could still be uncritically Hegelian as late as the 1930s—which does not correctly reflect the nature of Hegel's influence on Dewey. Dewey also remarks, in the same paragraph from which this quote was taken, about his drifting away from idealism in the 1890s and that "the form, the schematism, of [Hegel's] system now [in 1930] seems to me artificial to the last degree" (Dewey 1930, p. 12). Taken as a whole, this paragraph simply expresses a certain degree of respect for, but otherwise rejects, Hegel's views. Russell's remarks obscure the point that Dewey could abandon such a view and yet admire its subtlety or scope or elegance or forcefulness and openly acknowledge whatever positive influence it might have had on his subsequent thinking.

Russell later appears to temper his claim about Dewey's supposed Hegelianism (Russell 1945, pp. 820–1), agreeing that Dewey's naturalism does not fit well with Hegel's idealism. "Although the Hegelian philosophy influenced Dewey in his youth, it still has . . . its eternal world which is more real than the temporal process. [This has] no place in Dewey's thought, for which all reality [is not] the unfolding of an eternal Idea." Unfortunately Russell persisted in suggesting that Dewey retained some "unconscious Hegelian metaphysic" (Russell 1945, pp. 823–4).

It is the case that Dewey's theory of situations in particular, and his philosophical views in general, were a product of his early acquaintance with Hegel. But Dewey's later views were the result of a fundamental and pervasive shift of perspective, emerging in such a way as to render Hegel's views unworkable. Phillips (1971, 1976) and others have argued that Dewey's later thought (from the 1890s onward) was the result of not a point-blank rejection but rather a substantial transformation of Hegelian views. Influenced by Darwin, James, and a growing appreciation of the prospects for a scientific investigation of human nature, "Dewey was able to 'naturalize' all that he regarded as worthwhile in Hegel." But it is somewhat misleading to assert, then, that Dewey was constrained by some "unconscious Hegelian metaphysic," as Russell persistently claimed. Dewey openly acknowledged the influence and was quite aware of which of those aspects of his later thought were most directly derived from Hegelian themes:

> There were, however, also "subjective" reasons for the appeal that Hegel's thought made to me; it supplied a demand for unification that was doubtless an intense emotional craving, and yet was a hunger that only an intellectualized subject matter could satisfy.... [T]he sense of divisions and separations that were, I suppose, borne in upon me as a consequence of a heritage of New England culture, divisions by way of isolation of self from the world, of soul from body, of nature from God, brought a painful oppression—or, rather, they were an inward laceration.... Hegel's synthesis of subject and object, matter and spirit, the divine and the human ... operated as an immense release, a liberation. Hegel's treatment of human culture, of institutions and the arts, involved the same dissolution of hard-and-fast dividing walls, and had a special attraction to me.
>
> ... [T]he Hegelian emphasis upon continuity and the function of conflict persisted on empirical grounds [as an influence on my thinking] after my earlier confidence in dialectic had given way to skepticism. There was a period extending into my earlier years at Chicago when, in connection with a seminar in Hegel's Logic I tried reinterpreting his categories in terms of 'readjustment' and 'reconstruction'. Gradually I came to realize that what the principles actually stood for could be better understood and stated when completely emancipated from Hegelian garb. (Jane Dewey 1939, pp. 10–11, 17)

This acknowledgment of Hegel's influence only serves to highlight Dewey's divergence from an Hegelian view of things. By way of an analogy, it is one thing to say that Ptolemaic and Copernican astronomies share a common set of questions and problems or that the latter is an outright transformation of the former, and quite another to say that a Copernican is unconsciously Ptolemaic. No one would defend this second claim except in a qualified sense. But Russell essentially makes the same sort of claim regarding Dewey and Hegel— calling for substantial qualifications which Russell did not supply.

Russell's attempt to contrast his own British analytical bias with Dewey's supposed Continental leanings is therefore hardly appropriate. Dewey was not at all constrained by "Continental synthetic philosophy," though he aimed to develop a view of things which essentially *synthesized* what was right in these (and other) apparently divergent philosophical perspectives. This was a guiding principle for Dewey throughout his career—the principle, namely, that equally viable but mutually incompatible views (including, for instance, "Continental synthetic philosophy" versus "British analytic philosophy," or "holism" versus "atomism," or "existentialism" versus "essentialism") call for finding a perspective from which the given dichotomy is only apparent or is otherwise resolvable (see Dewey's *Experience and Nature* (1926), for instance, pp. 40–48, for one of many discussions of this antidualist stance). Dewey's antidualism (in whatever guise the dualism might appear) was no doubt influenced by his early study of Hegel, but without need for maintaining a "Hegelian metaphysic." This distaste for unresolvable conceptual dualisms is just as intuitively and independently well-founded as is the intuition which compels us to reject formal contradictions. One need not embrace Hegel's way of thinking in order to reject dualistic conceptual schemes, just as one can understand the nature of tautology and contradiction without embracing Aristotle's or Frege's philosophy of logic.

This charge of maintaining an Hegelian viewpoint would by itself be largely irrelevant if it were not for the fact that Russell repeatedly employs it as if it were a definitive and wholesale criticism of Dewey's views. Russell (1945, pp. 827–8) ultimately associates Dewey's instrumentalism with Marxian dialectical materialism (Russell 1939, p. 143), characterizing it also as a Fichtean "power philosophy" (whatever that is supposed to mean)—on the basis of this initial, purportedly innocuous claim about an implicit Hegelianism in Dewey's logical theory. But these associations pigeonhole Dewey unfairly and in a misleading way.

When we actually look at which of Dewey's statements in *Logic* are supposed to reveal this Hegelian influence, we find Russell citing Dewey's descriptions of a *situation* as a "qualified existential whole which is unique, . . . extensive, containing within itself diverse distinctions and relations which in spite of their diversity, form a unified qualitative whole" (Russell 1939, p. 139). Before examining Russell's discussion of such remarks, we should be clear about what Dewey meant by a *situation*.

2.2 Situations

As Russell is quick to point out, Dewey followed Peirce in focusing his logical theory around the epistemological notion of *inquiry*, rather than on a study of syntax and formal proof procedures. Dewey defines inquiry as follows:

> Inquiry is the controlled or directed transformation of an indeterminate situation into one that is so determinate in its constituent distinctions and relations as to convert the elements of the original situation into a unified whole. (Dewey 1938, pp. 104–5)

In particular, the notion of a *situation* occurring in this definition is a full-fledged technical notion in Deweyan logic. Dewey was able to employ this notion as a device for introducing factors of *context* as well as *direct reference* into logic and into his philosophical views at large. In later chapters I will address Dewey's views on more familiar logical matters; but it is important first to understand the naturalistic, ecological foundations of those views, encapsulated largely in his notion of a *situation*.

Situations, occurring in the ongoing activities of some given organism/environment system, are instances or episodes (or "fields") of disequilibrium, instability, imbalance, disintegration, disturbance, dysfunction, breakdown, etc. Dewey uses a number of such terms in various contexts. No single term covers everything we would want to mention here, due to the generality of the terms 'situation' and 'inquiry'. These terms should apply to a wide range of organism/environment systems at virtually any level of evolutionary complexity. Inquiry, in a common mentalistic sense of the term, should be viewed as an evolutionary variation on what originally appears as an innate impulse of organism/environment systems to transform situations so as to counteract such instabilities. This view of inquiry is supposed to be general enough to explain not only the behaviors of simple biological systems but also those of, say, a human scientific research community. The term 'inquiry' commonly carries various cognitive connotations, and ultimately we should be able to give an account of inquiry as a special sort of cognitive problem solving. But it is a naturalistic, noncognitive, conative characterization of problem solving which grounds Dewey's logical theory.

The basic picture, generally speaking, is that of a given organism/environment system performing a wide range of operations as a normal matter of course—scanning, probing, ingesting, discharging, adapting to, approaching, avoiding, or otherwise moving about and altering things in routine ways, in order to maintain itself. This applies not just to simple biological systems but also characterizes an individual human being's normal activities—from simple things like moving a cup to one's lips to drink from it without dribbling liquid all over the place, or walking down a hallway without careening into the walls, to long-range activities like being in love, pursuing a career, owning a home, managing a budget. Each of these things is at bottom a balancing act. Such ongoing activities just *are* interactions which constitute some manner of organism/environment integration. *Situations*, then, occur as instances or episodes of breakdown or imbalance in this dynamic integration.[1]

---

[1] It should be acknowledged that the term 'situation' is ambiguous. To begin with, its ordinary bundle of meanings as an English noun by itself renders the term ambiguous. Secondly, it is used as a technical term in situation theory and situation semantics (see, in particular, Barwise and Perry 1981, 1983; Barwise 1989; Perry 1986). Third, it is used as a technical term in Dewey's theory of inquiry.

Dewey's use of the term is somewhat more specific than what is found either in common usage or in situation theory and situation semantics. When using the term 'situation' without a qualifier, I will be using it in this third sense.

This is not the appropriate place to try to relate Dewey's conception of situations to the theory of situations offered by Barwise and Perry. Any similarities are neither apparent nor easy to explain, once you get past the relatively trivial characterization of a situation as a "context" of some sort. It is noteworthy though that Dewey conceives of situations primarily in organic terms, in contrast to Barwise and Perry, whose treatment of situations as "parts of the world" is motivated largely as a reaction against various formal and metaphysical features of possible-worlds semantics. On the other hand, a central theme of situation theory and situation se-

As a simple illustration, before looking in more detail at Dewey's ecological characterization of situations, consider a case where you leave your office and get into your car just in time to go pick up your friend at the airport, only to discover that the car will not start. This simple event becomes the focal point of an increasingly complicated situation.

That is, following out your normal routine would otherwise consist in successfully carrying out or undergoing or being subject to a number of interdependent, properly related activities incorporating both organismic and environmental features of your overall "constitution." All goes well on any given day as long as your basic daily schedule is met and as long as each of the activities in this schedule is carried off successfully. Dewey's relatively loose use of the term 'equilibrium' is applicable in this case where all of these activities are compatible and proceed unproblematically.

The system of activities and events which make up your day is of course a highly nested system. One can take a rather large cut and describe the whole day in a relatively short list of things to do. Taking finer and finer cuts, any single item in any such list can itself be resolved into an array of things to be done, virtually ad infinitum.

For example, at one point you will get into your car, pump the gas pedal, turn the ignition key, and the engine will hopefully turn over and fire into action. Seat belts and other such things aside, just this one action is a very complex phenomenon when you stop to think about it, requiring highly tuned bodily movements on your part and depending on quite complex regularities in your environment. Yet all of this is a mere detail in the larger schedule of routines you normally consciously orchestrate in making your way through the day.

---

mantics which is in line with Dewey's views is the idea of focusing semantic theory on the notion of *information*. See Section 5.1 below for a discussion of propositions and information in a Deweyan framework. Also, an attempt is made in Burke 1991b to read situation-theoretic ideas of partiality and perspectivity into Peirce's definitions of truth, and as well, to adapt situation-theoretic ideas to a pragmatist theory of meaning (as formulated by the so-called pragmatic maxim). Much of the discussion there is directly applicable to Dewey's views on logic and semantics.

Given the depth and complexity of this hierarchy of routine activities, breakdowns are sure to occur. You might have to pause to tie your shoe at some point; you may need to clean up a drop of coffee on your desk to make way for some papers; you might have to stop to regain your composure after knocking your knee on the corner of the filing cabinet; and so forth.

Taking a finer cut on things, many of the problems which occur on any given day are actually *constitutive* of the normal routines you expect to perform as a matter of course. Each time you stand up from your chair, that introduces a kind of kinematic disturbance which requires some sort of compensation. You have to make various bodily adjustments and otherwise utilize features of your immediate terrain in order to maintain your balance, in order not to simply fall to the floor under the impetus of the original standing-up motion. Or reading a newspaper consists in performing a wide variety of interdependent tasks, including simple little automatic "inquiries" such as identifying each of the letters and words on the current line of text you are now visually scanning.

Such examples indicate that situations can be quite tiny or mundane. But then they can also be large and urgently important—wars and armed conflicts, a worsening national debt, unchecked population growth, a deteriorating ozone layer, and otherwise all manners of flood, famine, and pestilence. For the sake of discussion, let us return to the middle-sized situation where you get into your car and it will not start. It is not unreasonable to think of this as an instance of "disequilibrium" insofar as the routine activities which would normally transpire at this juncture are thrown out of kilter. The complexity or "size" of the ensuing situation depends on subsequent events—on things like your mechanical abilities and on the nature of the car's breakdown. You might immediately grab your tool box, quickly fix a loose battery cable, and off you go, having essentially salvaged your overall schedule (regained your "equilibrium") with only a small delay. If the problem goes beyond your mechanical skills or if it is not possible in that instance to exercise those skills properly (e.g., a bad alternator needs replacing and you have neither tools nor auto-parts store at hand), then the situation can become increasingly complex. Problems can start to pile up, and disturbances can affect increasingly extended portions of your overall system of routines. You have to make various decisions dealing sooner or later with getting the car running again; and then there is your friend waiting at the airport, wondering where you are. Anything else you planned for the afternoon is probably seriously jeopardized. And so on and so forth.

Notice, though, that in spite of the incredibly deep and wide (and potentially deepening and expanding) nature of this particular situation, there are any number of things, near and far, which remain irrelevant to what is going on and so do not enter into the situation. What about that small meteor which just hit the backside of the moon? Or what about the ant you just crushed under your foot when you stepped out of the car? Who will be the 199th president of the United States? What is the cube root of thirty-seven, to forty-six significant digits?

Dewey's discussion of situations usually remained on a relatively abstract level, though focusing initially on biological and ecological considerations. He was aiming to get at what is common to all such examples. The basic picture of situations as fields of organism/environment disequilibrium is elaborated in Chapters 2, 3, and 6 of *Logic*. For instance, the following paragraphs occur early in the book:

> An organism does not live *in* an environment; it lives by means of an environment.... The processes of living are enacted by the environment as truly as by the organism; for they *are* an integration.
>
> It follows that with every differentiation of structure the environment expands.... [T]he difference is not just that a fish lives *in* the water and a bird *in* the air, but that the characteristic functions of these animals are what they are because of the special way in which water and air enter into their respective activities. (Dewey 1938, pp. 25–6)

This points to the fact that living agents are not just bundles of biological mushware encased in some kind of skin or shell, but rather are integrated systems encompassing both organismic and environmental processes. It is not quite correct even to talk in terms of a "tight coupling" between an organism and its environment, as this undermines the fact that such a system is a single integrated whole. Such unity is tighter than a tight coupling.

> With differentiation of interactions comes the need of maintaining a balance among them; or, in objective terms, a unified environment. The balance has to be maintained by a mechanism that responds both to variations that occur within the organism and in surroundings. For example, such an apparently self-contained function as that of respiration is kept constant by means of active exchanges between the alkaline and carbon dioxide contents of changing pressures exerted by the blood and the carbon dioxide in the lungs. The lungs in turn are dependent upon interactions effected by kidneys and liver, which effect the interactions of the circulating blood with materials of the digestive tract. This whole system of accurately timed interchanges is regulated by changes in the nervous system. (Dewey 1938, p. 26)

Such mechanisms for maintaining balance in a precarious world are fundamentally characteristic of living systems.

> The effect of this delicate and complex system of internal changes is the maintenance of a fairly uniform integration with the environment, or—what amounts to the same thing—a fairly unified environment. The interactions of inanimate things with their surroundings are not such as to maintain a stable relation between the things involved. The blow of a hammer, for example, breaks a stone into bits. But as long as life normally continues, the interactions to which organic and environmental energies enter are such as to maintain the conditions in both of them needed for later interactions. The processes, in other words, are self-maintaining, in a sense in which they are not in the case of interactions of non-living things. (Dewey 1938, p. 26)

Taken together, these remarks describe Dewey's conception of living systems as dynamic systems incorporating both organismic and environmental elements, with some sort of built-in impetus toward self-maintenance. Dewey's notion of equilibrium is of course not the classical thermodynamic notion. It is a notion rather of *dynamic* ecological equilibrium—not so much a state of balanced physical forces but rather a *phase* or *period* of compatible life processes and activities.

For an example of a simple biological system where the border between "organism" and "environment" is not so clear-cut, consider something like a sea anemone at the bottom of the ocean. We think of these creatures as having relatively complex internal workings, and also as subsisting within and as a part of some characteristic setting on the ocean floor. Whereas we humans have circulatory systems encased inside our skins, a sea anemone's circulatory system, or what amounts to the same thing, essentially includes the ocean water surrounding it. The ebbing and flowing of the seawater in which the anemone lives is as much a part of that system's constitution as are the workings inside its body. And, for instance, those currents are not always quite right (they are too fast or too slow, too hot or too cold, nutritionally deficient, etc.), in which case the sea anemone will move about in an effort to maintain a setting more appropriate to its needs. Dewey's theory of inquiry is able to explain this as a simple case of ongoing "proto-inquiry" on the sea anemone's part. In Dewey's words:

> When the balance within a given activity is disturbed—when there is a proportionate excess or deficit in some factor—then there is exhibited need, search, and fulfillment (or satisfaction) in the objective meaning of those terms. The greater the differentiation of structures and their corresponding activities becomes, the more difficult it is to keep the balance. Indeed, living may be regarded as a continual rhythm of disequilibrations and recoveries of equilibrium. The "higher" the organism, the more serious become the disturbances and the more energetic (and often more prolonged) are the efforts necessary for its reestablishment.
>
> Hunger, for example, is a manifestation of a state of imbalance between organic and environmental factors in that integration which is life.... A state of tension is set up which is an actual state (not mere feeling) of organic uneasiness and restlessness. This state of tension (which defines need) passes into search for material that will restore the condition of balance. (Dewey 1938, p. 27)

It is not necessary to restore the *same state* of dynamic equilibrium so long as *some* sort of dynamic equilibrium is maintained (p. 28). These disturbances and readjustments may occur virtually anywhere up and down and throughout a complex hierarchy of interactivities which constitute the organism/environment system as a whole—being centered in the organism perhaps, or in the environment, but in any case involving some localized part of the system as a whole. Such a localized instance of disequilibrium is what Dewey means by a situation.

For another example of a case where the line between organismic and environmental dynamics is hard to draw, consider the role of gravitation in affecting ordinary human physiology. This is a fairly straightforward and old observation going back at least to Galileo. Namely, much of the basic structure of the human body and many of its physical capacities are significantly affected by the fact that we live always subject to the Earth's gravitational pull. Our muscle structure, for instance, is designed to exploit the fact that we will often need to muster forces to lift loads but hardly ever need to exert effort to lower things. As you lift the coffee cup to your mouth, you are using gravity as much as you are using muscular forces to accomplish that feat. What this amounts to is that the field of gravity at the Earth's surface is as much a part of who you are as are the muscle sinews in your arms. One could do more easily without one's appendix and some other features of the human anatomy than one could do without the constant presence of this gravitational field.

Recent studies of bone development (Wong and Carter 1990, Carter et al. 1991) have shown that this dependency on environmental factors operates in the long term at the level of genetic design, not just at the level of learning how to lift coffee cups or move furniture. Consider a group of people who elect to try to live out otherwise normal lives on a space station orbiting the planet. It is understood that they will have to come to terms with living and working for an extended period of time in an environment where there is virtually no gravity. After a decade or two, as they do much of the hands-on work to build bigger and better space stations, they will hopefully be able to build an artificial environment which simulates, among other things, a constant unidirectional, terrestrial-type gravitational field. (Maybe this would actually be easy to do, but let's suppose it would be a major engineering feat which would take years to accomplish.) This is desirable since it is fairly obvious that after too many generations of raising children in zero gravity, the younger generation is going to start looking quite strange, and not just because of their coiffures. The surprising thing here is that the very first generation of zero-gravity children would have significantly altered anatomies, to the point of being entirely dysfunctional if shipped back to the planet's surface. Human evolution has known only the unrelenting constancy of terrestrial gravity, to the point of taking for granted that it will be a factor and may be exploited as such in musculoskeletal development. Taking away this gravitational pull would have effects as immediately drastic as would subtly altering a chromosome or two in one or the other gamete that contributes to the birth and growth of an individual person.

> The construction rules of developmental mechanics have evolved over hundreds of millions of years to produce organisms which are designed for this specific planet.... Studies of astronauts and cosmonauts have revealed an immediate atrophic response of the musculoskeletal system to space travel. Due to the elimination of Earth's gravitational field, all of the tissues experience a diminished stress history and the tissues [immediately] respond according to their mechanical construction rules.... If human space travelers or transported animals conceive offspring while in a weightless environment ..., their children would develop very different musculoskeletal characteristics than they would on Earth.... Since [mechanical] stimuli guide the architectural construction of most of the skeleton, important changes in the developed skeleton could be expected even though no genetic variations have occurred.... In addition to possible changes in other organ systems, there would be important changes in the skeletal system of the children in the immediate next generation.... In general, if the gravitational field were greater than Earth's the children would develop bones that were thicker and more dense than their Earthbound peers. In a lower gravitational field, the bones would be thinner and less dense. (Carter et al. 1991, p. 13)

Such studies evidence a tight functional dependency between anatomical and environmental factors which makes it just as odd to think of the human biological system without the usual environmental factors at work as it is to imagine a human biological system without a liver, for instance. Where folk genetics asserts that "gene x governs the development of physiological feature y, perhaps in the context and under the influence of genes x', x'', . . .," these results would have us assert rather that "gene x *operating in environment z* governs the development of physiological feature y, perhaps in the context and under the influence of genes x', x'', ..." Though you may not feel nervous pressures or twitches or pains when something breezes through your gravitational field the way you do when something brushes against your arm, nevertheless gravity is as much a part of you as your arm is. Of course, the Earth's gravitational pull is just one of any number of examples we could use to make this point. We might just as well be talking about ozone layers, air, water, earth, light, and many other aspects of our terrestrial "circulatory system."

Having discussed the naturalistic foundations of his conception of inquiry in Chapters 2 and 3 of *Logic*, Dewey tended to focus throughout the rest of the book on agents with relatively advanced "cognitive" capabilities. But we should not lose sight of the fact that he was trying to describe a theme or pattern in his theory of inquiry which is already laid down in the simplest living systems and which is nevertheless characteristic of the full range of human activities. When some sort of imbalance occurs in the ongoing inter-activities of a given organism/environment system, that system will have to adjust its current actions in some way in order to correct the problem. This restabilization might occur virtually instantaneously or it may be a long and drawn out affair, depending on the nature of the imbalance. This conception of situations applies to sea anemones avoiding nutritionally impoverished ocean currents as much as to office workers confronted suddenly with cars which will not start. Abstracting away from such specifics, Dewey's theory of inquiry was an attempt to describe and discuss the various stages and phases of the resolution of problematic situations in the most general sense.

It still remains to be explained what any of this has to do with *logic*. Before we go on to that, what is it about the notion of *situations* by itself which Russell found troublesome? Russell's actual argument that it commits Dewey to a some sort of holism is both sketchy and brief. Namely, Dewey's characterization of situations as qualitative wholes plus his "insistence upon continuity" are claimed to commit Dewey to the admission that "a situation can embrace no less than the whole universe":

> Data, in the sense in which many empiricists believe in them, are rejected by Dr. Dewey as the starting point of knowledge. There is a process of "inquiry" ... [which] is, in some degree, continuous throughout life, and even throughout the history of a cultural community. Nevertheless, in regard to any one problem, there is a beginning, and this beginning is called a "situation." A situation, we are told, is a "qualified existential whole which is unique."...
>
> The question arises: How large is a "situation"? In connection with historical knowledge, Dr. Dewey speaks of the "temporal continuity of past-present-future." It is obvious that, in an inquiry into the tides, the sun and moon must be included in the "situation." Although this question is nowhere explicitly discussed, I do not see how, on Dr. Dewey's principles, a "situation" can embrace less than the whole universe; this is an inevitable consequence of the insistence upon continuity. It would seem to follow that all inquiry, strictly interpreted, is an attempt to analyze the universe. We shall be led to Bradley's view that every judgment qualifies Reality as a whole. Dr. Dewey eschews these speculations because his purpose is practical. But if they are to be invalid, it will be necessary (so at least it seems to me) to give more place to logically separable particulars than he seems willing to concede. (Russell 1939, pp. 139–40)

This rendition of Dewey's view of situations immediately follows Russell's discussion of Dewey's purported "Hegelian metaphysic." Russell's argument rests moreover on the unexplained reference to Dewey's talk about the "continuity" of inquiry. Much of Russell's subsequent discussion (pp. 141–2) consists in arguing not against what Dewey actually says but against the *consequences* of the argument given above, as if to press home the absurdity and pointlessness of a view to which Dewey is supposed to be unwittingly committed (such as that inquiry must be "an attempt to analyze the universe").

In a somewhat biting reply to Russell's claim that his views are tacitly Hegelian, Dewey summarizes Russell's argument as follows:

> Mr. Dewey admits not only that he was once an Hegelian but that Hegel left a permanent deposit in his thought; Hegel was a thoroughgoing holist; therefore, Dewey uses "situation" in a holistic sense. I leave it to Mr. Russell as a formal logician to decide what he would say to anyone who presented this argument in any other context. The following argument answers perhaps more to Mr. Russell's idea of inductive reasoning. British philosophy is analytic; Dewey not only leans to the Continental synthetic tendency but has vigorously criticized British analytic thought; therefore, his identification of an experience with a situation commits him to "holism." (Dewey 1939a, pp. 544–5)

But to be more specific, to say that the moon and stars are part of *a* situation involved in an inquiry into the tides does not on the surface make them part of *all* situations. Even if we *were* to accept the claim that some situations encompass the whole universe (might we call such an inquiry "cosmology"?), we cannot validly conclude on that basis alone that all situations do. If we adopt a system of inference which allows us to universally generalize cases obtained by existential instantiation, then, yes, we can generate absurdities. But that is the logic of Russell's argument, not of Dewey's actual views.

But whether or not Russell's brief discussion of Dewey's Hegelian roots carries any weight in appraising Dewey's conception of situations, one must admit that there is a point to Russell's argument regarding the "size" of situations. Consider the following cleaned-up version of this argument:

(1) A situation is an instance of disequilibrium in the interactions between an organism and its environment.

(2) A situation instigates a process of inquiry, given the organism/environment system's impetus to maintain itself.

(3) Any action, fact, entity, or event which is relevant as such to the course of this inquiry is part of the situation.

(4) Any action, fact, entity, event, or process exists or occurs in a single continuum with, and hence is relevant as such to the causal history of, any other action, fact, entity, event, or process.

But then it follows that

(5) Any action, fact, entity, event, or process in the universe is part of the situation.

Premise (1) is Dewey's definition of a situation. Premise (2) reflects his definition of inquiry as the resolution of indeterminate situations. Premise (3) is clearly plausible, though "nowhere explicitly discussed" by Dewey. And Dewey's frequent mention of continuity (of inquiry, of judgment, etc.) presumably commits him to premise (4). These four premises together lead straight away to (5). This argument would make an unconstrained holist out of Dewey in that every inquiry yields a so-called judgment which is about (concerns, qualifies) the situation inquired into, which in every case will have to be reality as a whole.

For example, consider the problem of your having to go to the grocery store, because you are hungry or because you anticipate being hungry later. Insofar as you use your car to get to the store, the car and your action of using it are part of the resolution of this problem and hence are part of the given situation. Similarly, the fact that Neptune continues in its usual manner around the Sun is crucial to your getting to the store—as opposed to its careening off and disrupting the gravitational equilibrium of the solar system. This would clearly get in the way of your resolving the given problem. So Neptune, and the process of its maintaining a normal orbit, is causally crucial to your resolving the given problem and hence is part of the situation. Neptune's behaving itself, of course, is just an arbitrary example of virtually any natural process in the universe. It would seem that your grocery-shopping situation has no boundaries and must include everything.

Some of the examples considered earlier show that a situation can *potentially* be very large. Is there anything in principle to limit the bounds of the situation beyond an ad hoc stipulation that inquiries eventually come to an end? What is it in Dewey's theory which *explains* how it is that some aspects of the world remain irrelevant to a given inquiry while others count as parts of the given situation? Dewey says that situations are wholes which are transformed through inquiry until they are fully determinate; and he might agree (at least in a general sense, if not with respect to specific inquiries) that inquiry is "continuous" throughout the life of an individual and throughout the history of a cultural community, as Russell says. But then it seems to be the case that any given situation should ultimately encompass everything, insofar as anything would bear on anything else (and therefore enter into the given situation) in an ongoing, nonstop inquiry carried out to the fullest possible extent.

Note that in his reference to inquiry continuing throughout an individual's life or throughout the history of a cultural community, Russell appears to be conflating (*a*) the claim that an individual or community will continually be engaged in one inquiry or another, with (*b*) the claim that any single inquiry will be continually engaged in. The first statement is acceptable, whereas the second is not. Russell is not being careful about the order of the quantifiers employed in these two statements. Statement (*a*) says that for all times in the life of an individual or community, there is an inquiry being engaged in. This is oddly stated but otherwise acceptable, on the condition that we conceive of inquiry more broadly and as more of a foundational matter than Russell did (see Chapter 4 below). Statement (*b*) says that there is an inquiry such that for all times (after it begins?), the individual or community will be engaged in it. This is rather questionable. Even if it might be the case for specific communities or individuals, or unless we want to define life itself as an all-embracing inquiry, it seems in general to be contrary to fact. The two statements are in any case distinct. Nevertheless, the point now is to acknowledge that there is a plausible argument against Dewey here, whether or not Russell formulated it in the best possible way.

This same issue (discussed at length in Phillips 1976) arose in the 1960s and 1970s with regard to "general systems theory." The running dispute between holistic (vitalistic, synthetic) versus atomistic (mechanistic, analytical) views of things in fact has a rather extensive history. Russell apparently sees his bout with Dewey as part of this larger dispute, with Dewey supposedly wearing the holist trunks. If we accept the general-systems account of an organism/environment system as "a complex of elements in mutual interaction," and if we include in this conception anything to which such a system is causally linked, then it is hard to see how one can stop short of "contemplating the whole of reality" when it comes to characterizing such a system.

There are then several points to be made by way of mustering a defense against Russell's argument. Putting aside any misconstrual of Dewey's views by Russell, the long-standing arguments against an unconstrained holism cannot be ignored—though the issue here is not one of how to defend holism but rather to show that these arguments are arguments against something other than Dewey's views. It is not as if Dewey was a holist because he was not an atomist. These are not the only positions one can take. Rather, totally in character with his antidualist convictions, Dewey aimed to undermine the holism/atomism dichotomy (hence advocating the more moderate position recommended in the closing remarks of Phillips 1976). If we can show that he was successful in this regard, then we will have shown that arguments against holism do not constitute arguments against Dewey's views.

Note that one approach to a solution might be to appeal to certain cognitive notions, such as arguing that we can think of a situation "under a description" and thereby put boundaries of a sort on it. But this is contrary to what Dewey was trying to do with the notion of a situation. Dewey would relativize situations to organisms and environments, to particular dispositional perspectives, even concretely to particular instances of breakdown in organism/environment affairs. But it would beg the question to appeal to a cognitive notion of objects or situations "under this or that description" in the present context. The aim is to be able to make sense of cognitive intentionality, once we have recourse to the notion of situations, not the other way around. There is indeed a kind of behaviorist agenda at work in Dewey's views, which I would want to refer to as a behavior-based or operation-based view of things. George Herbert Mead was more explicit about the behavior-based character of a pragmatist philosophy of mind, although we can hardly equate it with the behaviorism of Watson, Skinner, or Ryle (see Section 6.3 below). What follows may seem like an odd path out of the problem of finding bounds for situations because it is a "pre-cognitive" one—i.e., one which by design does not initially have cognitive notions to appeal to. The argument here will be that situations are bounded by the reach, scope, or content of a living creature's experience, where the problem in the end is to explain "experience as situated," not "situations as experienced."

We have to show then that Russell's argument outlined in (1)–(5) does not hold up. There are two points to make in reply to this argument. First, it is necessary to examine Dewey's conception of the "principle of continuity" (which premise (4) does *not* express) in order to undermine an unacceptable reading of premise (3). Second, a more careful look at his characterization of situations as instances of disequilibrium yields an explanation of his "partialism" and otherwise shows how he is able to *avoid* rather than have to take sides in the atomism/holism stalemate.

As for premise (4), Russell's argument appeals to Dewey's notion of "continuity of inquiry," though Russell says little or nothing about what he thinks Dewey meant by that phrase. Premise (4), as stated, is an attempt to make explicit what Russell only hints at, and it does not adequately express Dewey's notion of continuity.

There are in fact two terms in the statements of (3) and (4), 'continuity' and 'inquiry', which warrant more accurate and more extensive discussion. Russell assumes a view of inquiry that is reminiscent of the view envisaged in Peirce's depiction of truth as the ideal limit of endless (continuous?) scientific investigation. But a reference on Russell's part to Dewey's "insistence upon continuity" is surely not enough to commit Dewey to a naive reading of Peirce's view of inquiry, particularly since Peirce lacked a clear conception of situations characteristic of Dewey's theory of inquiry.

So what *did* Dewey mean by "continuity of inquiry"? Does it commit him, as Russell claimed, to conceding that a situation necessarily encompasses the whole universe?[2] Dewey did in fact say a great deal about continuity (for starters, in *Logic* alone, one could work through the thirty or so references listed in the Index under the headings 'continuity, nature of' and 'continuum of inquiry'). His use of the term 'continuity' is uncommonly broad and perhaps so multifaceted as to be confusing. But we might be too hasty if we concluded that there is not a single idea at the core of his different uses of the term.

It is important to Dewey's view that any given inquiry will typically not just "go on and on," but to the contrary, will have a

---

[2]Though Russell accounts for Dewey's supposed holism in terms of an unconscious Hegelian-idealist influence, notice that identifying a situation (what it is that an inquiry is *about*) with the whole world just as readily brings to mind Frege's concept of "the True," which underlies the idea, now familiar yet enigmatic, that the references of declarative sentences are essentially truth-values. True sentences with otherwise completely different propositional contents nevertheless have the same *reference*, namely, "the True." In his criticism of Dewey's conception of situations, Russell was arguing that all inquiries (and the "judgments" which result from them) are ultimately about the same thing, namely, the whole world. If this were the case, it seems to be the case that Dewey would just as well be committed to something like a Fregean theory of reference so far as judgments are concerned (though, if we continue this line of argument, his theory of judgments is, on the other hand, verificationist, in which case his view of logic would fail miserably, etc., etc.).

This raises a number of issues which will not be discussed in detail here. Dewey's views are substantially verificationist, but he is not committed to a Fregean theory of reference, so this way of stating Russell's case has no force against Dewey. For the time being, I simply want to establish the point that Dewey's notion of "continuity of inquiry" does not commit him to a picture of situations as encompassing the whole universe.

beginning and an end. It will be necessary to look again at Dewey's conception of situations to establish this point. But we have to assume this momentarily just to clarify what Dewey *meant* by continuity of inquiry.

Phillips (1971, 1976) identifies two different senses of the term 'continuity' to be found in Dewey's writings:

> The principle of genetic continuity can be pictured as a theory of *vertical continuity*: a particular form in nature is continuous with preceding simpler forms, and is also continuous with succeeding and more complex forms. The organicism in Dewey's position becomes apparent when it is realized that he also held—from the 1880s on—a theory of *horizontal continuity*: a form is continuous with other forms existing at the same time. In this second version of the principle the term 'continuous' means 'interrelated' or perhaps even 'inseparable'. (Phillips 1971, p. 252)

It is perhaps the "horizontal" sense of continuity which is most pertinent to a discussion of Russell's argument. It incorporates and fuses both static and dynamic elements. On one hand, there is Dewey's notion of a situation as a "field" of experience—as opposed to a discrete set of objects and events. Continuity in this sense means something like "nondiscrete." On the other hand, continuity in a temporal sense means something like "ongoing" or "persistent." This temporal sense of continuity is an important part of what Dewey meant by the "continuum of judgment" (cf. Dewey 1938, Chapter 13). One might also consider a distinction, orthogonal to the two just considered, between *internal* and *external* continuity. A situation may be internally continuous, in terms of being both nondiscrete and internally stable. And a situation may be externally continuous in the sense that its relations with the rest of the world are stable and it is not carved off discretely from the rest of the world, any more than a knot is discretely separated from the rest of a rope.[3]

---

[3] The "vertical" sense of continuity is historical and hence temporal; but though the "horizontal" sense of continuity is an "orthogonal" notion of continuity (whatever that might entail), it does not follow that horizontal continuity is not also temporal

It is not clear if or how any of these distinctions is useful without knowing more about how situations fit into Dewey's overall logical theory. But perhaps it is no accident that Dewey often runs these various senses of continuity together as essentially one concept. Though we might find fault with Dewey's apparent failure to clearly distinguish the different senses of continuity which occur in his writings, it is just as likely that he was able to appreciate what was common to them all and often wrote from that perspective (in the same way that we often talk about "causality" despite its many different senses).

It would in fact be worthwhile to formulate a concept of continuity which is not limited to any one of the special cases so far mentioned but rather is general enough to cover all of them. A candidate for what Dewey meant by continuity of inquiry would be something like the following principle:

(4′)   The results of successful inquiries (to the extent that they are stable) tend to persist and carry over to other inquiries (in which they happen to be relevant).

The simplicity of this formulation of course hinges on the generality and perhaps obscurity of the phrase 'persist and carry over'. This will mean different things depending on what sense of continuity one considers. But a little thought indicates that it is compatible with both the spatiotemporal sense of horizontal continuity and the historical-evolutionary-genetic sense of vertical continuity.

> "[S]uccessful means operative in a manner that tends in the long run, or in continuity of inquiry, to yield results that are either confirmed in further inquiry or that are corrected by use of the same procedures. (Dewey 1938, p. 13)

---

in character, despite Phillips's particular choice of terms which seems to imply that. For an example, consider the standard fox-rabbit model of a dynamic ecological system. In any given stable phase, the cyclical covarying of populations is a temporal process, where we could say that all the different population states in any such stable cycle constitute a "horizontally" continuous system. The "vertical" dimension enters the picture when we consider the evolving character of the limit cycle in its own right.

For a mundane example, tying one's shoes is not something which has to be learned from scratch again and again—shoes and shoestrings and one's fingers and hands have a natural tendency to *continue* being in the present what they have been in the past, so one is able to interact with and use them in the same ways repeatedly and to master those particular sorts of interactions and uses to the point of virtual effortlessness. This principle of continuity is implemented innately as one visually scans a room or reads a line of text on a page. One could hardly locomote without trusting that visual inquiries yield temporally stable results. Reading would hardly be possible if one could not trust that the letters do not change before one gets to the end of the current line. One could hardly set a "trajectory" or formulate a plan except by taking such continuity of things for granted. Learning, habit formation, individual development, and even the evolution of species would not be possible without this natural tendency of things to persist in some regular and cumulative manner.

In fact, the principle of continuity supports, among other things, Dewey's way of handling the problem of induction, that is, of disposing of it as a pseudo-problem. More than just an ad hoc denial of the problem, this principle is rather a positive and independently motivated proposal which turns the problem of induction into a merely formal or technical riddle (see Dewey 1938, for instance, pp. 465–6; also Sleeper 1986, pp. 144–5). For instance, Goodman's 'grue' predicate, though a reasonable construction in some abstract sense and therefore presenting a formal problem of sorts, only serves to indicate that there is something missing in current formal conceptions of induction and inference. For Dewey, what is missing is not just a notion of "projective properties" but rather the more far-reaching principle of continuity—not in holistic terms but in a naturalistic, organic, ecological sense of continuity couched in "inquiry-theoretic" terms. It is not something to be proven or otherwise justified from first principles, but rather it is itself a first principle suggested (1) by its apparent independence from other first principles and (2) by its apparent correctness and usefulness in explaining our actual ongoing experience. One cannot even explain what experience is except by appealing to the principle of continuity and other basic features of a theory of inquiry.

The argument here is not unlike Kant's response to Hume. The theory of experience that Dewey was proposing presupposes certain principles—such as a principle of continuity—that undercut the grounds (e.g., Hume's overly simplistic epistemology) for the formulation of the problem of induction in the first place. Rather than a fact to be derived from experience, Kant spoke particularly in terms of a temporal continuity of perceived objects—their permanence or endurance—as a *condition* of possible experience.

> Permanence is thus a necessary condition under which alone objects are determinable as things or objects in a possible experience. (Kant 1781, A189/B23)

> The idea of a subjective experiential route through an objective world depends on the idea of the identity of the world through and in spite of the changes in our experience; and this idea in turn depends on our perceiving objects as having a permanence independent of our perceptions of them, and hence being able to identify objects as numerically the same in different perceptual situations. . . . Awareness of permanent things distinct from myself is therefore indispensable to my assigning experiences to myself, to my being conscious of myself as having, at different times, different experiences. (Strawson 1966, pp. 125–7)

When we look into the details of Dewey's account of experience, we find that the more or less technical answer to the riddle of induction, stated in terms of scientific inquiry, is that hypotheses guide data gathering, and that one continually selects and reformulates hypotheses in the context of testing prior hypotheses, not just from data analysis outside of some such context. This presupposes an enduring situation with some more or less secure features that one can come back to over and over again (if necessary) in an investigation guided by the formation and testing of hypotheses or expectations otherwise. The abstract problem of inductive inference (qua curve fitting) is otherwise rather special. It is not a prominent or typical problem in most practical problem solving. It is not characteristic of experience in general. Its "solution" is a necessary condition of the possibility of experience in the first place. Hypothesis construction and related data gathering is a dynamic, interactive, embedded affair in which the problem is not how to formulate hypotheses solely on the basis of given data (where we get the underdetermination problem) but how to *re*formulate hypotheses, based on given data *and* on prior hypotheses that suggested how and why to gather those particular data in the first place. Curve fitting is not so intractable when one already has a certain agenda to work with, which is how everyday experience usually works. (This dynamic interdependence of hypotheses and data in a given inquiry are discussed further in Chapter 5 below.)

In any case, to specifically address the point at hand, notice that there is no obvious way to couple Dewey's sense of continuity with the claim that situations are qualitative wholes, to come up with the conclusion that situations must be unbounded. Indeed this notion of continuity presumes in the first place that situations are bounded and that inquiries (as transformations of situations) have definite ends which can *then* persist and "carry over" as such to other inquiries. In this case, not only does premise (4) not express Dewey's notion of continuity but, by appealing to Dewey's notion of continuity, one actually *denies* the reading of premise (3) which makes the argument go through. We can now turn to that point.

Putting the concept of continuity to one side, we have to address the question of what it is in Dewey's theory which can independently account for the boundedness of situations in the first place. It is in fact Dewey's definition of a situation as an instance of disequilibrium which guarantees this boundedness. And this constrains how we interpret the phrase 'relevant as such' in premise (3).

Previous discussion has indicated how incredibly complex situations can be, but also how incredibly simple they can be. That is to say, Dewey's theory of inquiry has to be able to guarantee that inquiring into the tides, for instance, may directly involve the moon and stars, but dealing with a car which will not start or finding one's way to a grocery store probably will not. Simply put, such boundedness is entailed by Dewey's characterization of situations as concrete fields of organism/environment "life functions" subject to, and directed away from, breakdowns.

Dewey introduced the notion of a situation in order to be able to walk the line between atomistic and holistic conceptions of things. Confronted with this unreconcilable dichotomy between two equally extreme and unacceptable views, common reason says that there should be an intermediate conception of things. Viewing the unresolvable debate between atomism and holism as a virtual reductio against either position, one is lead to consider nonatomic things which are in any case less than the whole universe. Dewey happens to call these things "situations," which can be called anything you like so long as one is clear about what is being named. Besides offering this indirect argument in favor of them, he was able moreover to supply a positive characterization in terms of organism/environment life functions. The boundedness of situations when understood in such terms becomes not just an abstract rationalization but a concrete bit of common sense.

To support these claims, consider the following passages, which are essentially the bulk of Dewey's reply to Russell on this question of the size of situations:

> [Some] criticisms of my theory of experience are connected with the fact that I have called experiences *situations*, my use of the word antedating, I suppose, the introduction of the *field* idea in physical theory, but nevertheless employed, as far as I can see, to meet pretty much the same need—a need imposed by subject-matter, not by theory. The need in both cases—though with different subject-matters—is to find a viable alternative to an atomism which logically involves a denial of connections and to an absolutistic block monism which, in behalf of the logic of relations, leaves no place for the discrete, for plurality, and for individuals. In philosophy there is also the need to find an alternative for that combination of atomistic particularism with respect to empirical material ["data"] and Platonic *a priori* realism with respect to universals which is professed, for example, in the philosophy of Mr. Russell. According to the naturalistic view,

every experience in its direct occurrence is an interaction of environing conditions and an organism. As such it contains in a fused union some*what* experienc*ed* and some processes of experienc*ing*. In its identity with a life-function, it is temporally and spatially more extensive and more internally complex than is a single thing like a stone, or a single quality like red. For no living creature could live, save by sheer accident, if its experiences had no more reach, scope or content, than traditional particularistic empiricism provides for. On the other hand, it is impossible to imagine a living creature coping with the entire universe all at once. In other words, the theory of experiential situations which follows directly from the biological-anthropological approach is by its very nature a *via media* between extreme atomistic pluralism and block universe monisms. Which is but to say that [such a theory] is genuinely empirical in a naturalistic sense. (Dewey 1939a, p. 544)

And contrary to Russell's claim that this question is nowhere explicitly discussed in *Logic*, Dewey points out that

the pluralistic and individualized character of situations is stated over and over again [in the book], and is stated moreover in direct connection with the principle of the experiential continuum.... I lay no claim to inventing an environment that is marked by both discreteness and continuity. Nor can I make the more modest claim that I discovered it. What I have done is to interpret this duality of traits in terms of the identity of experience with life functions. For in the process of living both absorption in a present situation and a response that takes account of its effect upon the conditions of later experiences are equally necessary for maintenance of life. From one angle, almost everything I have written is a commentary on the fact that situations are *immediate* in their direct occurrence, [yet] mediating and mediated in the temporal continuum constituting life-experience. (Dewey 1939a, pp. 545–6)

These remarks are self-explanatory. Claiming boundedness but not atomic discreteness of situations, these statements require that inquiry be the sort of process which comes to a conclusion without having to address literally everything in the universe. Dewey's explanation of this is that situations are bounded because they are fields of so-called *experience*—domains within which the processes of experience are played out. That is, they are localized regions of imbalance or breakdown within a complex manifold of "life functions" constituting an organism/environment system. If there were any point in it, Dewey might have agreed that all things, including such life functions, are *connected* or otherwise *related* to everything else, but still not have to assert that such connectedness is fathomable, nor that it is worth trying to fathom, nor that inquiry is an attempt to fathom it. Experience is not typically unlimited in scope. Omniscience, omnipresence, etc., are not normal features of experience, suggesting that the grounds for such unbounded kinds of experience are not typical features of situations.

Consider the following analogy: as I repeatedly tap my pencil on the desk here in California, the sound moves through the air in and about this office, which is "connected to" and "continuous with" the air in and about Times Square in New York. The activity in the air in this office is therefore in some concrete sense connected to the activity in the air in Times Square. So, following an argument similar to Russell's, does one conclude that the sound here is part of what is happening in Times Square? According to certain ideas in chaos theory (related to the "butterfly effect"), this tapping could eventually radically affect the weather in Times Square. But certainly, on the other hand, any kind of audibility does not reach that far, though the medium through which the sound vibrations travel is unbounded and connected even to regions in New York. This is only an analogy, but situations, as disturbances in the manifold of life functions of some organism/environment system, are bounded in the same sense that sound vibrations are carried only so far through the air before dissipating. These vibrations and their eventual dampening may affect causal sequences which eventually affect New York's weather, but the sound vibrations themselves dissipate. A situation is like the field of sound vibrations in this example, which includes some but not all of whatever is causally affected by these vibrations.

So, for instance, in the case of Neptune and your situation of being hungry, the planets and their continued good behavior are not part of the *dis*equilibrium characterizing your being hungry, but rather are part of the background which remains in equilibrium before, during, and after the resolution of your problem. Hence Neptune is not part of that particular situation.

This brings us to the crux of the confusion. We want to say that mere causal connectedness to a situation does not guarantee inclusion in the situation. All of the things which are causally connected to a situation do not, just on the grounds of causal connectedness, count as part of the situation. If anything, if we may push the analogy with sound disturbances in the air a bit further, such causal connections serve, like a buffer, to put *boundaries* on the situation, namely, to concretely dissipate its effects and otherwise localize the problem.

The course of Neptune may eventually be minutely changed as an effect of your going to the grocery store rather than staying put. But it still is not part of that particular situation, because it and its motion were never part of the breakdown. Its current state of motion may have been affected by your past accomplishments, but it is not "off course" or otherwise "relevant as such" because of them.

The indictment of general systems theory for its failure to say enough about what a *system* is short of its encompassing everything (if it includes everything its parts are related to) does not apply, then, to Dewey because Dewey's notion of a situation is considerably more specific and concrete than that of a "system." An organism/environment system is perhaps a "system" in the sense of general systems theory, and Dewey in facts puts few constraints on what constitutes such a system beyond its being a locus of "life functions." The distinctions between an organism and an environment, and between a living organism/environment system and the rest of the world, are perfectly meaningful distinctions, though lacking sharp dividing lines—much like distinctions between various hues in the color spectrum. In the present context, it entails nothing of much significance one way or the other to allow that an adequate characterization of an organism/environment system requires that one ultimately "contemplate the whole of reality."

But in his discussion of inquiry, Dewey does not require the boundedness of organism/environment systems but rather the boundedness of situations—localized fields of disturbance within the manifold of processes and interactions which constitute the organism/environment system as a whole. An organism/environment system may well be said to include everything that it is causally linked to (though we may safely remain neutral about that), but not so for a situation. A situation may be causally linked to but not contain those parts of the organism/environment system to which the respective disturbance (and its eventual rectification) does not extend. In this sense, premise (3) is denied.

It hardly seems contentious to claim that disturbances to a system could be localized, not extending as such to the whole system. Such local disturbances to a system could not happen if there were not a larger system there in the first place; and there is nothing in principle to rule out disturbances which affect the system as a whole (for instance, clubbing a frog with a baseball bat could be said to disturb the whole frog system, by totally obliterating it as a distinctive living system). Yet what typically constitutes a situation is not the range of its causal linkages, but rather the range of the disturbance to what would ordinarily be characteristic of a balanced functioning of the organism/environment system. A locus of disequilibrium in any given instance involves only a finite amount of activity, and any accompanying reverberations will proportionally reach only so far, beyond which the response of the rest of the world is nil.

For another analogy, we might compare a situation to what happens when a pebble hits a safety-glass windshield: the breakage extends only so far as it extends. The breakage might expand under the influence of further stresses; and one could of course shatter the whole windshield with a strong enough blow, in the same way that one can completely overwhelm any given living system. But in terms of the disturbances which constitute ongoing experience, situations have bounded, if indeterminate, horizons in the same way that the breakage of a windshield extends only so far as it does under the influence of a colliding pebble.

Or again, for an example that is not just an analogy, the Vietnam War might have expanded to include the Burmese jungles; but it did not, so they never became part of that situation, to the extent that Burma continued being pretty much what Burma would have been even if the Vietnam situation had not occurred. Undoubtedly there were economic and political repercussions all over Southeast Asia due to the heavy U.S. presence in the region, but from many perspectives at many levels most of Southeast Asia other than Laos and Cambodia was *not* drawn into the conflict, i.e., was not part of the Vietnam situation.

On the other hand, increasing military expenditures by the United States in the 1960s will have adversely affected college professors' salaries, which may have encouraged a certain lack of blind patriotism on the part of professors and hence their students, which may not have discouraged the general air of discontent with U.S. involvement in Vietnam, which may have helped to bring about an earlier end to the war than would otherwise have been the case. One would then say that professors' discontent with their salaries became part of the Vietnam situation, not just because certain causal connections could be traced to them, but because they were eventually part of the overall disturbance.

As long as a situation remains "open" and unresolved, it is potentially expandable and liable to get increasingly out of hand. More resources may have to be diverted and otherwise brought to bear in order to undo a burgeoning problem. But that there is a potential for expansion does not mean that the expansion will actually occur. In any given case, it is a concrete fact that the disturbance goes only so far. A situation does not include what it might include but only what it in fact includes.

An analogy which might help to clear up some of the terminological confusion here would be to compare the reach (scope, size) of a situation to the "support" of a density function in probability theory. A density function defined on the set of real numbers has an infinite domain, but it may be zero-valued outside of some proper subset of that domain. The support of a density function is basically that region of the domain where the function has nonzero values. Because its integral over the real numbers is finite, a density function, if not zero outside of some finite interval, converges at least exponentially to zero. Then, in the same manner that a density function is defined everywhere but has an effectively bounded support, we might say that a situation is a "function" of the whole organism/environment system (and hence the whole universe?) but has an effectively bounded scope (because the sum of experience in any given instance is finite?). Without pushing the analogy too far, the point here is just that we should not confuse the "domain" of a situation, which is unbounded, with the "support" of a situation, namely, its size or scope.

Though the present focus is on Dewey's logical theory, it is worth noting that this has implications for his views in general regarding almost any issue he wrote about. In particular, the boundedness of situations is an essential aspect of Dewey's ethics and social philosophy. In *Reconstruction in Philosophy* (1920), for example, Dewey claims that too much ink has been spilled concerning different proposals as to the taxonomy and hierarchical arrangement of absolute and fixed standards of the good or the right. Dewey's claim is that such things have to be intelligently inquired into in each concrete situation as one comes to it. Lessons can and must be learned from one situation to the next—the principle of continuity applies here as much as anywhere—but each situation is at bottom unique and requires its own special attention. This statement is, of course, incoherent and says nothing useful if you cannot distinguish this situation from that, or if there is really only one big situation, namely, the whole universe.

So the idea of situations as bounded but nonatomic wholes is indirectly forced on us by the unresolvable conflict between atomistic and holistic conceptions of things. And more or less independently, this conception of situations is also presented as an empirical fact about the nature of experience—hence the repeated appeal to (and the force of) examples and analogies. We will be able to say more about this issue when we outline Dewey's conception of propositions (cf. page 226). For now we simply note that the boundedness of situations, and the fact that inquiries—as transformations of situations—eventually terminate, are evidenced by the finitude of our own experience and by the fact that actual organism/environment systems manage to survive in the world and to otherwise successfully maintain themselves.

We should then review Russell's argument and otherwise see where we stand. The two questionable premises are (3) and (4). Premise (3) is in fact ambiguous. One reading of it is acceptable to Dewey, but then it does not combine with (4) to yield (5). On the other hand, a second reading, which was behind Russell's asserting that (4) is the case, is not acceptable to Dewey.

The unacceptable reading is the following:

(3′)   Anything causally connected to a situation is pertinent to its resolution, and is therefore part of the situation.

Premise (4) is supposed to accommodate Dewey's "insistence upon continuity," where continuity between two causally connected events presumably guarantees that they are two features of a single whole. And (3′) and (4) together imply that no matter where you propose to draw the boundary around a situation, if its causal connections reach beyond that boundary, then that was not really a boundary. This argument would be applicable if one were to assume that a characterization of a given object, e.g., a situation, must include an account of its relations, including its causal relations, with everything else. This sounds like the old absolute-idealist theory that all relations are "internal," a claim which neither Russell (in later years) nor Dewey would want to endorse.

But the problem with (3′) and (4), besides the fact that they ignore Dewey's more general notion of continuity, is that they do not accommodate Dewey's definition of a situation as an instance of disequilibrium. The preferred reading of (3) would be something like the following:

(3″)   Anything which is part of the disturbance which constitutes a situation is part of the situation.

So far as the notion of continuity goes, we have seen that Dewey's notion, which I have tried to express in principle (4′), assumes the boundedness of situations, in the sense that inquiries typically come to an end. The idea is that inquiries yield stable results which one can usually depend on to persist in subsequent inquiries. And the boundedness of situations is guaranteed by Dewey's defining it as a breakdown in life functions—not a breakdown in experience as such, but a breakdown that contributes to and otherwise helps to constitute experience. The existence of causal connections between events is not enough to make them parts of a single whole, or at least not parts of a single situation. The question is not how far causal connections reach, since that is virtually boundless. It is rather a question of how far the breakdown in normal causal processes reaches. Causal relations (and other sorts of constraints, for that matter) may reach to things beyond the actual scope of the given field of disequilibrium. But that does not directly involve such things in the disequilibrium itself.

The bottom line is that premises (1), (2), (3′), and (4) may yield (5), but this has no bearing on Dewey's views. On the other hand, (1), (2), (3″), and (4′) more closely reflect Dewey's views, and they do not lead to (5).

Before proceeding to the next chapter, there is one last point to address so far as the notion of situations is concerned. In his argument that Dewey's position is holistic, Russell mentions that Dewey's purpose is "practical," as opposed perhaps to being purely analytical or theoretical, as if that were to account for some of the differences in their respective ways of thinking (see the quote on page 32 above). But the term 'practical' carries the wrong connotations in this context. In claiming that a theory of situations is "genuinely empirical," Dewey is saying that situations are objective, concrete things. They are actual fields of organism/environment activity, subsisting within the manifold of "life functions" of some particular organism/environment system. As such, they are concrete parts of a dynamic universe, as concrete as stones, though typically more complex; and they can serve as the subject matter of a systematic, empirical study. That such a study should lead to practical results, such as in education, psychology, linguistics, political theory, or wherever, is to be hoped for; but that is not necessarily what drives the theory.

One might counter that the empirical science to which Dewey was referring sounds more like psychology than logic. This brings us to one of Russell's more fundamental difficulties with Dewey's approach to logic. Russell's rejection of the idea of situations and his charge that Dewey's logic is in some way psychologistic stems from a misunderstanding of Dewey's use of the terms 'existential' and 'real'.

3

The Existential and the Real

One may misread Dewey's uses of the terms 'existential' and 'real' in two ways. On one hand, we may assume he uses these terms interchangeably. On the other hand, if we assume there is a distinction to be made, it is tempting to think that the distinction is essentially one of "appearance versus reality," along the lines of Bradley's *Appearance and Reality* (1899). But neither of these readings is acceptable. The distinction is more like Kant's distinction between objects of experience and things in themselves, but without the idealist overtones. We must clarify this distinction in order to address the question of whether Dewey's logic is psychologistic or subjectivistic.

3.1 Existence

Russell registers a complaint at one point that Dewey says virtually nothing about the world independent of the effects of inquiry:

> There are few further statements about what the world is apart from the effects which inquiry has upon it. For instance: "There is, of course, a natural world that exists independently of the organism, but this world is *environment* only as it enters directly and indirectly into life-functions." (The words "of course" here may be taken as indicating an underlying metaphysic.) Again: "existence in general must be such as to be *capable* of logical forms." We are told very little about the nature of things before they are inquired into; we know, however, that, like dishonest politicians, things behave differently when observed from the way in which they behave when no one is paying attention to them. (Russell 1939, p. 139)

It is immediately after this paragraph that Russell asks "how large" situations may be, the question reducing in Russell's view to one of how large a part of the world is if it includes everything that it is "continuous with"—as already discussed.

The point we will focus on here is the error in thinking of situations as parts of the world "apart from the effects which inquiry has upon them." That Russell is able to derive absurd consequences from such a view does in fact speak against this particular conception of situations, but this is not Dewey's conception of situations. It is true that situations are domains or universes of "existence" in Dewey's terms (1938, pp. 66–9, 125–31), but it is a mistake to think that, for Dewey, something is *real* if and only if it *exists*. In this case *the world* would comprise everything which is real, which is to say, everything which exists, and Russell's criticisms would then carry some weight. But though this wording may reflect common usage of these terms, it misrepresents Dewey's more specific use of the adjective 'existential'.

One cannot afford to claim that Dewey's uses of these terms always, from one decade to the next, reflect the distinction being drawn here. It is unfortunate that Dewey was not entirely consistent in this regard, since the distinction is fundamental to understanding his overall views. In particular, a direct and explicit explanation of this distinction is given in Dewey 1949. Earlier treatments of the distinction, with a somewhat different terminology, can be found in Dewey 1905a, 1905b.

By remarking that Dewey says too little "about the nature of things before they are inquired into," Russell is drawing a legitimate distinction between things as experienced and things independent of our experience. Neither Dewey nor Russell question the idea that there is a world out there independent of our experience. For example, Russell is of course correct to think that there was a time in the world before there were agents to experience it. Or making a different and somewhat subtler point, Kant is correct to say that there is a world independent of our modes of sensibility. In this same light, when Dewey talks about organisms, environments, interactions, or transactions among organisms and environments, and so forth, he is talking about certain aspects of the world outside of the contents and results of those agents' inquiries. In other words, Dewey is laying down a certain amount of conceptual framework on the basis of which he can formulate a theory of inquiry. Any actual process of inquiry is itself an objective piece of reality, insofar as it is something happening in the world. Dewey is therefore compelled to say something about the world independent of how it is manifested in specific agents' experience.

The divergence in their respective views rather concerns the question of what role such experience should play in logic. For Dewey, experience is a central concern, while for Russell (and up until recently, for the Fregean tradition at large) it lies outside the proper domain of logical theory. As this and subsequent chapters will try to make clear, Dewey can agree that our experience of the world is such that it consists more or less of objects having properties and standing in relations. But just how the world thus manifests itself to an agent will depend on that agent's operational perspective in the world. What this means is that the objects, properties, relations, and so forth which play a central role in semantic theory (in interpreting a language or stating truth conditions for sentences) should be treated as elements of our experience, i.e., as products and tools of inquiries, not as things given prior to or independent of experience.

For both Dewey and Russell, a certain amount of conceptual stage setting has to go on prior to presenting any such semantic theory. They differ rather in where the stage setting stops and logic in its own right begins. For Russell, we have to be able to make certain assumptions about the world independent of our experience of it. The world is in this view carved up into objects having properties and standing in relations, and we have only to open our eyes to note such facts. These facts are not products of our experience, but rather our experience is geared (faithfully or not) to such facts. A proposition is true if it states a fact, false if it does not. Otherwise, logic is the study of formal aspects of propositional or linguistic systems independent of determining or confirming actual truth values. The focus is rather on syntactic features of languages or propositional systems in the abstract. This is where logic begins and remains.

In disagreeing with this view of logic, Dewey claims not that syntactic theory is wrongheaded or inappropriate in itself but that what is wrongheaded is to think that this is the full extent of the domain of logical theory. For Dewey, one jumps the gun by a long shot by making certain independent and sweeping claims about the world in this manner. In taking this stance, one is less than a step away from embracing a view referred to by Dewey (in *The Quest for Certainty* (1929) and elsewhere) as the "spectator theory of knowledge," namely, the view that we can say something about the world (as it "really" is) independent of our participation in it. Russell commits himself, qua logician, to such a view to the extent that he assumes a world full of facts without questioning how we come to grips with such facts in our experience, opting to focus solely on the abstract study of propositional or linguistic systems. Russell assumes in effect that we can have an immediate grasp on things simply by "paying attention" to them, as if this permits basic and unrefutable knowledge of various facts. This is justified by the fact, he claims, that we are to a high degree able to maintain such a detached perspective. But he ignores the interactive character of "paying attention" to things. Indeed, many scientific disciplines, following the precedent established by Newtonian physics, take for granted a clean detachment between observer and the subject matter of observation.

Current discussions for and against Putnam's "internal realism" thesis (1983, 1987) address similar issues. Some of Putnam's critics, like Searle, take the view that either you have realism or else you have philosophical mush; and talking about *internal* realism is just a confused way of claiming realism but really having just mush. But this is a rather coarse way to view these issues. Putnam does not lose a direct handle on reality by asserting that *facts* as such are relative to (or internal to) some conceptual scheme. Consider an analogy. As you drive down the freeway, you note that the car next to you is moving roughly zero miles per hour relative to you. That is a simple and straightforward fact, as "real" as anything is real, though you are not in a position to say how fast that car is "really" going from some absolute reference frame. That the speed of that car is zero relative to you is no less a fact because you adopt your own position as the origin of reference. Conceptual schemes and operational perspectives in general are similar in this regard to kinematic reference frames. As long as a proposition contains at least an implicit reference to the operational perspective employed in its formulation, there is no way one can have any more of a fact than that. One cannot describe reality any more concretely than that (though one may describe it more and more extensively). There is no reason to think you are falling short of describing things as they really are by describing them from the perspective of a given conceptual scheme. There is no other way to do it and there never has been. This should be no more difficult to grasp than the claim that the Earth is not flat, or that humanity does not exist at the center of the cosmos.

Dewey's response to Russell on this particular point was the following:

> Any one who refuses to go outside [mere] discourse—as Mr. Russell apparently does—has of course shut himself off from understanding what a "situation," as directly experienced subject-matter, is.
>
> An almost humorous instance of such refusal and its consequences is found when Mr. Russell writes: "We are told very little about the nature of things before they are inquired into." If I have said or tried to say the tiniest bit about the "nature of things" prior to inquiry into them, I have not only done something completely contradictory to my own position but something that seems to me inherently absurd.... I plead guilty to not having written into my philosophical writings an encyclopedia of the conclusions of all the sciences. Whatever Mr. Russell may have meant by the sentence quoted, my position is that *telling* is (i) a matter of discourse, and that (ii) all discourse is derived from and inherently referable to experiences of things in non-discursive experiential having;—so that, for example, although it is possible to tell a man blind from birth *about*

color, we cannot by discourse confer upon him that which is had in the direct experience of color—my whole position on this matter being a generalization of this commonplace fact. (Dewey 1939a, pp. 546–7)

Of course, we have seen that Dewey does say a lot about the nature of things independent of inquiry, to set the stage for developing a theory of inquiry in the first place. He has overstated his position by claiming otherwise. But he does reiterate in this paragraph a point about the scope of logic which Russell persistently failed to appreciate, which is that a study of language and its meaningful use cannot be divorced from a study of experience.

Dewey does not deny that there is a world out there independent of our participation in it, but he holds that we have epistemic *access* to it only through such participation. Any reliable description of the world on our part is going to be colored by our operational perspective on it, that is, by our ways of participating in it. What we say about the world—what we talk about—are the actual things in our experience or possibilities extrapolated therefrom. The meanings of our terms are going to be determined by things as they do or might occur in our experience. We can always question what's really out there independent of our experience, but our experience itself is all that is ever immediately given to us.

It is just for this reason that one needs to distinguish "existential facts" from "reality."[1] We do indeed have direct access to existential facts—by paying attention to details of situations, that is, to the details of our "transactions" with the world—but it begs important epistemological questions to generally assume that such "facts" are unassailably true to reality by virtue of our attending to them. Such facts constitute in large part our grasp of reality; but our grasp of reality may fall short of complete or precise comprehension.

It therefore makes sense to distinguish the world in its *absolute reality* from the world *as revealed to us by virtue of our particular*

---

[1]This distinction is more explicitly addressed by Dewey in his reply to Reichenbach in the Schilpp volume (Dewey 1939a, pp. 540–3).

ways of operating in it. Contrary to Russell, Dewey holds that we cannot say much of anything for certain about the former in much detail, even if we may rationally speculate about it on the basis of the great amount we *can* say, and in significant detail, about the latter. By insisting that Dewey say something about the former prior to or otherwise independent of inquiry, Russell in effect turns Dewey's project on its head. When it finally comes down to talking about language and its use, Dewey does not say a whole lot about the world independent of inquiry because there is nothing to be said, other than that it is there, without importing question-begging assumptions into the matter. It is as if Russell accepts such question begging as unavoidable (see Russell 1939, top of p. 138, though one could argue that this paragraph is only a bit of introductory politeness, not the statement of a philosophical position), while Dewey finds it unacceptable and thinks it *is* avoidable. We do not deny that the world is out there by holding that we can know and say nothing reliable about it except as mediated through our transactions with it. Objects, properties, relations, etc., as they figure in a theory of semantics are, for Dewey, elements of our experience of the world, geared no doubt to the world in its absolute and independent reality, but also to our particular ways of operating in it.

Consider the following account of the essential role of an external world in objective experience:

> Experience, objectively construed, is a process that involves a large element of human activity and convention, but it also involves something else. We may or may not have the concepts required to formulate electromagnetic conjectures; we may choose to design an experimental set-up or not; we may choose to open our eyes in front of the voltmeter or not. But if we do these things, we are no longer free to choose to see the needle pointing at the number 4. In experience, as in the Wittgensteinian proposition, there is a constructive process in which the human will is in command and, at its end point, there is an encounter with a circumstance entirely beyond our will. In this resistance to or independence from our will, Dilthey had identified the very essence of our conception of an external world. It is this final stage that reveals, through its independence from us, the presence of a second

party in the epistemic process, the "external" world. Only the most extreme and less coherent forms of idealism will seriously put forth a theory of experience that does not allow for this extraconventional element. (Coffa 1991, pp. 366–7)

Dewey would surely endorse this statement so far as it goes, though it hardly says enough about what constitutes objective experience as such. As sensible as it sounds, this quote is deceptively simple in its depiction of what is involved in an account of objectivity. In contrast, Dewey's notion of objectivity is more like Kant's, in broad outline anyway.

Kant acknowledged that some such "independence from our will" is an important ingredient of our conception of objective experience, and yet in saying this he could deny that we should have a lot to say about the nature of things in themselves independent of experience. It is not enough simply to acknowledge some kind of external world to make sense of the idea of there being an "extraconventional" element in experience. For Kant, the manifold of sensory impressions that constitutes the basic subject matter of experience exhibits such resistance to or independence from our subjective states, but this particular sense of resistance or independence is not enough to yield objectivity as such. Objectivity is manifested rather in the systematicity or unity of the processes in which the manifold of sense is brought under various concepts—a unity of apperception, as it were (1781, A104/B142; Strawson 1966, pp. 89–92, 98, 118–52; see also the quote on page 42 above and the discussion on page 107 below). Objectivity is to be found in the overall systematicity of apperception, not solely by reference to some external world. This systematicity *also* shows a kind of resistance to or independence from our will—we cannot just decide over breakfast what is systematic and coherent and what is not, no more than we can simply choose whether or not a given set of sentence schemata in the propositional calculus is consistent. Insofar as such systematicity is independent of any subjective states, it constitutes the essence of objective experience. As such it may supply a sense of a world of experience independent of our subjective states, but it does not lead us to appeal to (beyond a bare acknowledgment of) an external world of things in themselves outside of the processes of apperception. The extraconventional element of experience that guarantees objectivity resides squarely within the processes of apperception.

Dewey espoused an equally refined account of objectivity and facticity, distinguishing objects of experience from things in themselves (as it were), but without endorsing anything that could be termed idealism or subjectivism, and without being bound to articulate an independent account of things in themselves, as Russell seems to require.

In any given situation, there *will be* a base level of information which one routinely acts upon and takes for granted as being directly indicative of the way things are. Such information helps to constitute the existential facts, and hence to determine the "directly experienced subject matter" of that inquiry; and there is nothing within our capabilities which is more directly indicative of the way things are. As we will see in more detail in the next section, Dewey talked about situations as being "capable of logical forms" and of objects being "produced and ordered in settled form" in the course of inquiry. Much in line with Kant here, objects (in the sense of concrete things existing independently of our subjective states) are none other than coherencies emerging in the experimental processes of inquiry. We might say that we are continually endeavoring to *regain* some kind of unity of apperception in this sense, insofar as we are continually faced with disunity. Unity of apperception, whether or not it is actually achieved, is rather the overall aim of every inquiry.

We may be entirely objective in our grasp of the facts of a given case, eliminating subjective factors of desire, appetite, preference, interest, and the like, and focusing entirely on systematicities emerging on their own terms within experimental processes of inquiry; but we cannot eliminate the operational perspectivity that's built into the very nature of experience. There is no way to step outside of a situation to absolutely check these facts against the way things *really* are in some absolute sense, an ability which the spectator theory of knowledge seems to unwittingly take for granted or otherwise tries to hold up as a practicable standard, but which is no more possible than is stepping outside of oneself in order to look oneself in the face.

We can devise and routinely exploit ways to *test* the reliability of what we take to be the facts. And we even tend to make our way through the world without deliberately questioning many of the facts we take for granted, not consciously distinguishing facts as we see them from the way things really, really are. But any sort of careful discussion of the issues involved here, such as in formulating a theory of logic, has to admit the distinction. Dewey adopts a terminology whereby he is able to effectively distinguish talk about existential facts of given inquiries from talk about absolute reality, in such a way that pursuing any kind of detailed talk about the latter falls squarely outside the range of his concerns (because it is not a viable project). He can admit the distinction and still avoid building into his theory of logic a duality of "things of experience and things-in-themselves concealed behind experience" (Dewey 1939a, p. 524) only to have to turn around and be puzzled about their "correspondence" or connection otherwise.[2]

If we think of reality as encompassing "everything," then a given organism/environment system (involving possibly a plurality of organisms) will be *part of* everything, that is, part of reality. Situations will occur as fields of organism/environment interaction, and as such are themselves part of reality. Then, existential facts occur as information within arenas of organism/environment interaction, i.e., situations, or what Dewey sometimes refers to as "fields of experience." Existential facts are in this sense features of situations.

---

[2]Dewey (1941) does in fact endorse a correspondence theory of truth, but not in such a way as to presuppose or entail such dualisms. The correspondence rather is between cognitive, discursive experience and sensory, perceptual experience, viz., between two kinds of experience. This is discussed further in Sections 5.1 and 6.1.

A situation in this view will not encompass everything but is rather a proper part of the world. It *is* fair to say that a situation determines an actual concrete perspective on everything. But anything beyond the reach of the agent's operational capabilities will remain insignificant, that is, outside of the situation. For example, processes of *perception* are interactive in that they involve some array of transactions with the world. An episode or phase of, say, visual experience, such as when you try to focus on some blurred object that you are unable to otherwise identify, is an example of a situation. The world is acting on you by bathing you in a flood of electromagnetic energy; and you are acting on it by methodically gobbling some of it up with your eyes. The situation in this case will be centered on a certain splotch of indeterminate visual activity occurring in the course of these floodings and gobblings. It is within such domains of interaction that "existential facts" are pieced together from qualitative data and otherwise *occur*.

Dewey's and Russell's different views of perception will be discussed at greater length in later sections. The point here is that situations, as domains of experience, are in the above sense "real" and as such constitute a viable subject matter for objective, scientific investigation. This investigation is in part psychological, but it bears as well on epistemology and logic. A study of situations and their transformation constitutes a study of the arenas within which information about the world *occurs* in and for some respective organism/environment system. That such realities exhibit regularities essential to the use of language positions this study well within the domain of logical theory and the philosophy of language. Facts, as potential contents of declarative statements, are not just in the head, nor are they just in an independent world outside of the head. Facts are experienced—facts are elements of experience—which puts them somewhere in the interactive interface between head and world. This domain of interaction is as real as anything is real, constituting the dynamic stuff or substance of a living agent's experience; and as such it can be studied objectively.

At the same time, one cannot step outside of *one's own* experience and view it in the detached manner which such a claim seems to require. The logician *is* an experiencer, which yields a distinctive perspective in logical theory wherein the observer/theoretician is also a sample specimen. Conflating or otherwise ignoring this distinction between theorist and specimen gives rise to what James referred to as the "psychologist's fallacy." It is an easy mistake to make because of the uniquely self-referential character of the cognitive sciences. Failing to distinguish existence and reality is one symptom of this fallacy at work, in the sense that one fails to acknowledge the operational perspectivity of factual information.

In the case of studying some independent organism/environment system—whether it be a group of frogs in a given pond or a community of English-speaking humans in Cincinnati—one may minimize this risk by being careful not to take one's own sense of reality for granted as the measure of what does or does not occur in these agents' experience. In developing and testing ways of explaining their experience, one is compelled to study their actions among themselves and in the world at large, monitoring their overt behaviors, whether they are catching flies or conversing in English. In the latter case, it is important for the purposes of logical theory to understand that agents' linguistic behaviors will typically concern (refer to, be about) what "exists" in their experience. Such things will exist within the situations, that is, within the domains of experience (perceptual and otherwise), in which this organism/environment system finds itself and which the linguist may directly observe by being part of that community and being involved in its situations. For Dewey, logical theory will anchor a theory of reference and meaning—to be tested against these or other agents' linguistic behavior—in this notion of "the existential," not "the real."

3.2 Objects in Context

We now turn to Russell's criticisms of Dewey's notion of "objects." By Dewey's account, epistemological problems arise if we fail to regard objects as elements of "existence" rather than as elements of "reality." Russell does not make this distinction and hence runs into difficulties with Dewey's talking about existence being "capable of logical forms" or of objects and events being "produced and ordered in settled form" in the course of inquiry.[3]

Some of the difficulties in this regard are due to Russell's not giving *inquiry* proper emphasis in his assessment of Dewey's views. In the course of transforming an indeterminate situation into one that is determinate, a given inquiry will often hinge on identifying and keeping track of singular things—objects[4]—as they occur within the situation. And since Dewey does not assume or attempt to provide a theory of objects independent of a theory of inquiry, it appears to Russell that objects in Dewey's sense are hardly more than fantasies created on the run as one finds one's way in a situation and from one situation to the next.

Russell's discussion of this issue in the Schilpp volume (Russell 1939, pp. 140–2) is intertwined with a discussion of several things, including Dewey's views on perception and what Russell refers to as "immediate knowledge." Russell's point in this sequence of paragraphs is that we perceive separable things in the normal course of experience, involving separable and mutually independent causal chains linking things in the world to utterances of words, and that Dewey's holism contradicts this commonplace view. We have already dealt with Russell's unacceptable projection of an unconstrained holism into Dewey's conception of situations. What is interesting in these passages are Russell's remarks about perception, revealing another basic difference between himself and Dewey.

---

[3]Much of Sections 3.2 and 3.3 is a rearrangement and expansion of a paper delivered at the 1991 meeting of the Society for the Advancement of American Philosophy, which appears in Burke 1991a.

[4]Dewey briefly summarizes his use of the term 'object' in *Logic* (1938, pp. 118–9, 520–22) and in the Schilpp volume (1939a, pp. 566–7), which is at odds with Russell's comparatively simple sense of the term. To fully appreciate Dewey's use of the term, we would have to explore his conceptions of knowledge and intelligence. I will not do that here, beyond some cursory remarks in Sections 5.1 and 6.3, but the differences between Russell's and Dewey's views should become clear in the following discussion.

Russell, as a matter of fact, initiates his criticism of Dewey's conception of *objects* by noting that Dewey denies that there is any such thing as "immediate knowledge," which is something Russell thinks one needs in order to ground a theory of knowledge. In place of nondefeasible sensory data, Dewey prefers to speak in terms of what he calls "apprehension," which involves direct recognition of objects "on sight . . . without questioning." Russell quotes a paragraph from *Logic* (Dewey 1938, p. 143) where Dewey defines apprehension as a sort of direct perception of objects which is nevertheless "mediated through certain organic mechanisms of retention and habit, [presupposing] prior experiences and mediated conclusions drawn from them." Russell claims to not necessarily disagree with this, but he also remarks that Dewey does not say enough about what he means by "organic mechanisms of retention and habit." Russell says nothing more about what Dewey did say about these things, but proceeds to offer his own account of how it is we come to recognize objects in the course of normal experience.

Focusing the discussion more specifically on the habits underlying our uses of words (particularly common nouns), Russell asserts that habit formation presupposes "frequent simultaneity" of objects of a given sort and instances of their names "as perceived objects" in their own right—claiming that habits of association are formed by virtue of repetitious associations, plus "the causal law according to which frequent simultaneity generates a habit." Russell's point here is that the causal chains involved in our using words on the basis of such habits are initiated not by the whole world but by singular features of the world—we use the noun 'book' demonstratively in association with singular objects which most often happen to be books. This fact that we use separable words, each usage linked via its own separable causal chain to separable starting points in real objects in the world, is thus supposed to undermine a holistic account of word usage.[5]

---

[5]"We must therefore suppose that natural processes have the character attributed to them by the analyst, rather than the holistic character which the enemies of analysis

> We have thus, when the common-sense belief is justified, a rather elaborate causal chain: book, light-waves, eye, optic nerve, brain, utterance of the word 'book'.... If the common-sense point of view is to be in any degree justifiable in ordinary circumstances, we must suppose that each visible object is the starting-point of a causal chain which remains, at least in some respects, independent of all the other simultaneous causal chains that lead to our seeing the other objects. (Russell 1939, p. 142)

At the same time, this discrete-causal picture allows that perception is not infallible, in that percepts can occur by means other than the usual associations one's habits are geared to—one can have bookish percepts where there is in fact no book. Hence Russell is led "to stress percepts as opposed to common-sense judgments" in his account of immediate knowledge.

The bulk of Dewey's response to these remarks by Russell on the nature of "apprehension" of discrete objects occurs in three relatively long paragraphs in the Schilpp volume (Dewey 1939a, pp. 568–71). Dewey begins by reiterating his claim that apprehension has to be understood in terms of its function in inquiry. By neglecting this functional aspect of Dewey's theory of perception, Russell is able to generate absurd readings of Dewey's views. According to Dewey, a given agent's particular apprehensions always occur with reference to the resolution of some particular situation. Presenting a view which he describes as a "*via media*" between Russell's "extreme atomistic pluralism" and the "block universe monism" which Russell argues against under the name of "holism," Dewey (1939a, p. 544) stresses that objects are indeed apprehended singularly in a way which should satisfy Russell's antiholism; *but* the significance of any such apprehension is derived from the context in which it occurs. The very idea of a situation is designed to provide a way to talk about such concrete contexts in which perceptions (and other activities) occur and have any significance, without

---

take for granted. I do not contend that the holistic world is logically impossible, but I do contend that it could not give rise to science or to any empirical knowledge." (Russell 1939, p. 142)

entailing the extreme sort of holism against which Russell argues at length. (Russell's argument cannot be, of course, that the separability of words implies that the "field" notion is in error. Otherwise why, Dewey asks, wouldn't this undermine the use of the idea of fields in physics? Words are separable, as are physical objects like chairs, trees, and stones. But this does not entail that the idea of continuous physical fields is mistaken.)

This issue deserves some attention. In what follows, I will discuss a series of passages from Chapter 2 of Dewey's *Logic*, which explain fairly well what Dewey meant by the "organic mechanisms of retention and habit." We will then see how this bears on his conception of "objects" insofar as they are alleged to be directly perceivable.

First, in his account of habits and their relationship to perception, Dewey's interest lies not in speculating about the physiological mechanisms of perception which Russell focuses on, but rather in trying to understand "the proper logical interpretation of direct apprehension." For Dewey what is important is to understand, first, how perception functions in inquiry, and second, how perception is, in its own right, a result of a kind of noncognitive proto-inquiry. These are the sorts of questions which bear on the problem of knowledge, immediate or otherwise, which are not adequately answered by a simple linear story about the causal production of perceptions.

> As far as causal conditions are concerned, it makes no difference to my argument what they may be, as long as it is granted that habits are formed that enable us to spot familiar objects on sight.... *If* I held a holistic view, [Mr. Russell's] reference to independent causal chains would be highly pertinent. But since I do not hold that position, and since in my own treatment, when I deal with the topic of causation, I expressly insist upon a plurality of sequences, I need only remark that Mr. Russell's considerations reinforce the point I have made about the logical aspect of the matter ... [namely] that causal issues should not be substituted for logical ones. (Dewey 1939a, p. 570)

If it is not a matter of analyzing or explaining such physiological mechanisms and causal chains, how are we to understand perception? Russell was perhaps right in remarking that, though Dewey was not necessarily wrong in what he did say, he did not say enough about the "organic mechanisms of retention and habit" and the "prior experiences and mediated conclusions" which characterize the perception of objects.

But then Dewey said a good deal more than Russell indicates. One series of passages which reveals a fundamental difference in Dewey's and Russell's views is worth discussing at length here, especially in response to Russell's account of the nature of habit formation as the result of "frequent simultaneity" (etc.).[6] These passages include Dewey's discussion (1938, pp. 29–33) of excitation/reaction events versus stimulus/response processes, and his discussion of how these distinctions bear on our understanding of habit formation. These themes were, of course, introduced and discussed by Dewey as far back as 1896 in "The Reflex Arc Concept in Psychology."[7]

Dewey's account of how excitations produce reactions is similar to Russell's description of the causal production of verbal utterances as initiated by singular objects, though the excitation/reaction distinction is more general in scope. In particular, an excitation/reaction episode in Dewey's view is "isolated and complete in itself." But does that tell us anything useful?

Russell treats an account of this excitation/reaction process as if it were an account of perception. And the only alternative to this discrete account of excitations and reactions which he considers is

---

[6] Russell's discussion of perception and knowledge in Chapter 8 of *An Inquiry into Meaning and Truth* (1940, pp. 144–70) is probably a better indication of his views than the brief passages in the Schilpp volume. Though certain aspects of his views there are more in line with Dewey's than he might want to admit, he continues to criticize "the Hegelians and the instrumentalists" (p. 154) on various grounds.

[7] See also Dewey's "Conduct and Experience," an article written in 1930 addressing, among other things, Dewey's disagreement with certain aspects of behavioristic psychology. He devotes a few pages to his conception of the stimulus/response distinction, in contrast with the "S-R" conception of early experimental behaviorism.

an unconstrained holism whereby such excitation/reaction events are *not* isolated and complete in themselves but rather encompass the whole world. This latter view does not seem like a workable position. Hence, compelled to choose between these two supposedly exhaustive and exclusive positions, Russell of course adopts the view where excitation/reaction events are taken to be separable and largely independent, and attributes the opposing view to Dewey.

Advocating neither of these alternatives, Dewey takes a slightly more refined position where discrete, separable excitation/reaction events have a place, but where an account of perception requires more of a story than that. Giving an account of the causal linkage of singular excitations and reactions is not necessarily pointless; but, by itself, it falls far short of accounting for what perception is, at least at a level of analysis appropriate to psychology, epistemology, or logic. It is in this regard that we have to understand Dewey's treatment of the stimulus/response distinction, where the differences between stimuli and excitations, and between reactions and responses, are pronounced.

For example, suppose a lion is subject to some particular excitation, such as an array of fluctuations in its visual field, as directly affected by some distant object, perhaps a gazelle. This may or may not instigate some sort of reaction, but in any case it presupposes some sort of preexisting ongoing activity in the context of which the excitation is made possible and might have any kind of significance to begin with.

> The particular sensory excitation occurs, but it is coordinated with a large number of other organic processes—those of its digestive and circulatory organs and its neuro-muscular system, autonomic, proprioceptor and central. This coordination, which is a state of the total organism, constitutes a *stimulus*.... The pursuit of prey is a response to the total state of the organism, not to a particular sensory excitation. Indeed, the distinction between what has been called stimulus and response is made only by analytic reflection. The so-called stimulus, being the total state of the organism, moves of itself, because of the tensions contained, into those activities of pursuit which are called the response. The stimulus is simply the

earlier part of the total coordinated serial behavior and the response the later part. (Dewey 1938, p. 30)

This neither advocates nor entails the unconstrained holism which Russell argues against, though Dewey does view stimuli as functions of the whole organism. We might think of this as a kind of localized holism, perhaps along the lines of a gestalt-psychological account of perception (see below), but that is just a matter of terminology.

The important thing for present purposes is to understand the difference between stimuli and excitations, and between responses and reactions. Stimuli and responses involve coordinated complexes of excitations and reactions whose causal links are potentially diffuse, variable, and so intricately intertwined as to not be individually traceable.

> When the stimulus is recognized to be the tension in the total organic activity (ultimately reducible to that between contact activities and those occasioned by distance-receptors), it is seen that the stimulus in its *relationship* to special activities persists throughout the entire pursuit, although it changes its actual content at each stage of the chase. As the animal runs, specific sensory excitations, those of contact and those that are olfactory and visual, alter with every change of position; with every change in the character of the ground; with changing objects (like bushes and rocks) that progressively intervene; and they also change in intensity with every change in distance from the hunted object. (Dewey 1938, p. 30)

It is not difficult to also see similarities, at least in broad outline, between this view of how multiple excitations and reactions are processed and principles underlying "connectionist" modeling in recent computer science—though connectionist theory has a long way to go yet to accommodate Dewey's treatment of the stimulus/response process.[8] So far as the standard mind/computer metaphor is concerned, it is as if Dewey was anticipating the difficulties which AI research would encounter in its treatment of perception and ac-

---

[8]See Rumelhart and McClelland 1986 and McClelland and Rumelhart 1986 for an early introductory survey of this approach to AI modeling.

tion in simple terms of inputs (excitations) and outputs (reactions) mediated by some sort of syntactic processing.

> If [this difference between stimulus/response and excitation/reaction] is ignored, the sequential character of behavior is lost from view. Behavior then becomes simply a succession of isolated and independent units of excitation-reaction, which would be comparable, say, to a succession of muscular twitches due to a disordered nervous system. (Dewey 1938, pp. 30–1)

The problem here is not the separability and independence of excitations and reactions, which Dewey accepts and which Russell nevertheless feels compelled to argue in favor of, but rather that these are not always properly distinguished from stimuli and responses in Dewey's sense—hence the one distinction in Russell's hands is forced to do the work of two distinctions in Dewey's. In Russell's case, this generates an impoverished theory of perception—one that is unable to account for the coordination of all the separate excitations and reactions it posits—and ultimately results in a misunderstanding of Dewey's views.

> The theory which identifies stimuli with a succession of specific sensory excitations, cannot possibly account for such unified and continuous responses as hunting and stalking prey. On that theory the animal would have to make at each stage a new and isolated "response" (reaction) to everything that came across his path. He would be reacting to stones, bushes and to changes in the levels and character of the ground in so many independent acts that there would be no continuity of behavior. He would forget, as we say, what he was after in the multitude of separate reactions he would have to make to the independent excitations. Because behavior is in fact a function of the total state of the organism in relation to environment, stimuli are functionally constant in spite of changes in specific content.[9] Because of this fact, behavior is sequential, one act

---

[9] This claim about the functional constancy of "stimuli" supports the idea that the situation transformed in inquiry (from stimulus to response) remains the same situation over the course of the transformation—in the same way that your mother remains your mother over the course of your respective life spans—in spite of many changing features. The alternative is to view inquiry as a process of moving

growing out of another and leading cumulatively to a further act until the consummatory fully integrated activity occurs. (Dewey 1938, pp. 30–1)

One can see similarities here with gestalt psychology. But while the comparison of a Deweyan situation with a perceptual "gestalt" may appear to be straightforward, the latter is a narrower notion pertaining primarily to the psychology of perception. It is not clear if there was a substantial historical tie between Dewey's work and gestalt psychology. It would be interesting to know if any of Dewey's earlier work, such as the "Reflex Arc" paper (1896), had any influence on German psychology around the turn of the century, and conversely, whether there was any influence the other way. It is more likely that Dewey and Wertheimer (et al.) were both influenced by James's *Principles of Psychology*, but not so much by each other (Ross 1982, p. xxvi). There are no references to gestalt psychology in Dewey's writings, except for several footnotes and one mention in the text of a work he published jointly with Arthur Bentley in the late 1940s (Dewey and Bentley 1949). The references there are exclusively to Wertheimer's work, and one might suspect these are due more to Bentley than to Dewey. The traditional notion of a gestalt does not carry with it the same emphasis on the initially problematic and resolvable character of situations. If anything, a gestalt could be viewed as the end product of a perceptual resolution process—i.e., a resolved "whole." As such, it is no longer a situation but rather an "object" in Dewey's sense of these terms, as we will see shortly. This is consistent with the mention of the gestalt idea in Dewey and Bentley 1949. More generally, some important

---

from one situation to the next, from one which is indeterminate to one which is "fully integrated." One might think these two ways of thinking about inquiry are equally viable, so that the difference is merely terminological—a matter of how to use the term 'situation'. But Dewey's view, as indicated in this passage and elsewhere, would seem to support the idea that the distinction is worth maintaining and that the two conceptions of inquiry are not equivalent. Inquiry moves through various phases, from "stimulus" to "response," but it is one given situation which undergoes transformation.

philosophical issues (involving realism, relativism, subjectivism) were handled by Kohler and Koffka in a way that does not reflect Dewey's views, so we want to be careful to distance an account of Dewey's views from gestalt psychology in this regard. The notion of a gestalt has a largely mentalistic flavor to it, which does not comport well with the ecological nature of situations.

By distinguishing stimulus/response processes from excitation/reaction processes, Dewey is able to explain how he conceives of habit formation and how habits function in stimulus/response processes. The natural impetus to proceed from stimulus to response is what gives organic behavior its "direction and cumulative force." As an elementary unit of experience, a stimulus/response process is a movement away from an initial phase of "tension of various elements of organic energy" (namely, a stimulus) toward "the institution of integrated interaction of organism and environment" (namely, a response).

> This integration is represented upon the organic side by equilibration of organic energies, and upon the environmental side by the existence of satisfying conditions. In the behavior of higher organisms, the close of the circuit is not identical with the state out of which disequilibration and tension emerged. A certain modification of environment has also occurred, though it may be only a change in the conditions which future behavior must meet. On the other hand, there is change in the organic structures that conditions further behavior. This modification constitutes what is termed habit. (Dewey 1938, p. 31)

This account of habit formation will of course sound odd if, following Russell, we think only along the lines of standard explanations of conditioning in terms of repetitive association. Dewey's view rather entails that a habit can be formed on the basis of a single stimulus/response episode. Each such episode involves the stabilization of organismic and environmental modifications which constrain subsequent behavior. In this view, there is a common pattern underlying an account of routine modes of behavior—habits—which one develops in coming to terms with and staying in step with the world, and, on the other hand, an account of singular perceptions as results of stimulus/response episodes.

For example, an account of how you gain your bearings in an unfamiliar city, and an account of how you manage to see a tree as a tree, are going to be variations on a single theme. The process of becoming habituated to a city may take weeks if not months, and the process of perceiving a tree may take seconds if not fractions of a second; yet each of these kinds of experience is explainable in common terms of the basic pattern of inquiry.

We can view the process of becoming familiar with a new city as a long and large process of eventually coming to know the city as a singular object. Initially, a new city makes up a complex and unfamiliar "situation." As you gain familiarity with it, and by virtue of the stability of many of its features, it becomes more like a routine object incorporated into your behavior patterns, helping to fill out the background of what come to be finer-grained problems in current experience.

Similarly, we can view the perception of a given tree as the result of a rather complex process of becoming familiar with an initially unfamiliar situation, namely, of coming to terms with some unidentified locus of features in one's immediate environment. This will generally be part of some larger process of exploring and otherwise moving through a given spatiotemporal terrain. Once that locus of features is identified as an individual instance of a familiar kind of thing (namely, a tree), it gains the status of being an objective, unitary part of the background taken for granted in the course of further exploring the given terrain. The apprehension of that tree as a tree becomes incorporated into your subsequent behavior, constituting a short-term habit, but a habit nonetheless, in the sense that it constrains and otherwise helps to establish your subsequent behavior in regard to that particular object in that part of the world.

This account of habit formation has as much to do with the modification or re-formation of habits in the course of ongoing experience. But it does allow that habits, in the usual sense of that term, can be formed or re-formed on the basis of singular experiences, that is, without need for repetition. One could, for example, gain the habit of avoiding open flames on the basis of a single painful experience of being burned. The point that is especially interesting in this regard is that it is habits which make consistently coherent (e.g., repetitive) behavior possible, not the other way around:

> Habits are the basis of organic learning. According to the theory of independent successive units of excitation-reaction, habit-formation can mean only the increasing fixation of certain ways of behavior through repetition, and an attendant weakening of other behavioral activities.
>
> Developmental behavior shows, on the other hand, that in the higher organisms excitations are so diffusely linked with reactions that the sequel is affected by the state of the organism in relation to environment. In habit and learning the linkage is tightened up not by sheer repetition but by the institution of effective integrated interaction of organic-environing energies—the consummatory close of activities of exploration and search. In organisms of the higher order, the special and more definite pattern of recurrent behavior thus formed does not become completely rigid. It enters as a factorial agency, along with other patterns, in a total adaptive response, and hence retains a certain amount of flexible capacity to undergo further modifications as the organism meets new environing conditions. (Dewey 1938, pp. 31–2)

Indeed, singular one-time behaviors, though they have never occurred before, can nevertheless be attributed to the operation of habit: "A man with the habit of giving way to anger may show his habit by a murderous attack upon someone who has offended. His act is nonetheless due to habit because it occurs only once in his life" (Dewey 1922, p. 42).

To understand how habits are formed, one has to understand the general features of inquiry, since inquiry *is* in effect the determination and stabilization of viable manners of conduct in concrete situations. In the next two chapters we will examine the basic pattern of inquiry as Dewey explained it. It turns out that inquiry is, in part, "cyclical" and therefore repetitive, but in the sense that an inquirer considers possibilities, tests them, reconsiders, tests again, etc., until some sort of stable result is attained. Inquiry in this sense could be said to involve a sort of conditioning, but in the context of solving some problem by successively modifying conditions, not just repeating them.

> The view that habits are formed by mere repetition puts the cart before the horse. Ability to repeat [e.g., to know one's way around a new city, or to see a tree as a familiar kind of object] is a result of a formation of a habit through the organic predispositions effected by attainment of a consummatory close. This modification is equivalent to giving some definite direction of future actions. As far as environing conditions remain the same, the resulting act will look like a repetition of a previously performed act. But even then repetition will not be exact as far as conditions differ. Sheer repetition is, in the case of the human organism, the product of conditions that are uniform because they have been made so mechanically—as in much school and factory "work." Such habits are limited in their manifestation to the rather artificial conditions in which they operate. They certainly do not provide the model upon which a theory of habit formation and operation should be framed. (Dewey 1938, pp. 32–3)

It follows that appealing, as Russell does, to "the causal law according to which frequent simultaneity generates a habit" explains little or nothing about what generates a habit. In Dewey's view, it is inquiry (or noncognitive stimulus/response proto-inquiry) which generates habits, characterized by a cyclical pattern of designing and testing possible modes of conduct in concrete situations characterized by need or felt deficiencies. Even pigeons, dogs, and other animals used in standard conditioning experiments learn behaviors only as ways of feeding themselves, avoiding pain, or otherwise satisfying felt needs. Inquiry moves through various phases, from "stimulus" to "response," and the eventual result is the formation of a habit which, with some degree of plasticity and sensitivity to changing conditions, constrains subsequent conduct.[10]

---

[10]See also Dewey 1911/1933, p. 117, for another statement of this view of habit formation.

The divergence between Dewey and Russell on the nature of habits and perception is obviously pronounced. Dewey's theory of perception will be discussed further in the next section, but the point of the present discussion is to see how Russell's theory of habit formation is geared to a different conception of "objects" than is Dewey's.

With hindsight we can more objectively evaluate the metaphysical agenda underlying Russell's views. By 1940, Russell's epistemology was designed to accommodate, and was otherwise secondary to, an already established view of logic which imposes certain constraints on how to think about objects. Russell's "unconscious [Fregean] metaphysic" requires *positing* a full-blown universe of objects because that is how the formal apparatus of predicate logic is designed. Russell was pressed to make epistemology and metaphysics accommodate this formal setup, initially geared as it was to the needs of mathematics rather than of natural language and ordinary experience. Extrapolating this framework to ordinary experience was allegedly a straightforward affair. So we hear something like the following: "The universe is carved up into objects, each having in fact many properties and standing in many relations; and we can directly discern such facts simply by opening our eyes and paying attention. And sometimes we may want to consider a restricted universe of objects. (And now that that's settled, let's get down to doing some serious logic and be done with this Hegelian silliness.)"

The irony is that Dewey's logical theory can provide the sort of conceptual framework Russell would like to be able to work with,[11] but from the perspective of an independently motivated epistemology. Each situation, if and when it is sufficiently determinate to contain discriminable objects, generates universes of discourse. Dewey's theory of properties and relations is more refined than Russell's (see Section 5.2 below), but Russell's extensionalist scheme can be

---

[11]This is a claim I would have to argue for in detail elsewhere, but see Section 6.2 for further discussion of Deweyan logic and formal semantics.

embedded, at least superficially, in a Deweyan framework. What is distinctive about Dewey's approach is that he provides a framework for talking about the generation and transformation of universes of discourse, and of transitions from one to the other, claiming that this sort of concern is a crucial part of the subject matter of logic. In any given instance in the course of an inquiry, but especially as things start to settle out in a stable way, one may take the present state of things as providing one or more domains of discourse in some classical model-theoretic sense—but it would be ludicrous to confine logic to the study of such instances independent of their context in inquiry, once existence of such contexts is acknowledged.

The alternative view of objects and domains of discourse which Dewey presented will be discussed in more detail as we proceed, but by no means adequately. His view is decidedly operationalistic, but in an unprecedented manner which calls for careful analysis. For now, we can say simply that so far as ground-level logical theory is concerned, instead of requiring a fixed universe of objects, Dewey's primitive notions include "modes of action" or "operations" (relative to and constitutive of some given organism/environment system) and their qualitative "results"; and he builds up a theory of objects and properties on the basis of those notions.

It is worth mentioning here that, once Dewey became acquainted in the 1940s with Tarski's work, the one thing that Dewey found most questionable was Tarski's taking the notion of "objects" as primitive in his definitions of logical satisfaction and truth. Dewey did not pursue it at length, but some of what little he did say about Tarski's views can be found in the correspondence with Bentley (Ratner et al. 1964, pp. 251, 587–8).

At a foundational level, domains of logical objects are not just given once and for all (which is *not* to say that a world full of "things in themselves" is not out there, independent of the experiencer), but rather it is assumed that nonabsolute domains of objects of various kinds, limited in scope on the basis of the capabilities of the given agent, will be progressively uncovered and otherwise determined in the course of and as a result of each inquiry. This evolving "universe of experience" corresponds to what Dewey (1938, p. 68) means by the *situation* unique to a given inquiry.

From this operation-based perspective, different (kinds of) agents classify and categorize things differently depending on those agents' different repertoires of ways of acting in the world. Ordinary perception, for instance, involves processes of interaction among an agent's perceptual systems, things in the world, and various connecting media, both in the world and in the agent, by means of which information is conveyed here and there. A frog's eye works differently from a human's eye, and consequently, if for no other reason, these two kinds of agents surely see the world differently, even if they are "eying" the very same piece of it. Exactly how they see the world differently is not something we can properly address here, if at all. But the point is that how we classify things in the world depends on how we are able to interact with things in the world, that is, on how the various elements of our ecological constitution work. When some concrete thing appears to us as being of some kind or having some property or belonging to some class or category, it is because our interactions with it are yielding the appropriate sorts of evidence characteristic of that kind, property, class, or category as determined (as *constituted*) by established habits. When we assert that something is of a certain kind (etc.), we are thereby committed to a range of possible evidence, based on our own operational capabilities, where different sorts of interactions with that thing should yield specific sorts of data.

An individual concrete object in a given situation, then, is a locus of coherent activity fitting specifications of some given habit (whether long-standing or newly formed). This activity will reflect a certain dynamic perspective on some real aspect or feature of the world—a peach, a dog, a cloud, the sky, the weather, or whatever. Concrete objects moreover will often be *stable* loci of activity. Stability is neither guaranteed nor required, but objects will generally have to exhibit some such stability in order to be around long enough to serve as subject matters of perception or discourse. It follows that the account of semantic models for (natural) languages which this framework supports does not require or assume fixed domains of objects. Rather, semantic models would be determined by modes of action, not by which particular objects these actions might evidence. This will allow that individual objects (and types of objects?) can be created or dispensed with or discovered or lost without necessarily changing the basic features of a given model—in some sense of the term 'model' yet to be clarified. In this view, semantic theory does not require an independent metaphysical account of what objects are, nor does it require a once-and-for-all taxonomical inventory of objects in the world. It is taken for granted that there *are* things in the world, and the world will support sustained interactions whereby individual things can be evidenced.

In effect, by developing his theory of habit formation and perception as he did, including in particular the distinction between the excitation/reaction and stimulus/response distinctions, Dewey was essentially, if perhaps intuitively, pursuing a strategy for avoiding the "frame problem" (as formulated in current AI research; see McCarthy and Hayes 1969; Ginsberg 1987) before it was even seen as a problem by most logicians (Dewey 1922, pp. 199ff). It is somewhat ironic that Hume (1748), over two hundred years ago, was pressing a similar point by arguing that neither immediate "impressions" nor "demonstrative reasoning" can account for those "operations of thought" which guide our everyday actions in the world. One must introduce a third element into the psychology of belief and action, namely, habit or custom. Dewey and Hume differ, of course, in their accounts of what habits are and how they might work to constitute the operations of thought. In working out a "hydrodynamic" view of belief (thinking metaphorically in terms of the steam-powered technology of his day), Hume characterized habits of association as results of experiencing "constant conjunctions" of events (which is essentially the view echoed by Russell, quoted above on page 67). Unfortunately, Hume's overly simple empiricist picture of experience compelled a retreat into skepticism. This is not the case for Dewey, who developed a naturalistic and constructive theory of experience that presupposed an account of habits in the first place.

Dewey's response to Hume is not unlike Kant's, preserving Kant's Copernican Revolution in epistemology but formulated in naturalistic rather than "transcendental-idealist" terms. Working from a Darwinian perspective, Dewey characterized habits as results of stabilization processes in concrete situations. This characterization supports a theory of objects, facts, and warranted belief that already takes for granted an intrinsically dynamic view of experience guided by established habit. In other words, habits (like Kant's forms of intuition) are a necessary "condition" of experience, not something in addition to it. This difference aside, both Dewey and Hume saw habits as natural features of ongoing experience, constraining our reasoning but not typically being products of reasoning (alone, or as applied to given empirical data).

3.3   Ecological Psychology and Direct Perception

Before responding to the charge that Dewey's logic is psychologistic, in this section I will focus on connections between Dewey's views on perception and recent developments in ecological psychology as developed by J. J. Gibson and others over the last few decades. The point of this comparison is to consider the previous discussion of objects from a psychological perspective and to otherwise discuss the relevance of Dewey's views to psychology, without having to conclude that Dewey's view of logic is psychologistic.

If we must put a label on Dewey's particular approach to logic, we would want to say that it is not psychologistic but "ecologistic." That this term is appropriate should be obvious from our previous discussion. It is also suggested by the fact that Dewey's views are similar in many respects with so-called ecological psychology, a twentieth-century movement in psychology inspired by the work of J. J. Gibson (1966, 1971, 1977, 1979, 1982).

Gibson's views are frequently criticized because he endorsed a theory of direct perception. This negative reaction is largely due to some confusion about what it means to say that perception is "direct." The following discussion will suggest a way to avoid this confusion by appealing to some ideas found in Dewey's logical theory.

In contrast with a classical empiricist view of perception (involving so-called sense data, sense impressions, stimulations of nerve endings, irritations of body surfaces, and so forth), ecological psychology emphasizes a different array of theoretical concepts: one being the concept of "invariants" and another the concept of "affordances." These are basic elements in a theory of perception which purposely does not appeal to manipulations of internal representations or to mental computational processes in any fundamental way.

Ecological psychology treats the perceiving agent as a dynamic organism/environment system, continually engaged in various sorts of actions designed for exploring the world and utilizing its resources. Controlled sampling of the world gives evidence of possible uses of things (and of ways to orchestrate subsequent actions) by virtue of the agent's being attuned to lawlike relations which involve organismic and environmental variables and which govern stable associations of different sorts of possible experiences.

These lawlike relations are referred to as *invariants*. And perception, then, is not just a matter of registering data, but is a process of interacting with things in terms of their *possible uses* (or *affordances*, as Gibson would say) as determined by such lawlike relations to which the agent has become attuned. An agent does not construct and process representations in the head, but rather experiences the world directly by virtue of such attunements, insofar as the agent *is* nothing more nor less than a dynamic integration of constrained organism/environment interactions. Ecological psychologists focus their efforts on the discovery and investigation of such ecological invariants, i.e., lawlike relations at an ecological level of organization of living systems (see, for instance, Turvey, Shaw, Reed, and Mace 1981).

Critics of ecological psychology often question this commitment to the idea that perception is direct (e.g., Fodor and Pylyshyn 1981). The idea that perception is not mediated by internal mental processes seems to be at odds with recent cognitive psychology and

AI research geared to a mind/computer metaphor. Opponents of ecological psychology insist that some sort of internal computational *mediation* must be involved in processes of perception. How else are we to explain our experience of Necker cubes, duck-rabbit figures, or other visual-gestalt puzzles which clearly evidence a "projective" aspect of perception? Marr's *Vision* (1982) or Pylyshyn's *Computation and Cognition* (1984), for instance, include good expositions of this view that perception requires some sort of "construction of enriched representations through the 'epistemic mediation' of knowledge, expectations, memories, or inferences." Perception in this view is *not* direct, insofar as it involves such internal computational mechanisms and processes.

This disagreement about the nature of perception echoes some aspects of the debate between Dewey and Russell presently under discussion. Specifically with regard to the question concerning the direct versus indirect character of perception, notice first that Dewey and Russell both claim that perception is in some sense direct. Their disagreement concerns what it *means* to make such a claim.

The conversation between Russell and Dewey goes something like the following. Russell asserts that at least some knowledge is immediate and basic, consisting of atomic sensory experiences. Dewey, meanwhile, wants to say that all knowledge is the result of directly experiencing things in the world; but such experience is *mediated* by established habits and so is not properly said to be "immediate." Dewey's main charge against Russell is that sensations by themselves do not count as pieces of knowledge, though they have a role to play in achieving knowledge. Russell charges in return that if no piece of knowledge can be simple and direct, then any piece of knowledge must be inaccessibly holistic. And that is essentially the extent of the discussion.

So the two were talking past each other. But it is worth noting that Russell was advocating a view of direct perception that is now generally considered unworkable (see Fodor and Pylyshyn 1981). The arguments usually arrayed against the claim that perception is direct are in fact arguments against this Russellian view of direct perception. See, for instance, Perkins 1983 for a carefully constructed philosophical discussion in this vein.

On the other hand, Dewey's (and Gibson's) views are immune to these criticisms. That is, in line with Dewey's distinguishing excitations and reactions versus stimuli and responses, notice that there is a more refined set of distinctions involved in the current debate about direct perception than is generally realized. It is simplistic to see this issue as concerned with whether or not perception is mediated by mental or computational processes. There are instead two questions here. There is the question of whether perception is immediate or not. This is the question painstakingly addressed by Perkins (1983), who thought by mistake that he was arguing against a Gibsonian view of perception. But second, on the assumption that it is not immediate, there is the question of just *what* it is which mediates perception.

First of all, if ecological psychology is on the right track, we should think of sense impressions as something other than simply pointillistic stimulations of nerve endings. We should think of them as local, temporary stabilities, registered as results of the operations of sensory systems. Even the simplest immediate sensory stimulation, in this case, is a registration of particular concrete constancies, as immediate results of automatic "averaging" processes or some such thing.

This builds a kind of temporal stability into a theory of perception at the most basic level of analysis, without the need to view the world statically. The idea that one registers particular *constancies* rather than pointillistic nerve firings presupposes in the first place a capacity for controlled variation of one's interactions with the world, in the course of which stable features of things can be evidenced. Rather than static sense data, on the basis of which an internal picture of the world is constructed and processed and used to initiate behaviors, these constancies are usable *products* of ongoing processes of interacting with and exploring the world.

We should think of such stabilities as basic building blocks of perception; but these alone do not constitute instances of perception, atomic or otherwise. Such sense impressions are as immediate to experience as anything can be, though they are *results* of controlled organism/environment interactions. Immediate sensory stimulations, in this light, would be what Dewey refers to as "excitations." Though causally complex, they are *psychologically* simple and existentially immediate, treated as functional primitives in a theory of experience.

Invariants, on the other hand, are lawlike relations among different dimensions or modes of activity (involving social and cultural as well as physical and biological factors in a full account of these matters). According to ecological psychologists, these are the proper focus of the psychology of perception, as opposed to a study of sensory data and internal representational computation. Invariants, at an ecological rather than merely "physical" level of behavior, are such as to be *embodied* or *engrained* in the agent (not necessarily "cognized"), constituting the basic gears and drivetrains of what Dewey refers to as "organic mechanisms of retention and habit." That an organism/environment system is attuned to this or that invariant is simply to say that its constitution has been organized (by evolution, education, etc.) to accommodate and exploit that lawlike relation. Rather than a computer program that takes sensory inputs and produces correct behavioral outputs, an invariant is more like a function that constrains courses of events in a domain of organism/environment conditions as a whole—i.e., inputs as well as outputs are distributed across both the organism and the environment in question. Hopefully this kind of setup is amenable to computational simulation, and there is no reason in principle why robotic machinery cannot be built using ecological design principles; but this is not the kind of information-processing setup one traditionally finds in the AI literature.

As an illustration, consider examples such as birds diving to catch prey, pilots landing airplanes, drivers approaching red traffic lights, or long jumpers approaching a takeoff board. Lee (1980) outlines a general treatment of cases where a moving agent has to be able to perceive its precise distance from some looming object and act appropriately. It is essential in these cases neither to stop short nor to plow abruptly into the approaching object. How do such agents know the time of contact so precisely, particularly in the many cases where the dynamics of the situation are so fast-moving as to not allow for extended "computations" involving internal representations of changing external circumstances?

We need not go into the details here, but Lee's relatively short paper describes several lawlike relations involving various retinal parameters (such as distances and speeds of retinal excitations) and various environmental variables (such as distances and speeds of environmental objects). Lee presents these lawlike relations by way of a surprisingly simple geometrical argument.

The analysis Lee outlines is arguably one of the best illustrations of what ecological psychologists mean by "invariants," though he would be the first to admit that his model is somewhat *too* simple in its details. Unlike invariants such as Newton's law of gravitation in a two-body point-mass system, which involves purely environmental variables, the equations which Lee presents include *both* organismic and environmental parameters. The ecological "laws" represented by these equations do not describe what a bird's brain *computes* in preparing to land on a tree limb, any more than Newtonian physics presupposes some cosmic computer calculating numerical values of relevant variables prior to or separate from moving physical objects around in an orderly fashion. A planet just moves, directly manifesting lawlike behavior which physicists attempt to model mathematically in order to understand that motion and the principles of natural orderliness it evidences. Similarly, an agent just perceives; and Lee's equations purport to model the natural orderliness manifested in those organism/environment interactions, involving features of the world at large as well as features characteristic of the given agent's constitution.

The problem of knowing precise times-to-contact will have been solved not by independent computational processes carried out in each particular case, but rather in general by a natural evolutionary process which has structured the organism/environment system so as to fit the specifications of, i.e., to be attuned to, such lawlike relations.[12]

Such capabilities or manners of perceptual competence are more than just computational, in Marr's sense (1982) or in any other sense that does not include environmental activities as an integral part of the "computations." Not that he deserves to be singled out, but Marr did not understand properly what information processing is, which led him to seriously underestimate the ecological complexity of vision and the consequent subtlety that is necessary in describing it. To see is to know what is where by looking, but this is not to say that vision is the process of discovering from images what is present in the world (Marr 1982, p. 3). The detection of and attunement to invariants is exactly and precisely an information-processing problem, but Marr vastly underrated the amount and range of organism/environment machinery that is involved in such processes. The information processing involved in vision and probably any other kind of natural perceptual activity is not simply "data processing" or "image processing" (Marr 1982, pp. 29–30). The information processing involved in visual perception is not carried out simply over representations in the eyes and head, but is an orderly activity taking place as much in the environment as in the head. Ecological laws of perception purport to describe this orderliness, and as such to directly describe perceptual processes.

The point that examples like Lee's help to make is that perception occurs not simply by registering and transducing arrays of sense impressions, but by virtue of the fact that the barrage of sense impressions which one is registering accords with this or that invariant to which one is attuned. Recognition of familiar objects, e.g., looming objects, is in this regard spontaneous and direct, by virtue of the stability and continued operability of such attunements.

This notion of attunement is what lies behind Gibson's notion

---

[12]Other examples of ecological invariants can be found in Turvey, Shaw, Reed, and Mace 1981, an article written in reply to Fodor and Pylyshyn 1981.

of *affordances*. It is by virtue of our attunements to invariants that we recognize objects as familiar objects from one concrete situation to the next. We recognize objects primarily in terms of the modes of interaction they allow, that is, in terms of their "unattained possibilities," as Dewey would put it:

> What a physical event immediately is, and what it *can* do ... are distinct and incommensurable. But when an event has meaning, its potential consequences become its integral and funded feature. When the potential consequences are important and repeated, they form the very nature and essence of a thing, its defining, identifying, and distinguishing form. To recognize the thing is to grasp its definition. Thus we become capable of perceiving things instead of merely feeling and having them. To *perceive* is to acknowledge unattained possibilities; it is to refer the present to consequences, apparition to issue, and thereby to behave in deference to the *connections* of events. As an attitude, perception or awareness is predictive expectancy, wariness. (Dewey 1926, p. 182)

The attunements underlying one's grasp of such "meaning" will include physical as well as social and cultural attunements developed from infancy over the course of extended and continuing experience.

Indeed, Dewey's answer to the frame problem (see page 82 above), stated in terms of perception processes, is that one's grasp of affordances guides sensory activities, and one continually monitors affordances in the context of testing prior affordances, not just on the basis of internal processing of sensory excitations given outside of some such context. Like the riddle of induction in scientific inquiry, the frame problem is rather special and odd; it is not a prominent or typical feature of ordinary perception. The monitoring of affordances and the guidance of sensory activity is a dynamic, interactive, embedded affair where the problem is not how to grasp affordances solely on the basis of given sense impressions (where we get an underdetermination problem as well as a persistence problem) but how to *re*formulate one's grasp of current affordances, based on given sense impressions *and* on a prior grasp of affordances which were guiding one's sensory activities in the first place.

A proper response to the frame problem is not a matter of explaining in some principled way how or when to stop sensing and do something like inductive inferencing and vice versa. The usual unembedded view of intelligence works with some manner of internal information processing divorced from acting, only to be stuck with the problem of how to fit the two together. This translates into a problem of deciding when to stop acting and start figuring out or deciding how best to act, and how to stop such decision processes and start acting, and back and forth it goes. The theoretical and technical difficulties of this view are familiar by now. An ecological theory of perception offers an alternative picture. We do not really stop acting while engaged in "information processing," nor do we stop processing information while engaged in action. The two are inextricably bound up with one another in living agents. The problem is not in deciding which action to perform based on given data; but rather the ongoing task of perception lies in deciding how to maintain and modify current actions, based on the stream of results one is getting from current actions as well as on "unattained possibilities" indicated by one's attunements to regularities in one's interactions with the world.

In this regard, perceptions are not necessarily immediate, though they are a matter of directly experiencing the world, insofar as they are mediated by such attunements. That is to say, we should allow that perceptions are direct but not immediate. They are direct insofar as they are mediated, not by internal re-presentational processes connecting up inputs (sensations) and outputs (interpretations), but by some repertoire of established habits of the given agent by means of which objects are simply *pre*sented.

We should therefore distinguish three kinds of processes: (*a*) immediate stimulation, (*b*) inference, and (*c*) direct perception. The debate in current cognitive science literature bats around (*a*) and (*b*), and often confuses (*c*) for (*a*), not realizing that (*c*) is a third thing altogether different from either (*a*) or (*b*) alone or in combination.

When ecological psychologists talk about an agent's "attunements" to invariants and so forth, they must have in mind something like the following analogy, which we can use to informally explain this three-way distinction. We can think of perceptual systems as musical instruments, and we can think of perceiving objects in the world in the way we think about musical tunes being played on these instruments. We can distinguish (a) sounding a few notes, and (c) the playing of a tune as a constrained collage of sequences of note combinations. Perceiving an object is like (c) the playing of a tune—no representation is involved, but the tune is simply instantiated. More than just strings being plucked or notes being blown, the whole instrument functions in a complex, intricate, dynamic fashion. The structural and causal story one could tell about the playing of any given tune is complicated—all the different aspects of the instrument have to work together coherently in complex temporal sequences. But this complex dynamic process either just happens, involving the whole instrument all at once, or it doesn't happen at all. That all-at-once-ness of the instrument's involvement in playing the tune is the analogue here of the directness of perception. More than just causing sense impressions (plucking strings), the world "plays" objects on perceptual systems, in much the same way that a person plays tunes on musical instruments,

Playing a tune involves (a) some kind of ordered registration of sequences of note combinations, requiring that the instrument be structurally "(at)tuned" to the harmonic and rhythmic particulars of the given tune. A European piano cannot play certain traditional Japanese sounds, much less Japanese "tunes" (if that is even a meaningful thing to say), because it is not structured appropriately— not attuned in a way that is appropriate for traditional Japanese music. By analogy, a frog's visual system doesn't work like a human's and cannot sustain perceptions typical of a human, and vice versa. This is primarily the result of structural differences between a frog's visual system and a human's, having little or nothing to do with the probable fact that frogs don't think about what they do whereas humans do often think about what they do.

A musical instrument, in playing a tune, does not have to (b) manipulate representations of those sequences of note combinations.

Perhaps it stretches the analogy to try to make anything of this fact, namely, that a musical instrument does not represent sequences of chords to itself, mulling over representations of sequences of note combinations (e.g., musical scores), comparing and contrasting such representations, surveying the structure of given representations, creating new ones, and so forth. But this fact would seem to support the present point about the nonrepresentational character of perception. The instrument has to be able to instantiate instances of those sequences, but it need not represent them as part of playing the tune. Playing a tune is more than just (*a*) instantiating a few notes, but one need not (*b*) process representations of the tune in order to (*c*) instantiate the tune as such. Perception is like the mere instantiation of tunes, and the operational habituation of a perceptual system is like the structural "attunement" of the musical instrument by means of which they are instantiated.

The debate about whether perception is direct or not is based on the mistake of confusing the question of whether or not perception is mediated by internal representational processes with the question of whether or not it is mediated at all. Ecological psychologists and Dewey share the view that perception is not mediated by internal representational processes, which is not to hold that it is not mediated by *something*. Perception is mediated, rather, by established attunements to lawlike relations among ways of acting in the world, that is, by habits. Perception is direct in that (i) it does not require manipulations of internal representations, and (ii) it occurs as (or simply *is*) an integral part of coordinating the ongoing conduct of given agents in an integrated system encompassing both organismic and environmental activities.

This view suggests a shift in the focus of psychological theory construction—away from questions about internal/external correspondence and representation and toward a study of the more fundamental nature of organism/environment interactivity. While many critics of ecological psychology stress the importance of understanding the alleged role of internal representational processes in perception, it is just as reasonable to turn that around and argue that perception is an intrinsic and essential element of representation. The theoretical shift suggested by ecological psychology entails not that perception is mediated by representational processes, but to the contrary, that representational abilities are dependent on and driven by perceptual processes. One must first understand the ecological character of perception before one can begin to presume to know what is even meant by "internal representational processing." (This perspective on perception and representation is pursued further in Chapter 5.)

The computer-functionalist position which Fodor and Pylyshyn defend is more than just a theory of perception. It holds that mental experience in general is just such internal representational processing. This is a dominant view in recent philosophy of mind, subsequent to the invention of computers, which is nevertheless a variation on a recurrent philosophical theme where mind and subjectivity are placed at the heart of human nature and perceptual experience is something happening somewhere (somehow) at its outer reaches.

Quine's web metaphor (1951) is a version of this perspective on the nature of mind. The direct-perception position, in effect, wants to turn this web inside out. What is at the *periphery* in Quine's analogy, namely, the interaction of the agent with the rest of the world, is *central* in an ecological framework. Thinking is not performed "internally" and quasi-independently of this interaction. As a relatively recent natural phenomenon with a long evolutionary history, "mind" is instead a particular species or manner of agent/world interaction (designed primarily to handle invariants involving communication and the coordination of group conduct, as it turns out; but that is another story).

In this regard, the distinction between "direct" and "indirect" should not be treated as a distinction between "immediate" and "processed." The debate over whether perception is direct or indirect is rather a debate about what is central and what is peripheral to the constitution of intelligent agents.

In this view, when pressed about the nature of mind and thinking, as opposed to perception, we would find that we cannot think of the human mind as an entity separate from an environment. Perception and cognition in general do not happen somewhere up in the head, but rather they involve an interactive information-processing mesh that cuts across a simplistic organism/environment distinction. Thinking, as opposed to mere information processing, is a kind of organism/environment interaction in its own right, as a process of rehearsal of possibilities and formation of plans, that runs parallel with noncognitive (e.g., perceptual) activities that also constitute the organism/environment agent. Just as one does not stop acting in order to process sensory impressions so as to perceive things, one does not stop acting in order to think. Thinking is instead a kind of reflective monitoring and manipulation of ongoing activities. This dynamic correspondence between thought and action is further outlined in Section 5.1 below. We have to understand mentality as a feature not of brains or organisms, but of agents consisting of organisms embedded in environments. This would require an information-processing view of mind which takes the mind out of the brain alone and embeds it also in the world. As a feature or characteristic of an organism/environment system, mentality is essentially and fundamentally and directly driven as much by regularities and forces in the world as in the head.

On this view, an ecological perspective on mind and perception need not be antirepresentational. Dewey was a representationalist of a sort but in a sense different from the way, for instance, Fodor is. The notion of representation was not theoretically fundamental for Dewey even though it was an important idea that played a definite role in his logical theory and in his philosophy of mind. We do not want to give up the notion of representation, but we do want to give up Fodor's way of using it in a theory of perception. The point is not to eliminate a concern for representation and correspondence but to give a different, ecologically grounded account of such matters. Representation is something to be accounted for—the fact that we represent things to ourselves and to others is undeniable—but as such the notion of representation does not have to be the starting point for a theory of perception. An ecological philosophy of mind will yield a possibly unusual account of representation (of facts), correspondence (e.g., of thoughts and facts), and so forth, but it will involve a shift in what is traditionally taken to be theoretically basic.

It is true that, in developing an ecological view of mind, Gibson overstated certain claims against a representationalist, information-processing perspective in psychology. But he was reacting to versions of that perspective which entailed an internalist view of mind. In opposing an information-processing or computational view of mind, it should be kept in mind that what Gibson meant by that in the 1960s and 1970s is not necessarily what we mean by it today. Effken and Shaw (1992) outline an approach to robotics that shows how far ecological psychology has come since Gibson's work in the 1970s when the optimistic claims by AI researchers were still way out of control and Gibson's counterclaims were equally and unnecessarily extreme. Similarly, Gibson might sound as if he would like to have any reference to cognition eliminated from psychology altogether, which of course is absurd. But we could also take him to be saying that psychology should not take for granted unanalyzed cognitive notions, since that just begs the question. This is not to say that there is no room for cognition and mentality in Gibson's view, but simply that references to such things cannot be just pulled out of a hat as needed. The same goes for representation—it is something to be explained, and only then is it something that can be used to explain other things. Perhaps this is a more sympathetic way of reading Gibson than many would care to allow, but his work makes more sense that way. Representation, computation, internal processing, cognition, mentality, etc., need not be eliminated in an ecological approach to psychology, but only put in proper perspective.

3.4 Experience and Subjectivity

The two previous sections addressed Dewey's theory of perception and the perspectival nature of objects, and the section prior to those addressed the mistake of using the words 'existence' and 'reality' interchangeably. We will now consider the charge that Dewey's logic and epistemology is subjectivistic.

It was claimed that what plays the part of a universe of discourse in Dewey's view is a "situation," which he refers to occasionally as a "universe of experience" and which is otherwise very definitely agent-relative and yet constitutes the range of what "exists" in a given inquiry. Even if it is understood that what "exists" in a given situation is not what is unreservedly "real" from an absolute perspective, and if logic is concerned with what "exists" in this sense and not with "reality," then, call it what you may, logic in this view is concerned not with "the truth" but with something which seems very much of the agent's own making. Dewey's view begins to sound psychologistic, idealistic, subjectivistic, even solipsistic.

It is to Dewey's credit that he was able to avoid these positions in his logical theory without buying into what one might assume is the only alternative, namely, a "Russellian-Fregean metaphysic." Granted, psychologistic logic, as defended for instance by Mill (in *A System of Logic*) in the nineteenth century and as effectively criticized and rejected by Husserl and Frege, is unacceptable. "A proposition may be thought, and again it may be true; never confuse these two things" (Frege 1884, Introduction). Or the allegedly subjectivistic character of Kant's transcendental idealism (in whatever sense that, e.g., *space* and *time* are "in us") is equally unacceptable as the basis of a theory of logic. But to go to the other extreme to conclude that psychology, epistemology, and related concerns have nothing at all to do with logic is neither acceptable nor necessary. Dewey was able to maintain an even keel in this regard.[13]

Russell's initial criticisms along these lines (1939, pp. 147–9) revolve around thinking of inquiry as "the allaying of *doubt*." First,

---

[13]It could be argued that it is Russell's views which are more in line with a psychologistic position. For instance, Carnap (1950, pp. 26–7) criticized Russell's empiricist characterization of propositions as "mental events." See also Coffa 1991, chap. 5, and Kaplan 1989a, pp. 603–4 (quoted on page 247 below), for similar discussions of the psychologistic character of logical-empiricist treatments of sense data. This issue will be addressed further in Chapter 5 below.

Russell draws an analogy between the removal of doubt and the allaying of hunger, stressing that the latter is a bodily concern while the former is a mental and even intellectual process. He does not quite attribute this characterization of inquiry to Dewey, though he suggests that it "seems" to be his position. Admittedly, Peirce (1877) characterizes inquiry as the removal of doubt and, concomitantly, as the "fixation of belief." Dewey fully acknowledged his indebtedness to Peirce in regard to making inquiry a primary concern of logic. But if inquiry is simply a matter of being rid of an uncomfortable attitude like doubt, then suicide or perhaps enough alcohol, Russell points out, would seem to be among the more effective means of inquiry. "To say that one man is a better inquirer than another can only mean that he allays more doubts, even if he does so by a brass band and ingenious spot-lighting. All this is not what Dr. Dewey means; but if it is not to follow from what he says, inquiry will have to have some goal other than the removal of doubt."

One of Dewey's own accounts of the mistake of defining inquiry as the removal of doubt can be found in *The Quest for Certainty* (1929, pp. 227–8). In the latter book, he explains how his epistemology *avoids* a subjectivist bias precisely by organizing it around the notion of inquiry: "The fundamental advantage of framing our account of the organs and processes of knowing on the pattern of what occurs in experimental inquiry is that nothing is introduced save what is objective and is accessible to examination and report" (1929, p. 229).

Nevertheless Dewey does at times consider the special case of inquiry where the initial indeterminacy is (or is accompanied by) an attitude of doubt. "If inquiry begins in doubt, it terminates in the institution of conditions which remove the need for doubt." For Dewey, this is not a definition of inquiry, but a conditional statement about a particular sort of inquiry, namely, the sort which "begins in doubt." But Russell suggests that this passage provides a solution to the problem inherent in defining inquiry as removal of doubt (implying, mistakenly, that this is how Dewey defined it).

Namely, if we think of inquiry instead as the removal of the *need* for doubt, then this anchors matters in objective facts. The need for doubt exists as much in worldly conditions as it does in the agent's inability to discern what those conditions are. If you get in your car and it will not start, then, regardless of your state of mind, there is "need for doubt" that it is working properly and that it does not need fixing. The subsequent inquiry in this case would be as much a matter of determining objective facts about the car as a matter of alleviating your doubts about what to do. Granted, claims Russell, the inquiry may be mere trial and error, "like that of an animal trying to get out of a cage, and may have just as little intellectual content." But Dewey would be able in this way to avoid the charge of subjectivism.

This line of reasoning is an interesting maneuver on Russell's part since his suggestion of how to salvage Dewey's position against the charge of subjectivism ultimately serves as the groundwork for an attack on a pragmatist notion of truth. Russell proceeds to address pragmatists' emphasis on consequences of actions, in the end claiming that, in the pragmatist view, "A hypothesis is 'true' when it leads the person entertaining it to acts which have effects that he desires." So while suggesting how to salvage the notion of inquiry, he manages to build some kind of subjectivism back into Dewey's alleged views—namely, into what he claims is Dewey's theory of truth—in the form of "satisfaction of desires" as a measure of truth. These matters are discussed further in Sections 5.1 and 6.1 below.

Dewey's reply in the Schilpp volume to the charge that his view is subjectivistic occurs in basically two places, one of these consisting in some general remarks about "the dualisms forming the stock problems of modern epistemological theory" (Dewey 1939a, pp. 523–7), while the other is addressed directly to Russell's discussion of inquiry as the removal of doubt (pp. 571–2).

As for the former, it should go without saying that the subjectivism Russell argues against is inherent in his own reading of Dewey, not in Dewey's actual position. Referring to the initial phase of inquiry as "doubt" is too narrow for the level of generality at which Dewey is working. Focusing exclusively the way Russell does on doubt may be more or less in line with some of Peirce's remarks about inquiry when taken out of context and forced into a Deweyan mold. But this is not Dewey's conception of inquiry, despite the fact that his theory of inquiry was derived in part from Peirce's views (Dewey 1938, p. 9n). It allows Russell to import a subjectivistic bias into the discussion, which he then attributes to Dewey, but which Dewey in fact successfully avoided.

Russell implicitly assumes a strict subject/object duality (Russell 1939, pp. 139–40, 143–4), apparently with no cognizance of the fact that such a duality is one of the central issues at hand, not a given fact. Rather than a minor detail to be taken for granted, Dewey was developing a view in which this duality would be dissolved. There are perhaps elements of what Dewey says about situations and experience which would allow a confirmed dualist to see a kind of subjectivism there, but that would be based on a failure to appreciate Dewey's aim. Replying to other contributors to the Schilpp volume besides Russell, Dewey writes:

> It is to me a very curious fact that some of my critics take for granted a mentalistic view of experience; so they cannot help attributing to me that view when I speak of experience. In addition they so largely ignore the difficulties inherent in their own subjectivism:— difficulties that are recognized by Santayana, and that drive him into complete skepticism, tempered by a sudden and unmediated practical jump of pure faith into the things of nature—a kind of arbitrary pragmatism from which I shrink. (Dewey 1939a, p. 526)

One finds over and over again in *Logic* and in Dewey's other writings an insistence that we should let go of outmoded ways of thinking that, though they have played a major role in our intellectual history, yield unresolvable difficulties. Two such problems in particular, says Dewey, have plagued the development of modern thought. One is the lack of integration between our beliefs about the world, particularly as affected by natural science, and our beliefs "about the values and purposes that should guide [our] conduct." The other concerns our lack of a proper understanding of the relation between the world as science describes it and the world as we have it in ordinary experience (Dewey 1939a, pp. 523–4). A case in point is Locke's difficulties in getting philosophical flesh to stick to the bones of Newtonian physics.

> It [the second problem] involves, however, a somewhat distinctive set of [more technical] problems, connected with the pre-experimental and pre-technological leisure class tradition, according to which the characteristic object of knowledge has a privileged position of correspondence with what is ultimately "real," in contrast to things of non-cognitive experiences, which form the great bulk of "ordinary experiences." Most of the dualisms forming the stock problems of modern epistemological theory have originated, as I have tried to show, out of the assumptions which generate these two problems. If, however, the philosophical theory of experience is brought up to date by acknowledgment of the standpoint and conclusions of scientific biology and cultural anthropology and of the import of the experimental method in knowing, these problems, I have argued, are "solved" by recognition that they depend on premises inherited from traditions now shown to be false. Some of the gratuitous dualisms done away with, I have argued, are those of the objective and subjective, the real and apparent, the mental and physical, scientific physical objects and objects of perception, things of experience and things-in-themselves concealed behind experience, the latter being an impenetrable veil which prevents cognitive access to the things of nature. (Dewey 1939a, pp. 523–4)

The problem is not simply a matter of being unable to reconcile "the objective" and "the subjective" but rather consists in having separated cognitive experience from other modes of experience to begin with, leading in different hands either to a disparagement of the latter or else, in an effort to justify the latter, to "assertion of a super-scientific, supra-empirical transcendent *a priori* realm." The error is not with recognizing the special character of cognitive experience but rather with the idea of *isolating* it and then either underestimating or overestimating its "access to the things of nature" in contrast with ordinary experience more generally. As distinct from subjectivistic psychology,

[t]he biological-anthropological method of approach to experience provides the way out of mentalistic into behavioral interpretation of experiencing, both in general and in its detailed manifestations. With equal necessity and pertinency, it points the way out of the belief that experience as such is cognitional and that cognition is the sole path that leads into the natural world. Anybody who accepts the socio-biological point of view is bound, I think, to raise sooner or later the questions I put forward in *Studies in Logical Theory* about the relations between dominantly esthetic, moral and affectional modes and subject-matters of experience and the cognitional mode and its subject-matter.... I believe the conclusion of any serious analysis will make the cognitional mode intermediate between an earlier, less organized, more confused and fragmentary sort of experienced subject-matter and one more ordered, clearer, freer, richer, and under better control as to its occurrence. (Dewey 1939a, p. 526)

These remarks reflect Dewey's emphasis on the *continuity* between our biological and cognitive natures—not a reducibility of one to the other, but a continuity which calls for a constructive rather than a reductive theoretical treatment. In this regard, cognitive experience is an integral part of the broader experience otherwise referred to as inquiry (inquiry understood in biological and anthropological terms). Cognitive modes of experience cannot be understood in isolation from their function in inquiry. Cognitive modes of experience are instead intermediary modes of experience brought to bear in processes of stabilization and reintegration of disordered organismic and environmental forces. This is not to say that all inquiry involves cognitive activities, but where the latter do occur, it is in service to carrying out specific inquiries.

In two later paragraphs (pp. 571–2), Dewey too quickly but more directly addresses Russell's discussion of inquiry as removal of (need for) doubt. Dewey first points out that Russell misunderstands the role of "consequences" in the confirmation or disconfirmation of propositions in a given inquiry. This has nothing to do directly with satisfaction of desires but rather with conformity (or not) of *actual* consequences of actions with *expected* consequences of actions in the course of resolving some specific problem. This is an important topic involving Dewey's conceptions of judgments and propositions, discussed in more detail in Chapter 5. By discussing inquiry in terms of the removal of personal doubt or the satisfaction of desires, Russell misses the point that it is not the doubt or the desire but the doubt-or-desire-ridden *situation* which initiates and is otherwise transformed in inquiry. Situations are *concrete* fields of ongoing activities (as concrete as stones, etc.), and the removal of doubt or satisfaction of desire is at best an unreliable litmus test (and in many cases not even that) for the success of some inquiries.

Russell's response to this in *An Inquiry into Meaning and Truth* (1940, pp. 405–8) is characteristically witty and unyielding. Perhaps because of his focus on subjective doubt rather than on concrete situations, it appears that he continues to underestimate Dewey's point about the relative significance of consequences of actions only as "these consequences are operationally instituted and are such as to resolve the specific problem evoking the operations." Russell confesses that the proviso that consequences be "operationally instituted" (in a given situation, if they are to have significance in that situation) remains obscure to him, which is unfortunate since that is a rather pervasive theme throughout Dewey's *Logic*. Saying nothing more about it, Russell proceeds instead to puzzle over Dewey's reply to him insofar as it seems to entail that "a doubtful situation could exist without a personal doubter." This would make sense, claims Russell, only if by a "doubtful situation" Dewey means that it is doubtful not to the inquiring agent but in the "purely hypothetical" sense in which "mankind" or "the experts" would be doubtful as to how the agent should proceed if they were able to observe the situation in a detached and objective manner. This "spectator theory of lack of knowledge" of course runs counter to Dewey's aims.

In his article "Propositions, Warranted Assertibility, and Truth" (1941, pp. 348–52) Dewey presents a more extended response to Russell's discussion of inquiry as removal of doubt. In particular, Dewey *does* want to say that a problematic situation can exist without a personal doubter insofar as what makes a problematic situation problematic is a condition of imbalance or disequilibrium in ongoing organism/environment interactivities, something which occurs not as a "feeling" necessarily but in any case as fragmented or disjointed activities. Generally speaking, a situation does not have to be characterized by doubt per se; it might instead be a matter of "pain" or "cold" or "hunger," not to mention "wonder" or "mild interest." Disequilibrium can be manifested in any number of ways, so why focus particularly on doubt? Even in those cases where there are feelings of doubt associated with a situation, those feelings are not something occurring over and above the situation, such as in a "mind" which is witnessing but is otherwise separate from the situation.

> [A]ny view which holds that man is a part of nature, not outside it, will hold that this fact of being part of nature qualifies his "experience" throughout. Hence the view will certainly hold that indeterminacy in human experience, once experience is taken in the objective sense of interacting behavior and not as a private conceit added on to something totally alien to it, is evidence of some corresponding indeterminateness in the processes of nature within which man exists (acts) and out of which he arose. Of course, one who holds, as Mr. Russell seems to do, to the doctrine of the existence of an independent subject as the cause of the "doubtfulness" or "problematic quality" of situations will take the view he has expressed, thus confirming my opinion that the difference between us has its basic source in different views of the nature of experience, which in turn is correlated with our different conceptions of the connection existing between man and the rest of the world. Mr. Russell has not envisaged the possibility of there being another generic theory of experience, as an alternative to the pre-Darwinian conceptions of Hegel, on the one hand, and of Mill, on the other. (Dewey 1941, p. 351)

It must be understood that Dewey does not dispense with mentality in his view of experience as organism/environment interactivity. To the contrary, his *Experience and Nature* (1926) is a lengthy development of a naturalistic, evolutionary conception of mind and consciousness, based squarely on the notion of organism/environment systems motivated to maintain some kind of integral balance. But Dewey wants to avoid an account which isolates the "subject" from the rest of the world. Moreover, Dewey's theory of experience allows for processes of experience which neither amount to nor presuppose the occurrence of "personal feelings." The "energies" involved in the particular activities which constitute a given problematic situation are just the ordinary energies involved in being alive. Dewey's theory of experience is supposed to be able to cover an account of what it is like to be a paramecium, say, which is most likely not going to involve talk about feelings of personal doubt on the part of the paramecium. In such cases, talking about allaying doubt or even the *need* for doubt is almost certainly irrelevant, while Dewey's talking about maintenance of equilibrium is very much in order. At the same time, in cases involving "higher organisms," where it is appropriate to say that the situation is "doubtful" (in other words, where the imbalance or disequilibrium constituting the situation involves psychological attitudes of doubt on the part of the agent in question), the doubtfulness is a feature of the ongoing organism/environment interactivities constitutive of that situation—that is, it is an integral part of the objective situation rather than something occurring over and above the situation. Situations in Dewey's technical sense are concrete insofar as organism/environment interactivities are indeed pieces of reality. Associated with living beings, such interactivities may or may not include psychological elements, depending in part on what sort of agents one happens to be talking about.

A significant task for Dewey in fact is to build any kind of subjectivity into his naturalistic picture *at all*. Rather than a presupposition, a reasonable account of sufficient conditions for the existence of subjectivity is one of the *goals* of his epistemology. This of course turns a phenomenological, Cartesian epistemology on its head. In particular, Dewey does not *start* with the cogito, to see what one might establish on that basis, but rather he pursues an analysis of certain principles and presumed facts about the world in order to uncover sufficient naturalistic *conditions* for the existence of such (evidence of) subjectivity. It is a different task altogether. That such subjectivity is undeniable only means that one *must* be able to give an account of it if one's epistemology is to be complete, and taking it as one's starting point is not the only way to account for it.

When Dewey claims that there can exist problematic situations without a personal doubter, he is of course not claiming that there could have been problematic situations "in astronomical and geological epochs before there was life," as Russell correctly remarks. Such epochs may figure into current situations by their affects on current organism/environment activities. In particular, there are scientists today who are interested in such remote realities, these realities therefore being the focus of some of those particular agents' inquiries. In general, such remote epochs are constituents of current situations only by their affects on the experience of living beings, i.e., organism/environment systems; and whatever can be justifiably said about such epochs "is of the nature of ... an extrapolation" backward or outward from current experience (Dewey 1941, p. 351). Otherwise it is not Dewey's project to engage in cosmological speculations about such epochs—the latter sounding more like the business of specific inquiries such as astronomy and geology, but not a general theory of inquiry, i.e., logic.

As for Russell's not seeing any point in the idea that consequences must be "operationally instituted" in some given situation if they are to have any significance, this is clearly a key aspect of Dewey's acknowledgment of the objectivity of situations and their transformation (in contrast with Russell's suggestion that this can be insured by talking about the removal not of "doubt" but rather of the "need for doubt"). Dewey's point in characterizing the role of consequences of actions in this way is precisely to say that situations, insofar as they are not just personal states of mind but involve concrete organism/environment interactivities, cannot generally be put in order simply by manipulating personal states of mind. What is required, assuming we are talking about an agent with mental capabilities in the first place, are concrete activities which test speculations and (possibly noncognitive) expectations about what the facts and possibilities are in given situations. This could sound confusing if one insisted on conceiving of inquiry only in terms of the allaying of doubt or otherwise as a purely mental process. From the perspective of an operation-based view of inquiry, maneuvers like getting drunk or committing suicide, rather than addressing a given situation, at best merely trade one kind of disequilibrium for another, getting rid of "doubt" perhaps but introducing other kinds of stress which carry no promise of insuring the dynamic stability characteristic of successful inquiry.

In this sense—in contrast, say, to Kant—we want to distinguish operational perspectivity from subjectivity. Aprioristic perspectivism, especially in Dewey's naturalistic and ecological sense where habits and attunements play more or less the same role in ongoing experience as would Kant's a priori forms of intuition (Dewey 1938, pp. 13–4, 17, 102, 530–2), is not the same as, and does not entail any commitment to, subjectivism. Experience is necessarily perspectival, relative to the operational capabilities of the given agent; but this is not to say that it is necessarily subjective.

On the contrary, both subjectivity and objectivity are to be understood together in an operational-perspectivist sense. All experience is perspectival; and for those agents for whom a subject/object distinction even applies, experience may be maximally objective just to the extent that it is minimally subjective—such as, ideally anyway, in scientific inquiry. But maximizing objectivity has nothing to do with minimizing operational perspectivity. As a matter of definition, experience is objective to the extent that any kind of agenda relative to peculiar needs and desires of the individual inquirer are relegated to irrelevance and have no functional role in that experience. But minimizing subjective elements of experience has nothing to do with stepping outside of one's operational perspective on the world—the latter simply cannot be done if there is to be any kind of experience at all.

This brand of perspectivism is not entirely inconsistent with the basic thrust of (some of) Kant's views. But we do not have to defend any kind of subjectivism or idealism, in a "transcendental" or otherwise qualified sense, in order to maintain this perspectival theory of experience. This avoidance of idealism is one of the strengths of Dewey's focusing on organism/environment interaction and stability as a foundational concept. What turn out to be the "a priori forms of intuition" in this view are "in us" only in the sense that "us" is an organism/environment system. Such a priori features of experience are built into the constitution of the environment as much as into the constitution of the organism, if we are to even have the latter distinction in the first place. Dewey's apriorism, if we may use such a term, is "ecologistic," not idealistic.

4

Inquiry as Concrete Problem Solving

Most of Russell's discussion in the Schilpp volume (Russell 1939, pp. 143–56) by his own account addresses different aspects of Dewey's "instrumentalism." Russell focuses in particular on Dewey's account of truth and warranted assertibility and how these affect his theory of knowledge. But Russell does not adequately address some important preliminaries to these larger topics, two of which are (1) Dewey's notion of inquiry, and (2) Dewey's treatment of propositions and judgments. Chapters 4 and 5 address these two topics in turn.

4.1 Russell's Concept of Inquiry

Russell's treatment of Dewey's notion of inquiry is based on some misconceptions which we have already discussed to some extent. He was mistaken to think of inquiry merely as a cognitive or mental process of "analysis" aimed at the removal of (need for) doubt; and, second, he did not conceive of situations properly as localized fields of organism/environment interaction (Russell 1939, pp. 139–40). By the time he explicitly addressed the notion of inquiry (pp. 143ff), it is not unexpected that he would find Dewey's account of it to be inadequate.

The following passage from *Logic* briefly explains what Dewey means by inquiry:

What is the *definition* of inquiry? That is, what is the most highly generalized conception of inquiry which can be justifiably formulated? The definition that will be expanded [in *Logic*] is as follows: *Inquiry is the controlled or directed transformation of an indeterminate situation into one that is so determinate in its constituent distinctions and relations as to convert the elements of the original situation into a unified whole.* [Dewey's italics]

The original indeterminate situation is not only "open" to inquiry, but it is open in the sense that its constituents do not hang together. The determinate situation on the other hand, *qua* outcome of inquiry, is a closed and, as it were, finished situation or "universe of experience." "Controlled or directed" in the above formula refers to the fact that inquiry is competent in any given case in the degree in which the operations involved in it actually do terminate in the establishment of an objectively unified existential situation. In the intermediate course of transition and transformation of the intermediate situation, *dis*course through use of symbols is employed as means. In received logical terminology, propositions, or terms and the relations between them, are intrinsically involved. (Dewey 1938, pp. 104–5)

Russell quotes the italicized part of this passage and then responds as follows:

I cannot but think that this definition does not adequately express Dr. Dewey's meaning, since it would apply, for instance, to the operations of a drill sergeant in transforming a collection of raw recruits into a regiment, or of a bricklayer transforming a heap of bricks into a house, and yet it would be impossible to say that the drill sergeant is "inquiring" into the recruits, or the bricklayer into the bricks.... Inquiry, it is evident, is some kind of interaction between two things, one of which is called the object and the other the subject. There seems to be an assumption that this process is more or less in the nature of an oscillation of which the amplitude gradually grows less, leaving it possible to guess at an ultimate position of equilibrium, in which, when reached, the subject would be said to "know" the object, or to arrived at "truth" concerning it. (Russell 1939, pp. 143–4)

Russell proceeds to question Dewey's conceptions of warranted assertibility in this light (Russell 1939, pp. 144–147) and then offers an allegedly improved account of Dewey's notion of inquiry in terms of the allaying of need for doubt (pp. 147–9), as discussed in Chapter 3.

Dewey's response to Russell in the Schilpp volume includes

little explicitly about the notion of inquiry. This is perhaps unfortunate since Russell's drill-sergeant and bricklayer examples have a degree of rhetorical force which Dewey could not afford to have ignored. These and other examples aimed at undermining Dewey's picture of inquiry are discussed below. But first, consider some general points.

Overall, Dewey's response seems to be weighted toward clarifying and otherwise stressing the nonsubjectivist character of his theory of *experience*. In this regard, and in light of virtually any of Dewey's writings since before the turn of the century, it would be inappropriate to attribute to Dewey the idea that inquiry is "some kind of interaction between two things, one of which is called the object and the other the subject." Dewey talked in terms of interactions between organisms and environments. But this is at best orthogonal to a subject/object distinction, which Dewey would rather put aside (Dewey 1939a, p. 524) in a development of logic as the theory of inquiry. It is fundamentally important for Dewey that an organism/environment system be thought of as *one thing*, namely, an agent. Such an *integrated* system will have two facets, which may be distinguished as *organism* versus *environment*, but we do not want to make a strict duality out of this distinction, which an unqualified subject/object distinction too easily connotes.

Russell's view of inquiry as a "subject" altering some "object" introduces a mind-based orientation which is inconsistent with Dewey's giving primary emphasis to singular organism/environment processes of exploration and experimentation. For Dewey, the notion of integrating and ordering fragmentary experience is fundamental; and cognitive modes of experience, if and when they enter into experience at all, occur "intermediately" within and in service to such integration processes (Dewey 1939a, pp. 526–7).

This disagreement between Russell and Dewey about the role of cognitive processes in inquiry is due largely to their having different ideas about what should be fundamental in a development of logical theory and what should be derived or considered secondary. Russell's logic requires that a certain amount of cognitive apparatus already be in place to supply meanings for linguistic expressions, while Dewey's logic is designed to supply a foundational theory of experience on the basis of which a principled philosophy of mind can be constructed. This difference in philosophical orientation becomes most apparent in Russell's response to Dewey particularly with regard to the nature of knowledge and its relation to inquiry.

In *An Inquiry into Meaning and Truth* (1940, pp. 400–10), the notion of inquiry receives attention from Russell in the context of his discussing the concepts of truth and warranted assertibility. He does not say anything about Dewey's notion of inquiry specifically which is essentially different from what he already said in the Schilpp volume; but he presses the question of how activities like house building, bricklaying, or recruit drilling are different from inquiries:

> So far as I can understand Dr. Dewey, . . . [a]mong the various kinds of activities in which mankind can engage, there is one called "inquiry," of which the general purpose, like that of many other kinds of activity, is to increase the mutual adaptation of men and their environment. . . .
>
> One difficulty, to my mind, in Dr. Dewey's theory, is raised by the question: What is the goal of inquiry? The goal, for him, is not the attainment of truth, but presumably some kind of harmony between the inquirer and his environment. I have raised this question before . . . , but have not seen any answer to it. Other activities, such as building houses or printing newspapers or manufacturing bombs, have recognizable purposes. . . . But "inquiry" is neutral as between different aims: whatever we wish to do, some degree of inquiry is necessary as a preliminary. . . . The question is: what happens as the result of my inquiry? Dr. Dewey rejects the traditional answer, that I come to *know* something, and that, as a consequence of my knowledge, my actions are more successful. He eliminates the intermediate stage of "knowing," and says that the only essential result of successful inquiry is successful action. (Russell 1940, pp. 401–4)

The commonsense view of inquiry which Russell is drawing on here is straightforward enough. We often have reason to stop and think about what we are doing, to do a bit of preliminary detective work in order to solve some problem—for example, to scope out the best way to ford a stream, to read the manual before we use a new appliance, to consult a map before we start a road trip, etc.—and the result is that we will then know or believe that we know how better to solve the problem. We will act more successfully on the basis of a belief formulated as a result of careful reasoning.

In contrast, the account of inquiry which Russell attributes to Dewey in this quote is certainly inadequate. Dewey developed a theory of inquiry on the basis of a fundamentally conative picture of experience, having a good deal to say about the nature of inquiry prior to any consideration of whether such basic drives (to maintain stability, etc.) are conscious or cognitive in nature. Russell concludes from this that inquiry by Dewey's account must be a mindless trial-and-error groping. Mindlessness characterizes the simplest and most basic kinds of experience, but it is not a fair rendition of Dewey's definition of inquiry in the broadest sense of the term (and it is an invalid universal generalization) to insist that this entails that all inquiry is mindless.

Dewey's view of inquiry is in fact more sophisticated than anything Russell was able to depict. In particular, inquiry is not, as Russell says, just one among many kinds of activities in which an agent can engage, at least not in Dewey's sense of the term. Rather, the idea of mutual adaptation of organisms and environments is *the* fundamental notion in Dewey's theory of experience, so that all of our activities are to be explained in terms of this fundamental notion. How far Dewey succeeds in the project of formulating a theory of experience on the basis of this fundamental notion is the question to be asked, whereas Russell appears not to realize that this is what Dewey's project is.

Notice Russell's unfortunate choice of words when he talks about "the mutual adaptation of [human beings] and their environment." Dewey would not explain inquiry in such terms, for the simple reason that a human being *is* an organism/environment system. It is conceptually skewed to talk about the mutual adaptation of an organism/environment system and its environment. That way of talking is not meaningless; but Dewey's notion of inquiry pertains to the organism/environment system in the first place, whereas there is no need to talk further about environments of such systems except to point out that not everything in the world counts as part of the environment of a given organism/environment system. Russell is in fact conflating two orthogonal distinctions, namely, between agents and the world at large, and between an organism and an environment, where agents *are* organism/environment systems, not just organisms. This may seem like so much nit-picking, but it shows how easily Russell was able to inadvertently distort Dewey's notion of inquiry by virtue of simple and apparently innocuous choices of terms. For Russell, inquiry is something which a human organism does in an environment, whereas for Dewey, inquiry is something that a human being qua organism/environment system does, period.

More generally, this quote again shows Russell's tendency to think of "knowing" as something separate and "isolated from continuity with the natural world." Russell surely allows that inquiry can be "experimental" and therefore can involve the performance of exploratory actions in the world. But in Russell's view, knowing, as the result of inquiry and for the sake of which inquiry is engaged in, takes place in the head, over and above the performance of these actions.

In contrast, Dewey's aim, rather than to eliminate "knowing" from the picture, is to give a constructive account of what knowing is, in which case he does not directly appeal to the notion of knowing in his description of inquiry since that would only beg the question. Russell views inquiry—a reflective, cognitive "witnessing" of things—as just one more element of our ongoing activities; whereas Dewey is trying to present a foundational conception of inquiry which is sufficiently concrete and still general enough to account for all aspects of animal experience—even those kinds of experience which cannot properly be said to involve cognitive modes of activity. Perhaps this sort of project does not interest Russell, but it seems that he did not acknowledge that this is what Dewey was attempting. Dewey's strategy is to organize this project around a *generalization* of the notion of scientific inquiry. The question

Russell should be asking is whether it is really the case that *all* kinds of experience are explainable in terms of a generalized theory of controlled experimentation continually aimed (from one episode of inquiry to the next) at the stabilization of life functions. In particular, is this a sufficient foundation for "framing an account of the organs and processes of knowing"?[1]

In Dewey's reply to Russell in "Propositions, Warranted Assertibility, and Truth" (1941), the notion of inquiry receives more extended attention, even if it does get second or third billing in Dewey's effort to clarify his conception of truth and warranted assertibility. In answer to Russell's "unanswered" question about his view that *the resolution of an indeterminate situation* is the goal of inquiry, and in an attempt to get the discussion back on track so far as his actual views are concerned, Dewey proceeds to outline in one long paragraph a general picture of the pattern of inquiry as he conceives of it. This paragraph is quoted almost in full here (with Dewey's italics):

[I]nquiry begins in an *indeterminate* situation, and not only begins in it but is controlled by its specific qualitative nature. Inquiry, as the set of operations by which the situation is resolved (settled, or rendered determinate), has to discover and formulate the conditions which describe the problem in hand. For *they* are the conditions to be "satisfied" and [are] the determinants of "success." Since these conditions are existential, they can be determined only by observational operations; the operational character of observation being clearly exhibited in the experimental character of all scientific determination of data. (Upon a non-scientific level of inquiry, it is exhibited in the fact that we *look* and see; *listen* and hear; or, in general terms, that a motor-muscular, as well as sensory, factor is involved in any perceptual experience.) The conditions discovered, accordingly,

---

[1]A discussion of this constructive orientation to the philosophy of mind can be found in Dewey's *The Quest for Certainty* (1929, pp. 223–37). See Goudge's "Pragmatism's Contribution to an Evolutionary View of Mind" (1973), and Chapter 3 of Tiles 1988, for other discussions of this topic. Mead (1934, 1956, 1964), a colleague of Dewey's at the University of Chicago, developed a similar evolutionary conception of mind (which is discussed a bit further in Section 6.3 below).

in and by operational observation, constitute the *conditions of the problem* with which further inquiry is engaged; for data, on this view, are always data of some specific problem and hence are not given ready-made to an inquiry but are determined in and by it. (The point previously stated, that propositions about data are not cases of knowledge but means of attaining it, is so obviously an integral part of this view that I say nothing further about it in this connection.) As the problem progressively assumes definite shape by means of repeated acts of observation, possible solutions suggest themselves. These possible solutions are, truistically (in terms of the theory), *possible* meanings of the data determined in observation. The process of reasoning is an elaboration of them. When they are checked by reference to observed materials, they constitute the subject matter of *inferential* propositions. The latter are means of attaining the goal of knowledge as warranted assertion, not instances or examples of knowledge. They are also operation[al] in nature since they institute new experimental observations whose subject matter provides both tests for old hypotheses and starting points for new ones or at least for modifying solutions previously entertained. And so on until a determinate situation is instituted.

If this condensed statement is taken in its own terms and not by first interpreting its meaning in terms of some theory it does not logically permit, I think it will render unnecessary further comment on the notion Mr. Russell has ascribed to me: the notion, namely, that "a belief is warranted, if as a tool, it is useful in some activity, i.e., if it is a cause of satisfaction of desire," and that "the only essential result of successful inquiry is successful action." (Dewey 1941, pp. 345–6)

There is a good deal packed into this passage which will be discussed more fully in the next chapter—particularly the remarks about propositions as "means of attaining the goal [of inquiry, namely] knowledge as warranted assertion," and the remarks about the role of inference in inquiry. But we can note several things in the present context. This passage explains how Dewey develops his conception of inquiry by generalizing the idea of scientific method. He is talking in this passage about an agent with cognitive abilities—i.e., one that can formulate hypotheses and reflect on possibilities. But inquiry, in the most general sense, is not just a matter of manipulating mental states, nor is it the *goal* of scientific inquiry to achieve "some absolute certainty . . . to the point of infallibility" (not that this is not possible in particular cases, but that it is not characteristic of knowledge in general). Rather, in a given situation instigated by some specific problem, a cognitive agent *acts* in accordance with certain expectations and registers the consequences of those actions in order to evaluate the relevance and viability of those expectations. Conjectures are both suggested by and evaluated on the basis of reliably obtained data. And a claim to knowledge, or rather warranted belief, is something which is achieved in the course of inquiry (not over and against it), embodied in the very process of instituting a determinate situation. This eventual result of inquiry *is* what warranted belief amounts to. In this respect, Dewey's account of inquiry does not involve an appeal to intuitive notions of knowing versus doubt (etc.), but rather is aimed at *generating* a description of what knowledge as warranted belief is by generalizing what is probably *the* canonical example of knowledge, namely, scientific knowledge. (As a result, much of the discussion of perception and noncognitive inquiry gets complicated, but is by no means thereby invalidated, in the course of generalizing this special case.)

Warranted belief, in Dewey's sense, is not an intermediate step between recognizing a given problem and then doing something about it, but rather it is a resulting state (of the inquiring organism/environment system) which is achieved by virtue of modifying one's ongoing activities until a solution to the problem is settled upon. Warranted belief is, among other things, a state[2] of stabilized activities which, for the cognitive agent, is achieved as the result of deliberate consideration and controlled exploration of possibilities suggested by details of a given situation. In this sense, Dewey *ac-*

---

[2]To talk about warranted belief as a "state" is misleading in this context, since believing is essentially a manner of conduct. Achieving a warranted belief, in this view, is not so much a matter of moving into a particular state but more like moving into a kind of dynamic "holding pattern." Such an accomplishment is of course a necessary but not sufficient condition for achieving warranted belief.

cepts a more or less traditional view that the inquirer comes to *know* something as the result of inquiry—but such that, *in the very process of knowing*, the inquirer's actions become more successful than they otherwise would have been. Knowledge as warranted belief is not an intermediate stage of inquiry but is its result, its goal; and it is achieved in a given situation only to the extent that successful action in that situation is stabilized. In this sense, Russell is not entirely wrong in saying that for Dewey the "essential result of successful inquiry is successful action"—not that such results are emphasized *in place of* knowledge but that such results are essential to what *constitutes* knowledge.

What is "intermediate" in an inquiry involving cognitive abilities, on the other hand, are formulations of proposals (propositions) articulating facts of the case as well as articulating what courses of action might be pursued by virtue of facts of the case. This calls for continual exploration of the situation as well as for deliberating (reasoning, reflecting, thinking) about the results and possible significance of those explorations. In this regard, our actions influence what we think about, and our thinking influences how we act, in a given situation. But this reciprocal acting/thinking process is intermediate and instrumental to stabilizing the given situation, namely, to achieving knowledge so far as that situation is concerned.

These intermediate processes of observation and deliberation in a given inquiry I_1 will no doubt draw on the results of past inquiries and thereby use if not strengthen established knowledge, both as a means of formulating what the facts of the present case are as well as what possible courses of action are possible on the basis of those facts. But this does not explain what knowledge is or how it is achieved with respect to the present inquiry I_1. A nuclear physicist will use basic knowledge about mathematics, about familiar features of macrophysics, even about some more or less resolved aspects of microphysics, in the course of inquiring into unresolved aspects of microphysics; but none of these more basic pieces of knowledge, alone or lumped together, constitutes knowledge about those unresolved aspects of microphysics as such.

The subsequent utility of given knowledge K in an inquiry I_1 is not what constitutes it *as* knowledge, in itself or with respect to the subject matter of I_1. Such utility tends to implicitly confirm the warrantability of K, but this is not what Dewey is referring to in characterizing the knowledge sought with respect to the given inquiry I_1. E.g., in the course of learning how ordinary real numbers work, one can come to know that $1+2 = 3$ pretty much independently of the utility of this fact elsewhere. One thereby knows a fact that happens to be used in quantum theory. But one does not thereby know a quantum physical fact *per se* until one pursues some kind of inquiry into the latter subject matter and establishes (explicitly or implicitly) that the arithmetic fact is relevant and can be taken for granted as such. (For instance, one cannot take for granted that decimal arithmetic is always appropriate, especially as subject matters become more and more epistemologically exotic, as in quantum physics.)

Knowledge about a given subject matter is achieved as the result of a given inquiry when what one suspects is the case with respect to the given subject matter is stably corroborated by the results of one's ongoing conduct with respect to that subject matter. We do not achieve knowledge in some intermediate stage of inquiry and *then* act in accordance with that knowledge in order to complete the inquiry, at least not in Russell's sense where that would be a definitive account of the role of knowledge in inquiry; but rather we achieve a state of knowledge in a given inquiry, as the conclusion of that inquiry, by stabilizing the situation (i.e., the subject matter) so that the consequences of current, ongoing actions (e.g., controlled experimentation) continue to agree with *given as well as expected* facts. Persistently successful action in this sense is what warrants and otherwise establishes a claim to knowledge. Further utility in other inquiries only strengthens such a claim, once established. But initially, ongoing actions serve as a Popperian test of such a claim; namely, actions prescribed by and constitutive of a given claim to knowledge are the test which establishes (though tentatively) the epistemological status of that claim.

It is clear in this context that conceptual coherence by itself is not generally sufficient to justify a claim to knowledge, but rather such a claim also requires *stabilization* and *empirical corroboration* of any such conceptual apparatus that is brought to bear in the given inquiry. It would be overly simplistic to say that Dewey presented simply a coherence theory of knowledge in his reference to inquiry as the transformation of an indeterminate situation into a determinate one. The coherence connoted by the notion of "determinacy" is not merely conceptual or theoretical but more broadly includes the practical coherence of theory and its active application to the given subject matter (in the given situation). Typically this will require a progressive refinement of thought and action until such stable coherence is achieved.

Admittedly, knowledge in general, like perception in particular, is potentially erroneous and hence defeasible. According to Dewey, we have to rethink what we mean by knowledge if what we mean by it disallows this defeasibility. Giving up the folk notion of "absolute" or "true" knowledge need not entail giving up a robust notion of knowledge, just as giving up a notion of absolute (Newtonian) position in physics does not mean giving up the notion of position.

Dewey does not say enough about the difference between knowledge and belief in this regard, preferring to talk instead in terms of warranted assertibility so as to avoid ambiguities associated with the terms 'believe' and 'know' (Dewey 1938, p. 7). To say more would require a more detailed theory of mind, including a treatment of belief as a cognitive attitude. Dewey did not take the latter so far in *Logic*, keeping the discussion of inquiry at a more general level, although he does pursue this to some degree elsewhere (in 1926, 1929, 1911/1933, and in various journal articles). These matters are discussed more fully but by no means adequately in Chapters 5 and 6 below.

Dewey's response to the criticisms in *An Inquiry into Meaning and Truth* unfortunately left Russell unswayed. In the chapter on Dewey in *A History of Western Philosophy* (1945), Russell's accounts of Dewey's views are largely a rehashing of earlier criticisms, though some of what appears there is presented more forcefully than before. In this third and final piece dealing with Dewey's logical theory, the notion of truth is the focal point of Russell's account of Dewey's views. Initially, Russell notes the unusual fact that "Dewey makes inquiry the essence of logic, not truth or knowledge." As harmless as this might sound, it is a skewed characterization of Dewey's point of view. Given that logic *is* (literally) the theory of inquiry and given that knowledge is the goal of inquiry, it follows that knowledge is a central consideration in Dewey's view of logic.

On the other hand, Russell is right in saying that the concept of truth, especially in Russell's sense of the term, is peripheral as a working concept in Dewey's logical theory. But Russell draws the wrong moral from this. In particular, he oversimplifies Dewey's definition of inquiry in order to then argue that it (inquiry) cannot be so central to logic as Dewey would have it be. Specifically, Russell argues that Dewey's account of inquiry is concerned only with pointless manipulations of things, with no goal or purpose (such as the attainment of truth or knowledge). He quotes Dewey's familiar description of inquiry as "the controlled or directed transformation of an indeterminate situation into one that is so determinate in its constituent distinctions and relations as to convert the elements of the original situation into a unified whole," noting also Dewey's statement that "inquiry is concerned with objective transformations of objective subject-matter." He then mentions his drill-sergeant and bricklayer examples again, concluding that these show Dewey's definition of inquiry to be inadequate. These are clearly not examples of inquiry, so "there must be an element in his notion of 'inquiry' which he has forgotten to mention in his definition" (Russell 1945, p. 823).

But does it follow from the two passages quoted that the essence of logic, by Dewey's account, is merely the transformation of a subject matter? Perhaps there are elements mentioned in the definition which Russell has not taken note of. For instance, one cannot properly present Dewey's definition of inquiry, much less produce counterexamples to any claims based on this definition, without saying more about what a situation is, since an inquiry by Dewey's definition is the transformation of a situation. Russell suggests counterexamples to Dewey's notion of inquiry—describing processes which would seem to fit Dewey's definition but which are clearly not examples of inquiry—yet they are presented without reference to a situation or even a *type* of situation. Russell does not mention Dewey's footnote appended to the definition he quotes, which refers to an earlier discussion of the notion of situations.

Russell may have been assuming that he had dispensed with the notion of situations in his 1939 review of Dewey's *Logic*, though there is nothing to that effect in the third piece written in 1945. Or perhaps the reference to Dewey's statement that inquiry involves "objective transformations of objective subject-matter" is apparently supposed to validate the situation-independent (thus objective?) character of the alleged counterexamples? But in juxtaposing Dewey's definition of inquiry with the reference to the objective character of inquiry, Russell presumes that these two passages are autonomous and self-explanatory, which they are not. Without reference to the notion of situations and their role in inquiry, one cannot do justice to what Dewey means by "objective transformations of objective subject-matter." Dewey's remark about the objectivity of inquiry entails a rejection of a traditional subject/object dualism which is characteristic of Russell's point of view (as discussed in Chapter 3) and which is built into the drill-sergeant and bricklayer examples. To simply pick out a piece of the world and transform it is in some sense to objectively transform an objective subject matter; but what is it that makes that piece of the world worth picking out, and why would one transform it in one way and not another? Russell's examples do not exemplify those aspects of Dewey's theory of inquiry which address these latter questions (in particular, that such a theory is ultimately grounded in the fundamental conative character of experience as directed away from imbalance and instability).

Russell goes on to claim that inquiry, "as conceived by Dewey, is part of the general process of attempting to make the world more organic" (Russell 1945, p. 823). He proceeds as follows:

> If I am given a pack of cards in disorder, and asked to inquire into their sequence, I shall, if I follow Dewey's prescription, first arrange them in order, and then say that this was the order resulting from inquiry. There will be, it is true, an "objective transformation of objective subjective-matter" while I am arranging the cards, but the definition allows for this. If, at the end, I am told: "We wanted to know the sequence of the cards when they were given to you, not after you had re-arranged them," I shall, if I am a disciple of Dewey, reply: "Your ideas are altogether too static. I am a dynamic person, and when I inquire into any subject-matter I first alter it in such a way as to make the inquiry easy." The notion that such a procedure is legitimate can only be justified by a Hegelian distinction of appearance and reality: the appearance may be confused and fragmentary, but the reality is always orderly and organic. Therefore when I arrange the cards I am only revealing their true eternal nature. But this part of the doctrine is never made explicit. The metaphysic of organism underlies Dewey's theories, but I do not know how far he is aware of this fact. (Russell 1945, pp. 823–4)

It is not clear what Russell means when he says that inquiry is "part of the general process of attempting to make the world more organic," though he attributes this to a "lingering influence of Hegel" on Dewey's thinking, thus returning to the theme that Dewey is committed to an Hegelian "metaphysic of organism." Russell again questions the idea that inquiry should result in "unified wholes," but again, with no mention of Dewey's concept of a situation. We have already discussed Dewey's conception of inquiries as being focused on and otherwise localized to given situations, and as being real, occurrent events in the life processes of some living system. According to Dewey, successful inquiry transforms an indeterminate situation into one which is determinate, thus stabilizing a discordant and unstable situation; but based on anything Dewey wrote, it is not clear why we should think that this will "make the world [any] more organic" than it already is. Perhaps "this part of the doctrine is never made explicit" by Dewey because whatever Russell means by it is not something which Dewey either endorsed or is committed to. But this is really a side issue.

The primary problem with the scenario involving the deck of cards and with other alleged counterexamples (bricklaying, recruit drilling, etc.) is that Dewey's definition of inquiry is misconstrued to say merely that X is an inquiry if and only if X is an objective ordering process. Russell's examples reflect what we might call a "spectator theory of inquiry," namely, that a part of the world (e.g., a collection of new recruits, a pile of bricks, a stack of cards) is "indeterminate" and warrants inquiry if and only if it is disorderly (by the standards, presumably, of some neutral spectator-observer outside of the given situation). But this cannot be right. "Orderliness" is not an absolute measure of determinacy, much less warrantability, at least not in the sense in which Dewey uses these terms. Instances of order can indeed be problematic and hence initiate inquiry, for instance, because they are inappropriate or out of context. Rank-and-file marching has its place, and otherwise it is out of place and potentially problematic, e.g., at a cocktail party as opposed to on the drill field.

Dewey does not actually talk about the "ordering" of a situation in the definition which Russell quotes, perhaps since mere ordering is not what inquiry is, at least not "in the most highly generalized" sense which Dewey is trying to formulate. Three pages after stating his definition of inquiry, Dewey writes that "[o]rganic interaction becomes inquiry when existential consequences are anticipated; when environing conditions are examined with reference to their potentialities; and when responsive activities are selected and ordered with reference to actualization of some of the potentialities, rather than others, in a final existential situation. Resolution of the indeterminate situation is active and operational. If the inquiry is adequately directed, the final issue is the unified situation which has been mentioned" (Dewey 1938, p. 107). Several pages later (pp. 110, 113ff), he discusses the role of reasoning in inquiry (whenever it is involved at all) as including the organization of facts (so as to "form an ordered whole in response to operations prescribed by the ideas they [the facts] occasion and support"). Still later (p. 118), he talks about the effects of experimentation as a "reordering" of existential conditions. And at the end of the chapter (p. 119) he refers to subject matters being "produced and ordered in settled form by means of inquiry." These references to ordering, especially when read in light of the fifteen pages of discussion in which they occur, carry neither the weight nor the particular connotations Russell appears to read into the definition. It is significant that these references to ordering are not part of the definition of inquiry, but rather arise in applications of that definition to a range of cases. And even then, the ordering involved in inquiry, according to these passages, pertains to the selection and control of one's actions in a given situation, and to the rational organization of facts and subject matters, whereas it is not clear that this will always constitute simply an ordering of some piece of the external world.

Tiles (1988, p. 15) quotes the following passage from Dewey's earlier writings (specifically Dewey 1916b, p. 299): "That knowledge grows from a confusedly experienced external world to a world experienced as ordered and specified would then be the teaching of psychological science, but at no point would the mind be confronted with the problem of inferring a world." Here we find a reference to the result of inquiry being a more orderly and comprehensible experience of the world; but the focus here is on the world as *experienced*, so that the presence or absence of order that is of relevance here is not just in the world but more inclusively in the agent's experience of the world. (See also Sleeper 1986, Chapters 3 and 4, regarding this same point.)

For instance, suppose you are building a wooden bridge and have just bought a truckload of 4×4 beams at a very low price. Because of the unusually low price and despite the fact that the lumber appears to be adequate for the job, you are suspicious that it may be defective. You decide to test a few of the beams. You have only the materials at hand, so you proceed in a crude but effective manner to determine the maximum weight which a single typical beam can hold. You lay a sample beam across two large stones so as to support its ends. Then, you successively stack 100-pound sacks of cement onto its center until it breaks. You repeat this test in an orderly way with two or three randomly selected beams, making sure to follow the same procedure each time, to conclude finally that the lumber is indeed suitable for building the bridge. In this inquiry, it seems that you have created a bit of disorder, at least so far as those broken beams are concerned. But you have done it in an orderly fashion; and you have thereby settled the question, at least to your present satisfaction, concerning the adequacy of the lumber for the job at hand. The situation is "closed" and "unified" (at the expense of creating a bit of disorder) insofar as you may now proceed with the bridge building. That is, your ongoing conduct is no longer impeded (dis-integrated) by the uncertainty concerning the materials you are working with. The lumber now fits well enough into your overall bridge-building conduct, where before it stood out as a potential source of problems and therefore halted progress.

Suppose then that we modify Russell's examples to pertain to ordering our experience or our behaviors rather than ordering objects in an external world. Even if it were not unreasonable to describe inquiry in terms of an ordering process (in the bridge-building case, for example, you ordered your actions), the most Dewey would say is that *if* X is an inquiry, *then* X is (in part) an ordering process. By claiming that his examples of ordering are not inquiries and so are counterexamples for Dewey's definition, Russell is in effect affirming the consequent of a conditional statement which in any case would provide only a partial characterization of inquiry.

But the problems with Russell's examples do not stop here. Russell is in fact affirming the consequent of a conditional statement which is *not* even a partial characterization of inquiry so far as Dewey is concerned. Dewey's hesitance to describe inquiry as simply an ordering process is in fact consistent with recent developments in the study of cellular automata and artificial life. Addressing the question of how information processing might have emerged spontaneously in physical systems, this computer-simulation work suggests "that the optimal conditions for the support of information transmission, storage, and modification, are achieved in the vicinity of a phase transition ... between highly-*ordered* and highly-*disordered* dynamics":

> These observations suggest that there is a fundamental connection between phase-transitions and computation. ... Perhaps the most exciting implications is the possibility that life had its origin in the vicinity of a phase transition, and that evolution reflects the process by which life has gained local control over a successively greater number of environmental parameters affecting its ability to maintain itself at a critical balance point between order and chaos. ... [T]otal disorder is just as "simple," in a sense, as total order. Complex behavior involves a mix of order and disorder. ... [S]ystems can be constructed in such a way that they manage to avoid either of the two primary dynamical outcomes by maintaining themselves on indefinitely extended transients. ... (Langton 1990, pages 1–3, 24–30).

In line with this view, Dewey's notion of inquiry suggests an ongoing process of a living system's securing and maintaining *balance* in a dynamic world, which does *not* reduce simply to its securing and maintaining *order*. As Russell's examples illustrate, maintaining order has no intrinsic value in and of itself. Dewey's focus on inquiry not as an ordering process but as a balancing process is corroborated by Langton's focus on the mix of order and disorder residing at the heart of life processes. Langton's picture of life "at the edge of chaos" supports a view of inquiry (qua maintenance of life processes) as walking the line between order and disorder, between freezing and boiling, and of avoiding the extremes of either total order or complete randomness.

We can see this on a large scale in our development and use of technology. Many of our activities as a species, in the interest of increasing our general comfort and security in a precarious world, are necessarily accompanied by "increases of entropy" in the environment, occurring in the form of toxic wastes or artifacts with deleterious effects otherwise. Though such effects occur as secondary products of our ongoing efforts to maintain ourselves (where in this case the inquiring agent is the human species, more or less), they may eventually become sources of problems which are worse than the ones whose solutions resulted in their production— in which case those earlier "solutions" are not adequate solutions after all. For example, according to one view, the gasoline-powered automobile is not so clearly acceptable as a way of solving the long-distance locomotion problem after all, though it has taken us a good deal more than half a century to begin to see the weaknesses in that proposed solution (as evidenced, for instance, in the worsening air quality in most urban areas around the world).

But before we get distracted, the point here is that Dewey does not characterize inquiry simply as an ordering process. Rather, inquiry will often involve the creation of disorder in the course of effecting a solution to a given problem, so that it is necessary to weigh costs and benefits of proposed solutions in that light. A solution to a problem is only a temporary if not unwarranted fix if it amounts to merely trading one difficulty for another. It does not do any good to avoid a left jab if it simply means running into a right hook. It is virtually inevitable that solutions to problems are going to come with certain costs. Every move is going to involve countermoves that may or may not serve our purposes.

We do not want to conclude that we should not solve problems for fear of creating disorder—that would be like committing suicide; but we do have to inquire as broadly and as deeply as we can, to be as sure as we can that any disorder created in the course of solving a given problem is not later going to undermine the given solution or otherwise serve as the source of other problems that are just as troublesome as the original one. The aim is not to maximize order *per se* but rather to achieve and maintain stable solutions whose benefits justify whatever costs might be involved.

Russell's counterexamples fail to accommodate this emphasis on inquiry as a *stabilization* process instigated by concrete disruptions in the ongoing course of affairs of the agent. Russell comes close to discussing the idea of stabilization when he describes inquiry as a process "more or less in the nature of an oscillation of which the amplitude gradually grows less, leaving it possible to guess at an ultimate position of equilibrium, in which, when reached, the subject would be said to 'know' the object, or to have arrived at 'truth' concerning it" (Russell 1939, p. 144). By talking about a position of equilibrium as something to be guessed at, Russell is presumably referring to the admittedly important role of hypotheses in inquiry. But in Dewey's view, hypotheses tend to pertain as much to the initial and intermediate details of a given inquiry as to the end result, formulating potential results of possible courses of action which may or may not effect some kind of solution to the given problem. Some hypotheses may deal with how to get a better perspective on the problem, but have nothing to say about a final solution until such a perspective is achieved. In this regard, it is not sufficiently clear in Russell's description that a solution may be had prior to or independent of any guessing at all, so that the solution would need only to be tested and confirmed. For example, while on a road trip, you may become lost and consult a map, only to discover that you are driving in the right direction after all according to what the map says and what the various road signs say as you proceed down the road.

Another weak point in Russell's description of inquiry as stabilization is that it does not explain the sense in which the "position of equilibrium" is something real and substantial, to be *achieved* and preferably *maintained*. Dewey's notion of equilibrium is not Peirce's notion of an ideal limit of inquiry. The process of knowing an object of inquiry *is* the concrete process of the achievement of equilibrium with respect to that once-problematic object, not just a secondary cognitive act of successfully guessing about such achievements or realizing in one's thoughts that one's guess is correct.

In addition to the point that inquiry cannot be defined simply as an ordering process, there is another point to be made concerning Russell's example of inquiring into the order of the cards. We all agree that we cannot order the cards any way we like and call that a solution. Just any method of investigation will not do, as Russell points out, if it does not address the problem at hand. Being obstinate does not guarantee that a given method of solution is acceptable. And doing what is "easiest" counts for nothing if it does not effect a solution to the given problem. There is nothing to guarantee that the apparently easy way out will not also be potentially a worsening of the situation—such as jumping off a cliff in order to come down off a mountain—so it follows that "ease" of solution is not an adequate measure of success. This bit of common sense is accommodated by Dewey's conception of inquiry insofar as he sees it as a natural phenomenon, embedded in and answerable to a world of natural events, whereby it is relatively rare that one can get away with "stacking the deck" in the game of inquiry.

Notice though that some sort of objective transformation of the deck of cards is unavoidable, even if just any objective transformation will not do. It is not likely that one could stare at the deck and know the sequence of the cards by some occult process. Rather, one must successively uncover each card and read off its value in turn. And that is all that Dewey is committed to. It is not that just any concrete activity will do, but that *some* kind of concrete activity, suited to the problem at hand, will nevertheless have to be carried out. Russell's argument is again an example of the fallacy of affirming the consequent. Or, to give him more credit, perhaps he is proceeding as if Dewey's claim were that a given series of actions in a situation constitutes inquiry *just in case* (if and only if) it effects an objective transformation of the given subject matter. But in stressing that inquiry is "active and operational," all that Dewey actually claims is that X is not an inquiry *if* X does not involve some objective transformation of the given subject matter. The implication goes just one way.

Russell does attempt next to find the element "missing" in Dewey's definition of inquiry that would provide a defense against the alleged counterexamples. He takes the opportunity to once again articulate Dewey's definition, as if to try to salvage it in some way. But he subsequently runs into a new set of problems having to do with the role of *truth* in logic. The topics of truth and warranted assertibility will be dealt with in more detail later (in Section 6.1). Of interest presently is Russell's further elaboration of what he thinks is Dewey's conception of inquiry:

> I think Dr. Dewey's theory might be stated as follows. The relations of an organism to its environment are sometimes satisfactory to the organism, sometimes unsatisfactory. When they are unsatisfactory, the situation may be improved by mutual adjustment. When the alterations by means of which the situation is improved are mainly on the side of the organism—they are never *wholly* on either side—the process involved is called "inquiry." For example: during a battle you are mainly concerned to alter the environment, i.e., the enemy; but during the preceding period of reconnaissance you are mainly concerned to adapt your own forces to his dispositions. This earlier period is one of "inquiry." (Russell 1945, p. 824)

Russell paints a picture of a military general receiving reports about enemy preparations and making counterpreparations, prior to actually engaging in a battle. This account of Dewey's theory starts to sound acceptable. But it is faulty because, for one thing, it manages to divorce action in the world (the actual battle) from preparation to act in the world (reconnaissance and redeployment of resources), where only the latter process constitutes inquiry. By this account, one inquires, and *then* one acts on the results of inquiry. This is just too simple.

It is not that Russell has not described one reasonable sort of inquiry, but he has not really presented the basic pattern of inquiry which can be generally extrapolated to all sorts of inquiry. Therefore he has not really stated Dewey's theory adequately.

This battle example is, after all, an analogy, where the general and his or her army corresponds to "the organism" while the enemy corresponds to "the environment." In particular, it tends to center the agent of inquiry too much in the organism (perhaps where we think of the general inside the bunker as being not unlike the inquirer inside the cranium?), and hence it skews Dewey's treatment of the inquiring agent as being not an integrated *organism/environment system* but rather, one-sidedly, as the *organism* in this or that environment. Russell may seem to be going out of his way to employ Dewey's terminology here, but when we try to generalize the analogy, the end result is that it too easily turns into a mentalistic or subjectivistic conception of inquiry. This ultimately imposes a subject/object (agent/world) duality onto Dewey's organism/environment distinction, which is uncharacteristic of Dewey's views (and which gives rise to too many other problems, such as with the concept of truth).

Before addressing this example in detail, let us get out on the table a second passage where this same problem arises, occurring a few pages earlier in the same text, where (perhaps for the first and only time in his debate with Dewey) Russell admits that a simple mind/body distinction is somewhat dubious as a serious working concept:

> Suppose, ... in descending a staircase, you make a mistake as to when you have got to the bottom; you take a step suitable for level ground, and come down with a bump. The result is a violent shock of surprise. You would naturally say, "I thought I was at the bottom," but in fact you were not thinking about the stairs, or you would not have made the mistake. Your muscles were adjusted in a way suitable to the bottom, when in fact you were not yet there. It was your body rather than your mind which made the mistake—at least that would be a natural way to express what happened. But in fact the distinction between mind and body is a dubious one. It will be better to speak of an "organism," leaving the division of its activities between the mind and the body undetermined. One can say, then: your organism was adjusted in a manner which would have been suitable if you had been at the bottom, but in fact was not suitable. This failure of adjustment constituted error, and one may say that you were entertaining a false belief. (Russell 1945, pp. 821–2)

This goes against the dualistic inclinations of Russell's other writings. And though it may start to sound like something Dewey should (at last) find acceptable, it is not acceptable because it merely shifts attention from a mind/body dichotomy to an organism/environment dichotomy. The distinction between organism and environment is an equally dubious one, as has already been discussed in Chapter 3;

and though both of these distinctions are useful in first-order meta-physical approximations, the real challenge which Dewey insists we face up to is to develop a manner of speaking which does not entail a hard and fast commitment to a strict mind/body/world separation. Russell should rather say that "the relations of an organism to its environment are sometimes satisfactory to the [*organism/environment system*], sometimes unsatisfactory"—satisfactory or not in the objective sense that results of organism/environment interactions may or may not fulfill felt needs or fit with deliberate expectations. Satisfaction as such is best thought of not as mentalistic nor subjective nor solely cognitive in character, but as constituting a kind of dynamic balance in organism/environment relations. Whether the adjustments ensuing from unsatisfactory relations are mainly on the side of the organism or on the side of the environment (they are never wholly on either side *because* we are talking about an integrated organism/environment life form) has nothing to do with whether or not they constitute "inquiry." Sometimes the alterations can be predominantly on the organism side, sometimes on the environment side, depending on the nature of the given situation; but they involve the integrated system as a whole in any case. (See pages 170ff below for further discussion of the notion of satisfaction in this light.)

For instance, in astronomy, especially before there were such things as telescopes or space shuttles, astronomers had to simply allow the celestial spheres to move through their regular cycles in order to be able to repeat similar observations. Such motions, though not "acts" on the part of the organism, are nevertheless transformations of the subject matter of astronomy which help to further astronomical inquiry (especially useful because of their apparent regularity). Such processes out there in the world do not in and of themselves constitute inquiry, prior to or independent of the fact that there are astronomers, but rather they are such only as they become "environment" to some "organism" (thus to constitute, e.g., an astronomer or two). While they are not acts of the organism, they become in some respects acts of the agent insofar as they help to constitute an astronomer's environment. The very same motions are probably irrelevant and extraneous to many other sorts of problem solving, constituting processes extraneous to the inquiring agent, such as when Russell tries to regain his composure after missing that last step on the stairs, when a frog searches for its next meal, and so forth.

More generally, an organism's "waiting and watching" can be a useful means of furthering an inquiry. It is often advantageous, if not necessary, for an organism to do as little as possible, at least temporarily, allowing the world to shift and reveal variations which would otherwise not be distinguishable from the effects of the organism's actions. Suppose you and a friend are walking in a forest busily chatting away and you suddenly think you hear something in the nearby foliage. What you might *do* in this case is to stop doing much of anything except to listen for the sound—to wait and watch—allowing the source of the sound to show itself. Obviously this abrupt "nonaction" on your part is yet a kind of positive "doing" or "acting." The point is that the inquiry in such cases hinges on allowing the environment to be a primary source of change.

In farming, for another instance, there is a good deal of reliance on the seasons and forces of Nature. Your role as a farmer is to know the course of the seasons and to predict and channel and redirect those forces—not like caging and otherwise taming them, but rather like learning to coexist with and benefit from their inevitable and often predictable nature.

In light of these other kinds of examples, Russell's example of planning a battle, as a device for illustrating basic concepts in Dewey's theory, is not presented as well as it could have been. In order to treat the planning of a battle as inquiry, or as part of an inquiry, it is important to describe it from an appropriate theoretical perspective. As with motions of the stars and planets, the planning of the battle as well as the battle itself may or may not be part of an inquiry, depending on how you consider it.

Russell leaves it up to the reader to imagine what the specifics of the situation are. It is conceivable that the planning of some battles may be rather routine (especially if the number of possible courses of action is small, or if one were proceeding much as if one were moving through some standard opening in a chess game), so that inquiry into the nature of one's enemy might not progress substantially until the actual battle ensued. This would be the case if actually engaging the enemy were the best or perhaps only way of gathering information about the enemy. This might also be contingent on having the resources and opportunities to engage the enemy repeatedly. Each battle in this case would be like performing an experiment whereby one would hopefully be able to better size up the enemy. Much in the manner in which experimental science proceeds, one's inquiry in this case would proceed over the course of several battles, not just in preparatory phases prior to each battle.

Russell has in mind a different kind of scenario where the battle is a one-time event and where a good deal of preparatory activity goes into (re)deploying one's forces. This is more obviously a speculative enterprise where one counts on being able to reliably predict the enemy's size, fire-power, movements, etc.—speculative not because such preparation is or is not concerned with altering the enemy versus one's own forces, but because it is oriented toward dealing with future conditions and actions (as contrasted with the immediacy of decision making in the heat of battle). Certain aspects of "deliberate" inquiry are more obvious in this case. But it is not necessarily any more or less a case of inquiry than is the sort of thing which takes place on the battlefield itself. One does not just stop inquiring and move into an action phase of battle, as Russell's example seems to suggest; but rather, the shift from reconnaissance and preparation to actually engaging the enemy is more like moving into a different phase of inquiry where plans and speculations are put to the test and new decisions may or may not have to be made. It would be unwise to close one's eyes and run on automatic at this point, but rather the more intelligent general will probably be sensitive to altering plans to fit changing conditions if and when the situation allows such flexibility. But all of this is just common sense, applicable to a wide range of human affairs other than military battles, and as such it serves to counter Russell's overly simple characterization of inquiry.

4.2 Dewey's Concept of Inquiry

This section will serve to consolidate and otherwise summarize an account of Dewey's conception of inquiry—in his own terms and without so much concern for having to counter Russell's various remarks about it.[3] We will put off the harder details about what a theory of inquiry has to do with *logic*, except for the following brief remarks.

It is not clear what Russell meant when he wrote that Dewey "eschews [metaphysical speculations] because his purpose is practical" (Russell 1939, p. 140), but such remarks probably derive from the fact that, in Dewey's view, logical theory should address not just a formal study of linguistic syntax but it should be grounded in a theory of experience. Dewey would even say that logic is *experimental*.

That is to say, Dewey wants to claim that *the theory of inquiry* is experimental. This is a claim about the "science" of logic, as viewed from the logician's perspective. Just what this means, and how Dewey could possibly make such a claim, will be discussed as we proceed. A quick explanation would be that logic, as the theory of inquiry, is concerned with general features of actual concrete realities happening out there in the world, that is, with general features of real inquiries consisting of concrete transactions going on between actual organisms and environments. Like any other empirical science, it stands or falls not *only* according to its internal coherence but also according to its empirical adequacy as it pertains to such concrete realities. In this sense, logic is still very much an abstract and even "formal" discipline—not quite in the way that Russell conceived of it, but more in the sense that mathe-

---

[3]Much of the following, along with parts of Chapter 5, is an extended version of material in Burke 1990.

matical physics is abstract and formal yet never quite divorced from empirical considerations.

This is to be distinguished from the claim that *inquiry*—the *subject matter* of logic—is experimental. That is, logic includes a study of natural processes which, from the agent's perspective, are exploratory and otherwise geared to consequences of controlled actions. This means that the formulation of an account of propositions, inference, truth, and other logical matters is going to be embedded within, and will otherwise draw upon, a more general account of various "empirical procedures" of exploration and deliberation on the part of inquiring agents. For instance, Dewey's quasi-technical treatment of propositions is not cast in what is now standard model-theoretic terminology but is rather geared to a study of various information-handling activities typical of inquiry (see Chapters 5 and 6 below). What is essential to distinguishing different sorts of propositions in this view are the various sorts of information they formulate and, respectively, the different functional roles they have in the furtherance of some concrete inquiry (Dewey 1938, pp. 287–8). The empirical character of inquiry (from the inquiring agent's perspective) is what Dewey is calling attention to when he talks about "the function of consequences as necessary tests of the validity of propositions, *provided* these consequences are operationally instituted and are such as to resolve the specific problem evoking the operations" (Dewey 1938, p. iv)—a point which Russell, as we have seen, did not see as having any relevance to logic.

Formulating a theory of logic in terms of inquiry rather than in terms of issues primarily involving the foundations of mathematics obviously yields a different conception of logic from what is now customary. The debate between Dewey and Russell is really a debate about what logic is; and Russell was able to accept hardly anything Dewey had to say about the matter because he was unable to see any point in Dewey's orienting his logical theory around a more general concept of inquiry.

Inquiries are in fact ubiquitous. Dewey's definition of inquiry is more fundamentally a definition of experience itself. The very idea of organism/environment subsistence free of instabilities would be a contradiction in terms, as if to conceive of an agent devoid of any experience. An innate compulsion to react against instability is a given fact of nature in Dewey's view. It distinguishes living systems from nonliving systems, and it is the foundation on which to build a constructive theory of intentionality and even consciousness (a main topic of Dewey's *Experience and Nature*, 1926). It is not as though situations were odd and occasional occurrences which are to be gotten rid of so that the agent might get back to subsisting in placid equilibrium. Situations are the very warp and woof of experience.

While it is a defining characteristic of living systems (versus, say, rocks or chairs) that they innately counteract and avoid instabilities, this does not contradict the fact that it is in the nature of living systems to seek out and *exploit* instabilities to counteract other instabilities. For example, consider the simple example of walking. Suppose you have to walk in some given direction if you are to avoid an oncoming automobile. What you do is create a forward imbalance in the given direction and then regain balance by moving your leg or otherwise allowing it to swing forward and stop your impending fall. Walking is a process of successively *creating* and dissolving this sort of situation over and over in a regular fashion, allowing the lateral component of the force of gravity upon your body to help move you in the direction in which you are leaning. Granted, this is a bit simplistic; but it is especially appropriate if you think what it is like to be a toddler first learning to walk. At first, the business of locomoting by utilizing gravity, ground, legs, and the rest of the body is puzzling and requires considerable attention. But it is soon mastered, having then no particular significance by itself, and is used as a *means* in subsequent activities (crossing a street, avoiding oncoming automobiles, etc.).

This example illustrates two important and closely related ideas in Dewey's theory of inquiry. First, there is the idea of inquiry as *habit formation*. Namely, inquiry is in part a process of mastering particular actions or otherwise becoming accustomed to certain manners of conduct, and it is by virtue of such mastery that reliable repetition of behaviors is possible. Habits are formed (and corresponding actions are mastered) in order to be exploited as *means* in subsequent experience.

In fact, the very notion of a capacity to *act* can be explained in terms of the fundamental conativity at the heart of Dewey's definition of inquiry. As a particular type of organism/environment system evolves (and as a particular individual develops), it acquires and continually modifies various capacities to act in distinctive ways. Such actions, prior to being mastered and hence prior to being *actions* as such, are initially unfamiliar stabilization processes. Various kinds of such processes may or may not be recurrent, but one sooner or later acquires capacities to deal with and ultimately exploit various sorts of instabilities in the world. According to this formula, a capacity to act in a certain way (e.g., to walk) is a capacity to orchestrate certain kinds of instabilities in a reliable way.

Playing on a merry-go-round—using one's foot to push against the ground in order to get moving—is a simple case of deliberately creating and exploiting instabilities for more general purposes, in this case, simply to move for the sake of moving. The same principle is at work when we push a stalled automobile off the road, say, to get it out of the way of oncoming traffic. In fact, the very same principle is at work when we push on the accelerator of an automobile which is in working order, to increase the flow of gasoline into the carburetor, ultimately to increase the intensity of the explosions in the piston chambers which push against the pistons and otherwise create the forces that turn the drive shaft and move the car along the road. These kinds of activities are made possible by having mastered the fact that pushing against things in the environment creates tensions which invite immediate responses from those things, responses which can often be controlled and exploited for purposes beyond themselves.

This first idea is a special case of the second and more general idea of the *continuity* of experience. In simple terms, this is the idea that the results of inquiries tend to cohere with and otherwise carry over into other current and subsequent inquiries. Walking is a more or less isolable action which is nevertheless almost always performed in coordination with other activities (looking, listening, talking, chewing gum) and for various more general purposes (moving to another room, crossing the street, going to the mailbox, taking a hike). This idea of continuity is central to a picture of experience as a complex hierarchical meshwork of inquiries.

So, for example, we have already discussed Dewey's characterization of a stimulus/response process as "a function of the total state of the organism in relation to environment" (see Chapter 3 above, and Dewey 1938, pp. 29–31) which suggests that even perceptions are episodes of inquiry (in the "most general sense" of Dewey's definition). Rarely do we perceive just for the sake of perceiving, but rather perceivings usually take place in service to other inquiries. Indeed, the fact that the results of perception often function in inquiry as "data" tends to obscure the relatively complex nature of perception as a kind of noncognitive proto-inquiry in its own right.

Both of these ideas—of habit formation and of continuity—are built into the basic definition of inquiry as being what an integrated organism/environment system does to maintain its systemic integrity. It is not appropriate to talk about some of these examples (walking, perceiving) as inquiries unless we take the term 'inquiry' to be a technical term which is consistent with but not to be constrained by common usage. In most general terms, inquiry is the resolution of uncertainty as it arises in concrete situations. A situation in Dewey's view is problematic insofar as it is a locus of uncertainty and insecurity within the overall conduct of normal affairs. Inquiry consists in transforming a situation into one which is no longer insecure. A situation is resolved just to the extent that one is able to reintegrate that experience into one's ongoing conduct.

Hence, as we have already pointed out in response to Russell in the previous section, inquiry has to be understood not simply as cognitive problem solving but, more generally, in terms of an adaptive stabilization propensity of organism/environment systems. Dewey's definition of inquiry, strictly speaking, presupposes no mind or cognitive capacities in particular, but rather it posits a fundamentally nonmentalistic, conative intentionality, in the form of an innate motivation to avoid insecurity. Dewey's theory of inquiry is at its foundations a general theory of how such systems counteract disintegrating influences and thereby maintain themselves. This will sound silly if all you have in mind is someone stumbling through the world being puzzled by everything. Dewey's notion of inquiry is rather more elementary than that, aimed as it is at providing a foundational account of experience itself, not just of some limited kinds of experience peculiar to agents with cognitive abilities that occasionally go awry. The basic scenario, to review the discussion in Chapter 2, is that of a given agent performing a wide array of actions as a matter of course. Problems are initiated by some localized, unsettling perturbations—due to excesses or deficiencies or conflicts or blockages or discrepancies of some kind. The resulting countermoves need not be "deliberate" or "reflective." Dewey's picture of inquiry describes general architectural and dynamic features of virtually any constituent subsystem of living animals, characterizing the simplest cellular life functions as well as the most complex motor activities. Indeed, this definition of inquiry is aimed at characterizing not only the microstructure of physiological behavior but also wholesale features of human sociocultural interactions. By this account, agents should be motivated to solve problems independently of whether or not they have *minds*. We do not need a theory of mental states, beliefs, desires, consciousness, or cognition prior to developing a theory of inquiry in Dewey's naturalistic sense. That would amount to putting the cart before the horse. This notion of inquiry rather is supposed to serve as the basis of a constructive account of these other matters.

In this same vein, we have seen already how it is a mistake to project some kind of subjectivism into Dewey's focus on organism/environment interactions. Dewey argues explicitly and at length against such a view, and it is not entailed by anything he says despite the claims of several critics. Dewey stressed that inquiry has to be in some sense experimental or exploratory if it is to be successful. This might involve some sort of anticipation or planning. But he was interested in understanding how such aspects of experience can be explained in nonmentalistic, nonsubjectivistic, naturalistic terms. Rather than presuppose some kind of subjectivity to begin with, things like distance detection (etc.) and the anticipation this affords should serve as the basis of an account of how a subject/object distinction might eventually have arisen as a feature of experience.

Organism/environment interactions and situations in particular should be thought of as pieces of reality, pieces of the world, which may serve as the subject matter of an objective scientific investigation. The foundations of this science revolve around trying to understand the different means and methods such systems use to successfully maintain themselves in the world at large. One prominent aim of this science is to generate a constructive account of mind on this situation-theoretic basis, rather than pursue a phenomenological investigation of mind based on the assumption of some kind of subjectivity or consciousness or mentality in the first place. Dewey would claim that such situation-theoretic concerns constitute the subject matter of *logic*. These sorts of considerations are in his view basic to a theory of propositional contents of utterances, inference, truth, and other notions that are central to logic and the philosophy of language.

The idea that living systems should be disposed to deal with disintegrating influences in as localized a way as possible seems like a sensible design principle for natural biological systems. The ongoing operations an agent performs are just the system of interactions (transactions) which constitute an integration of organism and environment. When some sort of perturbation or disintegrating influence occurs within this system of processes, the system moves to correct the problem by altering its actions in some way. Such an instance of disintegration constitutes a *situation*, where it is the business of inquiry to dissolve situations. The instability may be centered in the organism perhaps, or in the environment, but in any case it involves some localized part of the system as a whole.

How one might build this kind of focused stabilization propensity into a working robot, for instance, is not obvious; but taking this as a basic design principle would seem like a reasonable way to proceed if one wants the robot to operate like a semi-intelligent autonomous living system. So far as that kind of engineering problem goes, Dewey has surely gotten the priorities straight by trying to establish a principled basis for a constructive account of mentality, rather than have us presume that the folks over in the software department will be taking care of that some time in a near future which never seems to get any nearer.

Determining how best to modify current actions in order to dissolve a situation involves clarifying given details of the situation and being sensitive to what possible modes of action are plausible on the basis of those details. This does not require that such information be mentally represented—such information need only be *pre*sented, and not necessarily "mentally" (whatever that might mean). It does require actually implementing and testing different modes of action to see what the consequences are. The assumption here is that the agent has at its disposal a possibly extendable repertoire of capacities for action which can be employed from one situation to another. Such standard modes of action function as resources for transforming situations, not so much in the sense of articulating already established courses of action which fully determine the subsequent dynamics of a given situation, as in Russell's battle scenario, but more in the sense that Suchman (1987, pp. vii–x, 1–4, 49–67) talks about unavoidably ad hoc "situated actions" which fall into place in the context of concrete circumstances which cannot always be fully anticipated in advance of their occurrence: "we generally do not anticipate alternative courses of action, or their consequences, until *some* course of action is already under way. It is frequently only on acting in a present situation that its possibilities become clear, and we often do not know ahead of time, or at least not with any specificity, what future state we wish to bring about" (p. 52).

The most we can say in general terms is that inquiry is directed toward determining a course of action which stabilizes the dynamics of a given situation. Early phases of inquiry, beyond an initial sense of insecurity, are aimed at determining more precisely what the problem is; and the ultimate end of any given inquiry, broadly speaking, is to determine how best to act or be in order to counteract the problem. Intermediate phases of inquiry, whether by deliberation (reflection, thought) or by habit (perception, intuition) alone, involve the manipulation of information in such a manner that hopefully a fitting determination can be made.

For agents with cognitive capabilities (however we might come to understand that—there is still a constructive story to be told here) this pattern of inquiry is more elaborate but essentially the same. Under the control of expectations formulated on the basis of current facts and assumptions, or by virtue of established habits, or otherwise in an ongoing trial-and-error manner, a determination of how best to act will, in a sense, make itself in the process of the agent's securing some kind of equilibrium. Dewey refers to such determinations as judgments, or acts of judgment, to be more precise. An act of judgment, even for cognitive agents, need not be a process of deliberate decision making so long as it is a process of settling on a course of action or mode of being which effectively solves the problem.

At least in some cases, it will be determined that a particular array of actions is appropriate because those actions are in that instance being performed and seem to be working. This may be as simple as identifying some initially unfamiliar object or stuff—for example, the liquid contents of a given drinking glass, the source of some unusual noise, an object approaching from three hundred yards away, the layout of a darkened room—where such determinations enable one to regard or otherwise behave towards such things in familiar or otherwise appropriate ways. In other cases, such as in a court of law, or in planning a cross-country road trip, a judgment will be based on past experience but will necessarily be *speculative* before one performs many of the proposed actions. In *all* cases, judgments are *provisional*, given that what works now may soon break down and given that speculations warranted at one point may ultimately fail due to unforeseen contingencies.

Dewey describes judgments in this sense as having a (deceptively simple) subject/predicate structure. A judgment consists in attributing a predicate to some subject, both of which are determined (i.e., made determinate) as the result of inquiry. The terms 'predicate' and 'subject' are to be understood initially in a prelinguistic sense, without supposing that the given agent must deliberately articulate this distinction to itself. This is a distinction we make as theorists, not one which inquiring agents necessarily make as part of their inquiries.

The subject of a judgment will be the determinate subject matter of the respective inquiry. The subject of a judgment is that piece of the world which the judgment is about, that is, the situation transformed as such in the course of the inquiry, from one with an indeterminate character to one with a determinate character. The predicate of a judgment will be the process or course of action settled upon as being what is appropriate and fitting for that situation. The predicate of judgment is that manner of being by means of which the situation is made determinate in a stable way.

Determining what the subject and predicate of judgment are is of course an exploratory process in the manner already outlined. The pattern of inquiry should be understood in terms of the construction of judgment in this sense. In effect, a coherent *universe of discourse* is developed in the course of inquiry on the basis of the results of ongoing activities (Dewey 1938, pp. 68–9, 118–19, 313–14). An inquiry cannot be effectively completed—judgment cannot be effected—unless and until the facts of the case converge as a system to some such coherent limit. This limiting array of facts will constitute the *subject* of the judgment which terminates that inquiry. The *predicate* of judgment, on the other hand, consists in the possibly complex manner of action which has been tested and otherwise settled upon as a course of action which produces a stable solution to the given problem. The agent's concrete actions will in this case converge to some stable manner of conduct, the results of those actions eventually holding together as a coherent array of acceptable consequences. Otherwise the inquiry goes on.

This conception of the nature of subjects and predicates of judgments calls for further discussion. In the next section several examples are developed to illustrate various distinctions at work in Dewey's picture of inquiry. The next chapter looks in more detail at this conception of propositions, particularly in terms of his distinction between judgments and propositions. Much of their disagreement over the concept of truth is traceable to the fact that Dewey and Russell held different and not-very-well-articulated views about what propositions are. We have in the present chapter focused on the notion of inquiry, since propositions in Dewey's view can be properly understood only in terms of their function in inquiry.

4.3 Four Examples

The following examples of inquiry illustrate Dewey's conception of the role of propositions in inquiry and otherwise help to explain his distinction between propositions and judgments, as presented in the definition of inquiry quoted on page 109 above and the more extensive summary on page 115.

1. Consider an example of *scientific* inquiry—specifically, the example of Ptolemaic astronomers trying to understand the apparent motions of the planets. This is a special case of inquiry—not all inquiry is *scientific* inquiry—but it nicely illustrates the main features of Dewey's picture of inquiry.

What problematic situation was being transformed in this case? Unlike mundane activities such as walking or seeing a tree, this particular inquiry was presumably aimed at transforming a lack of understanding of celestial motions into some kind of coherent, positive understanding. A degree of uncertainty will have arisen out of an inability to fully comprehend a pattern where a pattern was otherwise called for (on scholastic metaphysical grounds, say) and was *almost* discernible.

The situation therefore seems to have been primarily of a cognitive or intellectual nature. But the emphasis on a lack of understanding should not obscure the fact that the situation was not just inside astronomers' heads, nor was it only out there in the heavens. It occurred rather in the objective interactions going on between some particular heads and what was out there in the heavens. That is, we still want to say that the situation will have been a field of experience, generated by some sort of local disequilibrium in organism/environment interactions. In this case of astronomical inquiry, it is appropriate to think of the disequilibrium as a lack of understanding. This of course begs some important questions, since it still does not explain what is meant by 'understanding'. But it locates where such an explanation is to be sought, at least in Dewey's view.

So we may select almost any given year back in fifteenth-century Europe, and we will find that the existing community of practicing astronomers had a more or less coherent view of things which at least tacitly included guidelines not only for how to collect data about the apparent motions of the planets but also for how to analyze and understand the data (in terms of Euclidean geometry, scholastic cosmology, and so forth)—whether or not there was an explicit cognizance at that time of anything like *scientific method*.

Examples of propositions in this collective inquiry into the nature of celestial objects will include things like classifications of various objects as planets or stars or comets (etc.), claims and predictions about positions and trajectories of various planets, and also explanations of those classifications and claims and predictions in terms of prevailing principles, tenets, rules, and laws of geometric, scholastic, and folk theory. Such principles, tenets, rules, and laws are themselves instances of propositions in this inquiry, albeit of a different sort than merely classificatory propositions or propositions about specific positions and trajectories.

Judgments, on the other hand, will consist of or otherwise bear on claims about the success, failure, or status otherwise of the inquiry as a whole—specifically, whether or not, and *how*, the inquiry might achieve a stable conclusion (Dewey 1938, p. 138). The default decision in the year 1450 to continue with an analysis of planetary trajectories using various geocentric systems of circular epicycles (etc.) amounted to a judgment that the overall gist of astronomical inquiry in terms of scholastic cosmology and Euclidean geometry was correct insofar as it was reliably producing substantial results. The contrary decision a century or two later to take the heliocentric view more seriously was apparently affected by a changing evaluation of the previous manner of inquiry—since, for example, increasing refinements and complexity of the geocentric view were by contrast affording no increase in explanatory value. The project of dispelling a lack of understanding was not being well served.

This is obviously different from Frege's conception of judgments. For Frege, a judgment is a determination of the truth or falsity of some proposition. For Dewey, a judgment consists in an assertion, explicit or implicit, about how to proceed with a given inquiry. A Deweyan judgment will address things like which of a number of possible exploratory efforts to follow out, where and how to allocate resources, and so forth—the sorts of things that agencies who evaluate research proposals are concerned with, as opposed to what researchers qua researchers do. A judgment concerns or is about the overall subject matter of the inquiry itself and is therefore only indirectly about specific details of what is being inquired into. In Dewey's view, propositions in a given inquiry serve to spell out facts of the case as well as possible actions and expected results of actions on the basis of accepted laws and principles. As such they are instruments for articulating the details of the subject matter of a given inquiry. Therefore lots of propositions are typically built into the formulation of a judgment, insofar as a judgment concerns questions about how the articulation and handling of a given subject matter is developing. But a judgment is not a determination of the truth values of those propositions.

Strictly speaking, it is not usually appropriate in Dewey's view to talk about the truth or falsity of propositions. Rather, propositions in a given context are said to be *affirmed* or *denied* (or neither, or both), on the grounds of their being confirmed or disconfirmed, being relevant or irrelevant, informative or uninformative, effective or ineffective, consistent or inconsistent, useful or not useful, and so forth.

The notion of affirmation, unlike truth, is, among other things, verificationist in character. But this amounts to a claim about what propositions are, constituting not a verificationist theory of truth but rather a verificationist theory of propositions. For Frege (1918), propositions are things "for which the question of truth or falsity arises," while for Dewey they are things for which the question of situated affirmation or denial arises, as it were.

Judgments, meanwhile, are said to be *warrantably assertible* or not—a third notion distinct from either affirmation or truth. We have discussed already what a judgment *is*. As for what *warrants* a judgment, a theory of inquiry will have to include a number of criteria for gauging the success of inquiries. Such criteria would include various epistemological and methodological considerations such as whether or not the subject matter of the inquiry is being articulated in a coherent way, whether or not the expected results of ongoing activities are satisfied, whether or not such coherence and empirical adequacy are stable, whether or not there are better ways to proceed, whether or not the results are useful or otherwise applicable to other inquiries, and so forth.

These sorts of considerations are measures of the success of inquiry insofar as the aim of inquiry is to transform an indeterminate situation into one which is determinate. Judgments are assertible, and while such assertions are not essentially linguistic in character, they are nevertheless *about* something, and they say something about what they are about. That is to say, a judgment has a "subject" and a "predicate."[4] What a judgment is about, its subject, is the

---

[4]Propositions in Dewey's scheme of things, on the other hand, come in a number of basic forms that are not easily reflected within the framework of a classical first-order language. So far as judgments are concerned, their subject/predicate structure obviously involves a kind of reference and attribution that goes beyond the simple function/argument idiom at the heart of Frege's "formula language."

situation being transformed through inquiry. And what a judgment says about the situation, its predicate, supports a claim about how to proceed in the inquiry so as to effect and maintain a coherent, empirically adequate, effortlessly stable conclusion.

2. As a second example, consider Dewey's discussion of the general case of judgment in a court of law (1938, pp. 120–2). Highlights of this discussion are given in the following quote:

> A literal instance of judgment in the sense defined is provided by the judgment of a court of law in settling some issue which, up to that point, has been in controversy. 1. The occurrence of a trial-at-law is equivalent to the occurrence of a problematic situation which requires settlement. . . . 2. [The] settlement or judgment is the outcome of inquiry conducted in the court-hearings. . . . On the one hand, propositions are advanced about the state of facts involved. . . . This subject-matter is capable of direct observation and has existential reference. . . . The decision takes effect in a definite existential reconstruction. On the other hand, there are propositions about conceptual subject-matter; rules of law are adduced to determine the admissibility (relevancy) and the weight of facts offered as evidence. . . . 3. The final judgment arrived at is a settlement. The case is disposed of; the disposition takes effect in existential consequences. The sentence or proposition is not an end in itself but a decisive directive of future activities. The consequences of these activities bring about an existential determination of the prior situation which was indeterminate as to its issue. A man is set free, sent to prison, pays a fine, or has to execute an agreement or pay damages to an injured party. It is this resulting state of actual affairs—this changed situation—that is the matter of the final settlement or judgment. The sentence itself is a proposition, differing, however, from the propositions formed during the trial, whether they concern matters of fact or legal conceptions, in that it takes overt effect in operations which construct a new qualitative situation. While prior propositions are means of instituting the sentence, the sentence is terminal as a means of instituting a definite existential situation. (Dewey 1938, pp. 120–2)

One should read the full text of the example in *Logic*, but these particular remarks, in Dewey's own words and in terms of a definite and familiar sort of inquiry, illustrate well enough Dewey's proposed distinction between propositions and judgments. The intermediate, "re-constructive" role of propositions in the process of inquiry is to lead eventually to the formulation of a final judgment. The concrete operational character of this formulation guarantees that an actual assertion of the judgment, the carrying out of the sentence, will alter the world in what is supposed to be a maximally (universally?) appropriate way.

3. As a third example, consider a mathematics student learning for the first time about square roots of positive integers.[5] At some point the student might wonder if $\sqrt{x+y} = \sqrt{x} + \sqrt{y}$. That is, do addition and taking square roots satisfy a distributive law? This question designates a problem to be solved and hence a subject matter to be explored. The average student will probably not try to prove or disprove the alleged equality from first principles, but might fix a few values for x and y and see if the resulting values on either side of the equals sign are the same. Picking x to be 0 and y to be 2, the equality holds. So far, so good. But picking x and y both to be 1, it does not. That settles the question. The equality does not hold in general. Such is the judgment which results from, in this case, an investigation of specific cases.

Meanwhile, a week later, the student might be solving some kind of problem in which it is possible to *use* the fact that $\sqrt{x+y} \neq \sqrt{x} + \sqrt{y}$, having discovered it only a week before. Perhaps the problem is to find two arithmetic operations which do not distribute, if there are any. Whatever the case may be, the point is that in this office as a fact to be used in solving some given problem, the inequality now formulates a proposition.

As the formulation of the result of a discovery process, in the instance of settling on that result, an assertion of the inequality is an example of a judgment; and as the formulation of a fact to be used in some other problem-solving process, it is an example of a proposition. It does not make any sense to ask out of the blue if this formula represents a judgment or a proposition, but rather such

---

[5]This example was suggested by Nel Noddings.

a designation depends on how the content of the formula relates to or bears on some given problem-solving activity.

4. To avoid overgeneralizing examples of inquiry which usually involve well-developed cognitive processes, consider a fourth example having to do with simple visual perception. Consider someone who enters a cluttered room, intending to do some routine house-cleaning. In particular, consider a brief inquiry into the identity of a certain item sitting on the floor next to a given chair. This inquiry, I_1, is embedded in the larger inquiry, I_2, of discerning the overall layout of the room and determining what to do in order to clean it. Part of this larger problem of discerning the layout of the room as a whole includes classifying various objects in the room in terms of things to be gotten rid of, things to leave alone, things to be rearranged, and so forth. Hence, embedded in this larger classification business will be otherwise independent inquiries into the identity of particular things.

Assume that the given thing sitting on the floor next to the chair is not one of the usual "fixtures" but occurs in an unusual place or manner. Identifying it will probably take all of a split second, in which case it is going to sound odd to dissect and analyze that experience; but let's do that, just to be able to distinguish propositions and judgments in regard to this particular inquiry. So perhaps for a split second, the person's visual activity is focused on the thing on the floor next to the chair. A good deal of information will be affirmed: shiny here, greenish there, letters F, i, z (etc.) here, cylinder shape there—in short, lots of evidence indicating that the thing is indeed another one of those often encountered Fizzy Soda containers. With regard to the inquiry I_1 aimed at identifying that thing, the judgment will be made that *that thing*, the subject matter of inquiry I_1, is a Fizzy Soda container. The predicate, which could be expressed linguistically in this case by 'Fizzy Soda container', attributes a certain familiar mode of being to the subject matter. This will of course serve as information in the larger inquiry I_2 into the overall layout of the room—so that a judgment relative to inquiry I_1 will yield propositional information in inquiry I_2. The propositional information in inquiry I_1, on the other hand, will have been the information about shininess, greenishness, etc., whereas the *judgment* that the object is a Fizzy Soda container will mark the termination of registering and focusing on such information, asserting in effect that inquiry I_1 has settled into a definite identification of the object, and indicating at the same time how to proceed with respect to that thing, namely, that it subsequently be treated and otherwise acted upon as is normally the case with loose Fizzy Soda containers in a tidying-up context.

This fourth example illustrates Dewey's conception of "objects" as "objectives" of inquiry, as discussed in *Logic* (1938, pp. 118–19, 520–22) and in the Schilpp volume (Dewey 1939a, pp. 566–7). At the end of Chapter 6 of *Logic*, Dewey briefly clarifies some terminology used in the rest of the book:

> Were it not that knowledge is related to inquiry as a product to the operations by which it is produced, no distinctions requiring special differentiating designations would exist. Material would merely be a matter of knowledge or of ignorance and error; that would be all that could be said. The content of any given proposition would have the values "true" and "false" as final and exclusive attributes. But if knowledge is related to inquiry as its warrantably assertible product, and if inquiry is progressive and temporal, then the material inquired into reveals distinctive properties which need to be designated by distinctive names. As *undergoing* inquiry, the material has a different logical import from that which it has as the *outcome* of inquiry. In its first capacity and status, it will be called by the general name *subject-matter*. When it is necessary to refer to subject-matter in the context of either observation or ideation [viz., in the middle phases of inquiry], the name *content* will be used, and, particularly on account of its *representative* character, content of propositions.
>
> The name *objects* will be reserved for subject-matter so far as it has been produced and ordered in settled form by means of inquiry; proleptically, objects are the *objectives* of inquiry. The apparent ambiguity of using "objects" for this purpose (since the word is regularly applied to things which are observed or thought of) is only apparent. For things exist *as* objects for us only as they have been previously determined as outcomes of inquiries. When used in carrying on new

inquiries in new problematic situations, they are known as objects in virtue of prior inquiries which warrant their assertibility. In the new situation, they are *means* of attaining knowledge of something else. In the strict sense, they are part of the *contents* of inquiry as the word content was defined above. But retrospectively (that is, as products of prior determination in inquiry) they are objects. (Dewey 1938, pp. 118–19)

It is tempting to think that Dewey is appropriating the term 'object' in a way that has little to do with normal usage. But the latter part of the passage just quoted clearly denies this. (See also *Logic*, pp. 520–22, where Dewey explicitly claims that his notion of "objects" is supposed to accommodate normal usage of the term.) He is talking about standard commonsense objects in the world around us—things like Fizzy Soda containers today, or for that matter, celestial spheres in 1450—though he is proposing a different way of thinking about them. Dewey intends that the extension of his term 'object' coincide with the extension of the term as commonly used; but its meaning is somewhat new and unusual by virtue of its characterization in terms of a theory of inquiry.

As the outcome of astronomical inquiry, our current knowledge of the physical universe is very easily taken for granted as a "background object" against which the "contents" of other inquiries are played out—whereas it does not enjoy this secure status when the inquiry at hand is astronomy itself, where it is the "subject matter" of inquiry. Similarly, once inquiry into the identity of the Fizzy Soda container is concluded, the outcome of that inquiry persists as a stable object within the larger context of subsequent cleaning actions (or else it would call for further inquiry).

In this sense, it should be understood that this terminology ('subject matter' versus 'contents' versus 'objects') does not introduce an absolute three-way distinction. Whether some given thing is the subject matter of, or an object within, a given inquiry is relative to the perspective of the inquiry. As the *subject matter* of an inquiry, a bit of "existential material" will serve as the *subject* of the respective judgment. But as the outcome of that inquiry, it may serve as an *object* within subsequent inquiries, helping to constitute part of the *content* of such inquiries. That subject matters may in this sense become "objectified" is an important aspect of Dewey's principle of continuity of judgment. This takes us back to the statement of principle (4′) in Chapter 2. In the present case, the Fizzy Soda container would then be just one more of the "things," one of the *this*es or *that*s, within the given subject matter and in terms of which information is propositionally formulated. It would now serve as a *means* for carrying out subsequent inquiries. (Compare a child's investigation into the nature and capacities of a hammer, as a subject matter, versus that same person's use of a hammer thirty years later, now as a familiar object and tool, in building a wood-framed house.) In this respect, to stress that there is a distinction to be made between judgments and propositions is not to say that the very same "thing" in the world cannot from different perspectives be the referent or otherwise a constituent of either.

One thing to note in regard to each of these examples, in light of criticisms of the alleged "experiential" or "existential" character of judgments, is that a judgment is made by an inquirer about an actual ongoing inquiry—specifically as regards the current success or failure of that inquiry in solving the problems specific to the given situation. Such evaluations of current experience can be warranted but where the warrantability is limited in scope by the boundedness of that experience. Hence a quite warranted judgment, as a currently justified "opinion," may fall short of asserting anything which one would want to call "the truth." The alleged Fizzy Soda container, for instance, might actually have been an expensive hyperrealist sculpture, which will not have been evident until one actually reached down to grab it in order to throw it into the wastebasket. Or, the default decision in 1450 to continue to pursue and develop an Earth-centered view of the universe was warranted by European astronomers' experience up to that point, given that the inappropriateness of that view either was not evident in anything they were doing at the time or else was legitimately overridden by other considerations. In this regard, then, in proposing a theory of warranted assertibility, Dewey was not proposing a definition of truth. He was rather dealing with a related but different matter which pertains to the evaluation of situations and which should be central to a theory of belief and knowledge.

5

Propositions and Judgments

Many of Russell's criticisms of Dewey's *Logic* centered around the notion of warranted assertibility. Russell regarded this notion not only to be inadequate as an account of truth but irrelevant to logic altogether. But Russell's criticisms are undercut by the fact that the notion of warranted assertibility was not supposed to be an account of truth. Russell did not see this, at least in part as a result of having overlooked Dewey's distinction between *judgments* and *propositions*. This latter distinction is an essential element in Dewey's account of warranted assertibility. Russell's criticisms fail to reflect Dewey's view that *judgments* are said to be warrantably assertible or not, while *propositions* are more properly said to be confirmed or refuted. Once this is clarified, it is not so difficult to understand and accept Dewey's claim that it is rather the notion of *truth*, not warranted assertibility, which should be considered secondary if not peripheral as a working concept in logic.

5.1 Propositions and Information

Judgments and propositions in Dewey's view have to be understood primarily in terms of their relation to and function in inquiry— *not* in terms of syntactic features of linguistic expressions, *nor* in Frege's sense in which judgments are determinations of truth values of propositions.

> Propositions are logically distinct from judgment, and yet are the necessary logical instrumentalities for reaching final warranted deter-

mination of judgment. Only by means of symbolization (the peculiar differentia of propositions) can direct action be deferred until inquiry into conditions and procedures has been instituted. The overt activity, when it finally occurs, is, accordingly, intelligent instead of blind. Propositions as such are, consequently, provisional, intermediate and instrumental. (Dewey 1938, p. 283)[1]

To understand Dewey's conception of propositions, we first need to understand the basic features of the pattern of inquiry, in as general a way as possible. In this section, I will propose a way to think about this pattern which will clarify in particular what propositions are in Dewey's view, hence to begin to explain how it is that we can think of logic as the theory of inquiry.

Though Dewey is nowhere quite so graphic, we may for heuristic purposes imagine that inquiry has the more or less helical pattern of a corkscrew. Thinking diagrammatically can sometimes be misleading if not dangerously simplistic; but the image of a corkscrew pattern is especially apt here.

This helical pattern of inquiry is resolvable into two orthogonal processes or dimensions of activity—a linear component and a circular component.

1. The linear, conative, teleological character of inquiry is depicted in figure 1. Successful inquiry is innately directed toward establishing some sort of stable conclusion, which is to say, toward construction of a warranted judgment. A judgment, in Dewey's view, consists in the attribution of a determinate "predicate" to a determinate "subject," though in the prelinguistic sense (introduced in Chapter 4) in which facts of the matter systematically converge to a coherent subject of judgment, while ongoing modes of action settle into a manner of conduct which constitutes the predicate. In this case, if the inquirer associates linguistic labels, say s and p, with these two elements of a judgment, then a sentence 's is p' (modulo appropriate grammatical constructions) is warrantably

---

[1]See Dewey's discussion of logical positivism in *Logic* (pp. 284–6) where he mildly applauds but mostly criticizes their emphasis on "sentences" and "words," versus propositions and terms.

FIGURE 1 The teleological component of inquiry

utterable. But otherwise, one *asserts* the judgment itself (not its sentential expression) by actually conducting oneself in accordance with the predicate *p* in that particular situation *s*.

Admittedly, this will seem like an odd use of the terms 'subject' and 'predicate'. But it reflects Dewey's attempt to supply naturalistic foundations for logic and semantics. Consider in this light the following quote from *How We Think*:

> In the case of the meaning of words, ... happenings, like sounds, which originally were devoid of significance acquire meaning by use, and that this use always involves a *context*. With children just learning to understand and use speech, the context is largely that of objects and acts. A child associates *hat* with putting something on the head when he is going outdoors; *drawer* with pulling something out of a table, etc. Single words, because of the direct presence of a context of actions performed with objects, then have the force that complete sentences have to an older person. Gradually other words that originally gained meaning by use in a context of overt actions become capable of supplying the context, so that the mind can dispense with the context of things and deeds. Speaking in sentences marks obviously a *linguistic* gain. But the more important matter is that it shows a person has made a great *intellectual* advance. He can now think by putting together verbal signs of things that are not present to the senses and are not accompanied by any overt actions on his part. (Dewey 1911/1933, pp. 144-5)

The interesting point here is that "predication," so far as judgments are concerned, is originally to be found in overt action, and only later (developmentally speaking) in the formation of sentences. Theories of grammar and logic more generally could afford to address such concerns, according to this view.

Theories of intentionality could also afford to address such concerns. This progressive, conative component of inquiry constitutes the basic intentional character of experience. Even the most rudimentary forms of experience involve a kind of reference and attribution, even if this reference and attribution is neither linguistic nor cognitive in nature. Any given episode of experience involves a simple form of indexical reference to the present situation as the "subject" of experience; and it involves the attribution of a "predicate" to this subject, in the form of an acceptance or rejection of the present course of activity (the content of the predicate) as being an appropriate response to the problem which gave rise to the "subject" in the first place.

2. The process of securing a judgment, in addition to having the linear component described above, has a progressive but essentially circular or cyclical component as well. In a nutshell, this circular aspect of inquiry looks something like the following: The agent observes the results of his/her/its actions, entertains possible courses of action and expected results based on those observations, experiments with the more feasible alternatives to test their viability, observes the results of such experimentation, and around it goes—a process of exploring facts of the matter and narrowing the range of possible actions one can take, until, hopefully, a solution to the initial problem is settled on.

But actually this circular component of inquiry is somewhat more complex than just sketched. The circular component of inquiry has a multifaceted structure, the complexity of which is correlated with the overall evolutionary development of the given inquirer. To facilitate a summary discussion of Dewey's taxonomy of propositions, we will focus on the two main facets of this circular structure, postponing an account of their evolutionary-developmental linkage.

As discussed in Chapter 3, inquiry may be entirely perceptual in character, as if to proceed in a largely automatic manner, or it may also involve reflective processes. In the first case, this means that perception by itself is a complete kind of experience. Hence the process of perception can be resolved into the linear and circular components characteristic of any complete experience.

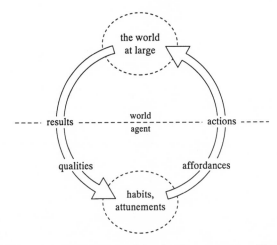

FIGURE 2 Perceptual aspect of the circular component of inquiry

Using the terminology developed in Chapter 3, we would say that an episode of perception is such as to spiral from a stimulus to a response by way of a process of registering sensory data (qualia) as results of motor activities which are guided by habits keyed to given sensory data (etc.). Figure 2 depicts this circular facet of inquiry so far as mere perception is concerned. It depicts a habit-guided interaction between an agent and the world at large, where qualities (registered as world-mediated results of motor activities) serve as cues to affordances of things in the given situation, as dictated by established habits. Perception "succeeds" in given instances to the extent that this circular interaction is stably coherent.

A notion of noncognitive rationality is suggested here, measured by the appropriateness of given habits in given instances. The rationality involved in determining which habits are triggered in a given instance and which are not is a function of the systematicity of the space of constraints and processes which make up the contents of various habits, matched against whatever actions and results are actually occurring in the present situation. We can say in this sense that a nonthinking animal's actions are rational or irrational by virtue of the appropriateness of various habits in various circum-

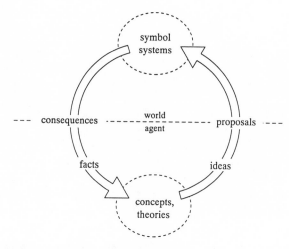

FIGURE 3 Reflective aspect of the circular component of inquiry

stances, independently of its exercising any cognitive abilities. This is a qualification we impose on the animal's actions from an external perspective, not that the animal has any choice in the matter.

Or, inquiry may in addition be conceptual in character, proceeding in a reflective manner, for agents that have developed the necessary mental abilities. But what does it mean to be "mental" or to reflect? However such abilities come about, inquiry is reflective insofar as the inquirer is able to at least partially back away from the concrete situation as given, to consider facts and possibilities in the abstract, becoming free to sift through given information and to speculate about possible courses of action without having to actually follow them out in every case. Possibilities can then be explored and perhaps eliminated with minimal vital commitment and expenditure. Costly mistakes or dead ends may be entirely avoided by virtue of the foresight afforded by speculative rehearsal of possible courses of action.

But now we are in a position to say what propositions are. Perception by itself does not involve the use of propositions, but rather propositions occur as formulations of factual and hypothetical information in reflective modes of inquiry.

Figure 3 depicts this reflective aspect of the circular character of inquiry. The process of reflection is also a kind of agent/world interaction, modeled on the structure of perceptual experience, but it is an interaction of the agent with a special kind of subdomain of the world at large, namely, with systems of symbols (e.g., with languages). In the course of reflection, actions are not directly executed, but merely proposed, by virtue of suggestions made on the basis of given facts formulated in terms of some conceptual framework. This reflective interaction will employ some kind of language or symbolic system to formulate and explore consequences of alternative proposals. Reflective experience is in this sense like an internal monologue concerning details and prospects of a given situation. Reflection "succeeds" in given instances (*a*) to the extent that this circular interaction is stably coherent, and (*b*) to the extent that the results comport with perceptual experience.

A notion of cognitive rationality is suggested here, as measured by the appropriateness of given concepts in given instances. The rationality involved in determining which concepts are triggered by certain facts and which do not is a function of the systematicity of the contents of the various concepts, matched against whatever proposals and consequences are actually derived in the present situation. We can in this sense say that a thinking agent's actions are rational or irrational, by virtue of the appropriateness of various concepts in various circumstances as manifested in the applications of cognitive processes in those circumstances. This is of course a qualification we impose on the agent's actions from an external perspective, not that the agent must be cognizant of acting rationally in order to act rationally.

On this view, thinking (reflection) does not take place solely inside the cranium. Habits and concepts serve to constitute the agent and hence in some sense are *in* the agent—as depicted in figures 2 and 3. But recall from earlier chapters that an agent is an organism/environment system, so what is "in" the agent is nonetheless as likely to be in an environment as in an organism. The organism/environment distinction is orthogonal to the agent/world distinction depicted in these figures. Even if thought were to take place solely within the agent, separate from the rest of the world, it does not follow that it would take place solely within the organism, much less inside the cranium. But the picture here is a bit stronger. Thought, in the most general sense of the term, does not even take place solely within the agent but rather is a kind of agent/world interaction. Thought takes place in the interactive interface between agent and world.[2]

The existence of these two aspects or modes of inquiry—perceptual and reflective—requires and presupposes some kind of connection and interplay between the formulation of propositions and the control of actions in the world. As discussed in earlier chapters, Dewey claims that an evolutionary continuity links these apparently disparate but complimentary aspects of inquiry. Conceptual abilities will have evolved out of more basic perceptual abilities in the first place. Evolutionary processes will have laid down their constitutive linkage by virtue of the fact that reflective capabilities have developed out of or on the basis of perceptual capabilities. But starting simply with these two distinct facets of experience as given, all we are interested in presently is their functional correspondence, not to try to tell this evolutionary story (but see page 260 below for some further discussion along these lines; also Burke 1994).

For a reference other than *Logic*, this twofold picture of the workings of observation and thought in inquiry is discussed informally but at length in *How We Think* (1911/1933, especially pp. 97–8, 102–118). Dewey is explicit there not just about the interdependence of thought and overt action but also about their constitutive similarity.

> Obviously the use of both methods [i.e., thought and action] of proving a proposed inference is better than one alone. The two methods do not

---

[2]An account of so-called "silent" thought requires objective awareness of a self as an entity in the world and the subsequent dialogue this allows: silent thought is talking to one's self, in the broadest not-limited-to-first-order-logic sense of the term 'talk'. This is an important issue that will not be pursued here. But see Mead 1909, 1924–1925, 1938, and Burke 1994.

differ, however, in kind. Testing in thought for consistency involves acting in *imagination*. The other mode carries the imagined act out overtly.... The original pattern of reflective action is set by cases in which the need for doing something is urgent, and where the results of what is done test the value of thought. As intellectual curiosity develops, connection with overt action becomes indirect and incidental. Yet it persists even if only in imagination. (Dewey 1911/1933, p. 98)

Presumably the symbol systems mentioned in figure 3 should be rich enough to express the workings of all kinds of imagination, not limited just to verbal representations. It should also be possible to invent ad hoc symbol systems on the run to fit current needs, such as when you grab a bunch of rocks and sticks (not usually thought of as elements of diagrams, linguistic morphemes, or meaningful symbols otherwise) to make a map on the ground, in discourse with your fellow campers.

Reflective capabilities in this view are like a clutch-and-transmission system, allowing an agent to disengage itself from concrete activities and adjust its conduct according to a changing foresight into possible consequences of feasible actions—foresight which is often worked out on the run, contingent upon given circumstances. The value of reflective thought lies in its allowing one to scope out possibilities on the basis of results of past actions and thereby to avoid troublesome alternatives and choose more promising ones. This clutch mechanism is engaged (thought proceeds independently) or is disengaged (the results of reflection, of "switching gears," are applied to current activities) as dictated by the circumstances and fortunes of one's ongoing conduct. The gear-systems that constitute this cognitive transmission system are *concepts*. As habits designed for handling symbol systems, concepts are not really learned by a cognitive agent until they can be used by that agent as means for solving problems and otherwise for making one's way through the world. The adjustments in one's conduct which are surveyed and tested in reflective thought are aimed at affecting transformations in the given problematic situation, presumably to move matters toward a solution to the given problem.

The value of reflection—of the use of concepts—lies in the capacity it affords the agent to back off from the world in the concrete and deal with it in terms of possibilities represented symbolically. Clearly the evolutionary value of an increased capacity not just to solve problems but to foresee and avoid problems is immense. One can thereby formulate and rehearse possible courses of action without being bound to suffer the actual consequences of those actions. This disengaged symbolic activity is useful, of course, only to the extent that one brings what develops in thought back into the concrete world. Though it may proceed independently more or less for its own sake, the primary function of thinking is to monitor and control actions in an efficient and effective way. Perception and thought are designed to work consistently with one another and in unison. This functional correspondence, by no means guaranteed, is a measure of successful inquiry.

Dewey would appear to agree with Kant (1785, 1788) at least in this one regard, namely, that an agent's free-agency (spontaneity, autonomy) is manifested in that agent's capacity to exercise reason and to apply the results of reflective thought to the control of its own conduct. The sense of freedom that we have as reflective agents is a sense that the choices we make and the actions that we perform on the basis of the choices that we make are able to affect the world in some independent sense—that the world is not just making itself over through us but that our own reflective decision-making processes take place and yield results autonomously in varying degrees. But this is precisely what is meant by likening thought to a clutch-and-transmission system. It is not that thinking does not have a naturally systematic character just like anything else in the world; but an agent's mental faculty is a piece of the world that is specifically designed to operate independently of the rest of the world. Thought (thinking, reflection, the use of reason) is a manifestation of our spontaneity in a universe otherwise driven by natural law—not that thinking is not as lawful as anything else, but that it is a free-running bit of machinery capable of engaging with and disengaging from (in varying degrees) everything else on the basis of its own operations. That we have such a capacity, especially as brought to light in uncertain situations, is what fosters our sense of free-agency and power in a world in which we otherwise seem to be buffeted by forces beyond our control. If there are differences between Dewey and Kant here, one would be that for Dewey our power of reason is explained by reference to our spontaneity (viz., our ability to initiate causal sequences), rather than vice versa (Kant 1785, chap. 3). And the story of how our spontaneity comes about lies in our social and cultural heritage—an evolutionary story I am not prepared to tell here (but see Burke 1994 for details). In this regard, we need not appeal to a noumenal self outside of the "laws of nature" in order to account for this free-agency (which is not to argue that there is nothing outside the laws of nature, but simply that we do not need to make such a move at this point).

The one thing that a free-running reflective faculty must nevertheless answer to is the practical application of its results in real problem-solving situations. Otherwise it has no reason for occurring in the first place. The drive and the need to correctly judge situations gives thought its free reign but also binds it to the world of "actual" activity. As Kant (1788) would have it, practical reason (the making of judgments, in Dewey's sense; determining the will, in Kant's sense) has primacy over theoretical reason (reflection; the formulation of propositions, in Dewey's sense; the making of judgments, in Kant's sense). The slippage between thought and perception which virtually guarantees the fallibility of reflective speculation and which otherwise generates all sorts of epistemic problems from one situation to the next is at the same time evidence of our freedom as cognitive agents.

Note the contrast between the picture we have just outlined and the classical picture of correspondence between propositions and facts characteristic of Russell's way of thinking. The classical picture is outlined in figure 4. Perception is depicted as a one-way causal process by which the world affects the mind, and the mind in turn affects the world by means of actions selected on the basis of one's beliefs, desires, and so forth. Several of Dewey's distinc-

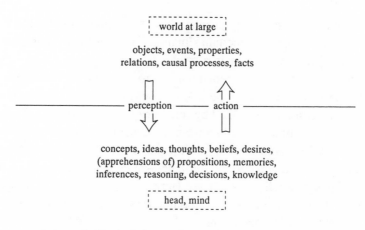

FIGURE 4 Classical picture of proposition/fact correspondence

tions will have been lost or collapsed or otherwise conflated and realigned to produce this simpler picture. According to the classical view, there are facts in the world, and there are propositions in (or at least entertained by) the mind; and these propositions either accurately describe the facts, in which case they are true, or else they do not and are then false. Inquiry, clearly a secondary concern here, is something that occasionally goes on in the mind, as the agent accommodates itself to the world at large. It is not clear where language belongs in this picture; but for Russell, a study of the syntax of formal languages—i.e., logic—is a study of propositional forms and formal features of propositional systems. This picture preserves classical epistemological problems associated with skepticism and an inability to explain connections among mind, body, and world (not to mention a realm of propositions).

Condensing and combining figures 2 and 3 into one figure and ignoring the teleological dimension of inquiry, we get Dewey's alternative picture of the relationship between perception and thought in figure 5. Perception and thought, just to be what they are in the first place, involve two different kinds of two-way interaction (with finer details provided in figures 2 and 3 respectively). In Dewey's picture, we are asked to consider a more complex, multidimensional

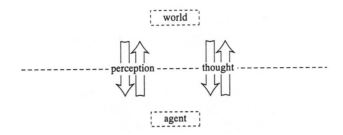

FIGURE 5 Alternative to the classical picture

treatment of correspondence, not just between the contents of the head and the outer world or between propositions and facts (in a classical sense of those terms). There are actually several distinct kinds of correspondence evident in these diagrams. For instance, proceeding in no particular order:

1. With respect to figure 3 by itself, if the interplay between symbolic and conceptual systems is disjointed, then processes of reflection are compelled to continue, to move inquiry along, toward some manner of reflective coherence. This coherence, occurring or not in specific cases, may be thought of as a kind of correspondence between the symbol systems and the conceptual systems employed in those cases.

For example, symbolic expressions such as 'round square' would not correspond to any single coherent concept in Euclidean geometry, whereas something like 'perpendicular lines' would. (An expression like 'two distinct straight lines through two given points' might count as corresponding to a coherent concept in Euclidean geometry, in some sense of the term 'coherent' which nevertheless allows that the concept may be inapplicable to any object. We do not need independent axioms to rule out round squares, but we do need axioms to rule in or out two distinct lines through two given points.) Outside of geometry, an English expression like 'Santa Claus' apparently would also correspond to a single coherent concept, but only to the extent that one can coherently conceive of flying reindeer and the like. More generally, translations between natural languages invariably raise questions of whether and how a given language is suited to expressing concepts as formulated in another language.

2. Similarly, with respect to figure 2, if the interplay between habits and the world at large is disjointed, then processes of perception are compelled to continue until some manner of perceptual coherence is achieved. For example, a lunchtime apple tasting like chopped liver would give one pause, whereas an apple tasting like an apple would be eaten routinely with minimal cause for attention.

3. With respect to both figures 2 and 3 taken together, there is the matter of what we might refer to as *empirical adequacy*— namely, reasonably sufficient and acceptable comportment between processes of reflection and processes of perception. The latter notion of correspondence—empirical adequacy of the results of reflection—perhaps best substantiates the basic intuitions under-lying a classical notion of correspondence such as one finds in Russell's views or in Tarski's truth criterion.

The notion of *satisfaction* has been discussed here in various ways: as fulfillment of needs (pages 28, 78, 133), as a balancing of organic energies and environmental conditions (pages 75, 131, 133), as fulfillment of desires (pages 99, 102, 116), as a matching of expectations and actual conditions (pages 102, 115, 133; see also pages 239–244 below), not to mention references to Tarski's definition of logical satisfaction (pages 80, 245). We may add one more notion to this list—satisfaction as empirical adequacy of the results of reflection—and point out that all of these different senses of satisfaction, while not identical, have a common basis in Dewey's treatment of organism/environment stability. It is neither inappropriate nor mere coincidence that Dewey should have begun a text on logic with a discussion of such concerns.

In particular, the fulfillment of needs is a specific case of the maintenance of organism/environment balance, where particular felt needs are instances of imbalance. The specific character of a given felt need is presumably determined by the constitution of one's habits and attunements, where organism/environment balance is dynamically gauged by a habit-mediated match between registered qualities and perceived affordances (cf. figure 2).

The fulfillment of desires is a further specialization of this same kind of thing, if we regard desires also as instances of imbalance, but where the specific character of a given desire is generated by the confluence of habit-driven experience and at least rudimentary forms of reflection. If we think of desire as a more or less reflective (cognitive) attitude, not merely a product of habit or a felt need, nevertheless the fulfillment of desires is a matter of securing organism/environment balance. More complex than merely fulfillment of needs, the satisfaction of desires would also involve the coordination of processes of reflection with habit-driven experience.

The notion of satisfaction as a match between expectations and actual conditions moves us more cleanly into figure 3. Being reflective in character, this notion is nevertheless patterned after the notion of fulfillment of needs. In this case, expectations would be determined by one's concepts, and organism/environment balance would be dynamically gauged at least in part by a concept-mediated match between conditions and expectations, i.e., between facts and ideas.

Then, the idea of satisfaction as empirical adequacy of conceptual processes would address the more or less substantial link between figures 2 and 3. That is, this idea pertains to the fit between processes and products of reflection and processes and products of perception, though it is a broader and more elaborate notion than those previously outlined. It is similar to the idea of satisfaction as fulfillment of desires insofar as it pertains to the fit between these two kinds of processes. But, taking scientific inquiry as an ideal if not canonical example of the sort of experience where this kind of satisfaction is most relevant, it would seem to assume fully operative if not refined reflective processes, and reflectively guided rather than appetite-driven perceptual processes (e.g., controlled experimentation). Satisfaction as empirical adequacy at least requires a kind of objectivity that is not presumed in satisfying desires.

At least in more rudimentary forms, though, such concerns are still relevant to the maintenance of organism/environment balance.

As a fact of evolutionary development, reflective capacities exist precisely because of their value in this latter regard. Reflection, as opposed to brute appetitive trial-and-error processes, serve to increase efficiency and efficacy of problem-solving efforts, yielding laborsaving foresight, allowing avoidance of foreseeable problems altogether, and so forth. As an evolutionary/developmental step forward, the existence of reflective abilities adds a new and distinct twist to the whole project of ensuring survival and maintaining some degree of well-being. As opposed to matching different features solely within the act of perception, and rather than matching different features solely within the act of reflection, satisfaction as empirical adequacy is a matter of matching wholesale perception processes with those of reflection. In the best of all possible situations, a good fit in this regard should correlate highly with, and would therefore serve as a gauge of, organism/environment balance.

Normally, one would hope for a correlation between *coherent* perceptual and reflective processes, though (as we might also have noted with regard to interactions of habit and desire) such coherence of each of these two processes is not guaranteed even if there is a high degree of correlation between them. Presumably, it is not impossible that disjointed reflection could fit quite well with disjointed perception. For example, we could regard Ptolemaic astronomy as the result of just this sort of thing. Alcoholism would be a similar example with regard to correlations between dysfunctional habits and desires. So the idea of empirical adequacy is not only independent of previous notions of satisfaction but is also not a foolproof gauge of organism/environment well-being. The criterion that this correlation should exhibit tested stability suggests that it may, with sufficient care, be a promising if not reliable gauge of organism/environment balance; but it is on such grounds only indirectly and conditionally indicative of successes or failures to secure the more basic kinds of satisfaction.

Finally, the idea of logical satisfaction, more or less in the spirit of Tarski's formulation, may be cast as a specific version of the preceding notion of the empirical adequacy of conceptual processes.

In the most basic case—such as in the base case for an inductive definition?—we would be interested specifically in *objects* as products of perception, and *concepts* as products of reflection, and the question of what it means to say that the former *fall under* the latter. The answer is found in what is essentially Peirce's pragmatic maxim. This introduces an array of technical issues that needs to be explored but which will not be pursued further here (though see Section 6.2 below for some further remarks along these lines).

4. Otherwise, continuing a survey of different conceptions of correspondence suggested by the present account of the pattern of inquiry: there is the question of point-for-point correlations between the different features of perceptual and reflective experience. For instance, what is the connection between habits and concepts? We might expect this connection to be fairly tight, due to an evolutionary/developmental linkage between perceptual and reflective capabilities. For that matter, what is the *difference* between them? It would seem that concepts are not simply habits, but in some sense they are habits. Some careful textual exegesis (of Dewey 1911/1933 and 1938, in particular) would be required to justify this claim, but what we would come to is two things. First, concepts are more or less self-contained habits that have names or otherwise are subject to representation within some symbolic medium or other (which is not necessarily verbal). As such, concepts are representations of habits—or more properly, habits-at-a-distance, capable of being held at bay by virtue of some kind of symbolic handle. As such, concepts have a different functional role in inquiry from mere habits. Habits and concepts both serve to sift and select possibilities in their own peculiar ways, but plain nonconceptual habits play this role in perception and in direct apprehension of things otherwise, while concepts function as such in processes of reflection. Concepts are sources of suggestions and tentative proposals (ideas), while plain habits are mechanisms for directly guiding actions by mapping out affordances of things in given situations.

But secondly, concepts *are* habits in a more straightforward sense—insofar as they are mechanisms for directly guiding reflective processes by mapping out ideas relevant in given situations. That is to say, insofar as at least some perceivable affordances will have been named or otherwise can be handled indirectly by some symbolic means, ideas *represent* affordances—in the sense that ideas are suggestions and support specific proposals about how to proceed in a given situation. In a different sense, ideas *are* affordances. Insofar as they pertain to the systematic use of representations, ideas point to lines of development by which reflective processes might work themselves out. In this sense, ideas are the affordances of reflection. And in this same sense, concepts are habits, but specifically with regard to agent/world interactions constituting the use of symbols.

5. Also, what is the connection between symbol systems, as *re*presentational media, and the world at large? Other than the fact that symbol systems are just subdomains of the world at large, the question here concerns the capacity of symbol systems to *represent* anything and everything, including other symbols. We might expect this connection to be fairly loose, evidenced by the linguistic diversity found within and across different cultures. This connection would probably be tighter in certain respects with standardized symbol systems that are pictorial or diagrammatic, looser with linear, verbal symbol systems. In any case, some degree of convention is involved in the design of any symbol system, such as when a linguistic community chooses to call dogs "dogs" or when we sit around the camp fire and refer to rock X as Mount Baldy as we plan the next day's hike.

The formulation of propositions in a given problem-solving context is not necessarily a formal-symbolic enterprise, but it will nevertheless employ some system of symbols as a way of handling information about what the facts are and what modes of action are possible and relevant to the case at hand. Systems of propositions, especially as formulated by means of one or more symbolic media, are devices for managing information pertinent to a given inquiry to the extent that they serve to register and organize actual *and* possible facts in the given situation.

Contrary to Russell's remarks about how the structure of the world is somehow mirrored in the structure of language (see Russell 1940, pp. 22, 437), we have no reason to believe that formal aspects of symbol systems constitute anything like a reliable guide to how the world is structured. There is obviously a connection between symbol systems and the world at large, but for the most part this connection is only indirect by way of the mediation of habits, particularly in their capacity to function as concepts and thereby underwrite the contents of our uses of symbols. Singular names are associated with singular objects, so far as that goes, but there is no reason to think that the bare formal properties of the language in which names function mirrors nomic properties in the situation in which the objects function.

6. As for propositions versus facts, we run into a terminological glitch. The question of correspondence between propositions and facts, in Dewey's sense of those terms, is basically meaningless. For Dewey, formulations of facts constitute one particular category of propositions. Facts *are* propositions, of one sort anyway. Facts are elements of information about concrete experience. Hypotheses about the prospects of concrete experience are another sort of proposition. In this sense, facts, while provisional, are not hypotheses, strictly speaking. As elements of reflective experience, they may be misleading or just wrong, like Ptolemaic data; but, up to some point, they will still be the facts of the matter.

Facts, formulated as propositions in given situations, come in a couple of varieties which are not simply reducible one to the other. In the course of a given inquiry, in response to some given problem, there will be facts concerning registered *qualities* of things in the given situation, and there will be facts about what *kinds* of things there are in that situation. Propositions of a third sort, namely, those formulating constraints among possible *modes* of action in the given situation, are not strictly *facts* in Dewey's sense of the term, though they nevertheless "hold" or "are the case" (or not) in the given inquiry. What distinguishes them from propositions formulating facts is that they are assumed to hold from one inquiry to the next, from one situation to the next (whether or not they actually do). Hence Dewey refers to them as "universal" (i.e., trans-situational) propositions, whereas facts are "existential" (i.e., situated) propositions. Universal propositions validate the formulation of possibilities (ideas, suggestions) in a given instance, insofar as they help to determine possible operational consequences of given facts in that instance.

As devices for representing various sorts of information, propositions are formulated in inquiry in service to the process of effecting judgment. The facts of the matter (actual and possible), both in terms of registered qualities of things as well as in terms of classifications of things as instances of various kinds, will almost certainly change due to the changing implementation of different modes of action.

It would appear then that, by treating propositions as "instruments" of inquiry, Dewey was ahead of his time in advancing a theory of logic built around the modern notion of *information*. That is, Dewey's logic essentially focuses on propositions as units of symbolic information in a given reflective inquiry. Whatever else information is, it is, in this or that context, *useful*. Symbolic information, moreover, is useful for representational purposes. "Instrumentalism" in Dewey's sense may be described as the view that logic should be built not around the study of syntactic form, but around the notion of garnering and using information in concrete problem-solving contexts, to map out possible conditions and consequences of current activities in order to control one's actions and otherwise one's fortunes in a dynamic world. In short, instrumentalism in Dewey's original sense views logic as the study of the nature and use of information.

5.2 Dewey's Taxonomy of Propositions

Following up on the discussion in the preceding section, we are now able to survey Dewey's taxonomy of propositions as presented in Chapter 15 of *Logic* (1938). It should be helpful to try to understand Dewey's conception of propositions in his own terms, before proceeding to consider Russell's views on the matter.

The project of vindicating Dewey's view of logic would not be feasible if one were to try to make sense of it solely in terms of classical predicate logic or otherwise employ the predicate calculus as a standard against which it were to be measured. Dewey was developing a truly alternative conception of logic.[3] Dewey's manner of distinguishing different categories of propositions is not geared to interpreting any particular language or symbol system (or to accommodating any particular approach to syntactic theory more generally), but rather is geared to delineating various sorts of information involved in determining the subjects and predicates of judgments. As a result, things turn out to be a bit more complicated than what one finds in extensional model theory.

Dewey discusses seven basic kinds of propositions. Due to his discursive, nonaxiomatic manner of presentation, this list may seem unprincipled if not haphazard. But it is actually rather sophisticated. Rather than basing a theory of semantics on structures consisting of fixed universes of individuals with properties and relations handled purely in terms of extensions in this given universe, Dewey develops his logic in terms of a different array of basic ideas.

In particular, he works with *three* sorts of attribution rather than one. Besides registering *qualities* of things, or classifying things as being of this or that *kind*, we consider relations among different *modes-of-being* and judge situations to be of this or that mode-of-being. These three sorts of attribution, not to mention the taxonomy of propositions Dewey presents on the basis of this three-way distinction, make sense only in the context of their function in inquiry. We should not think of qualities, kinds, and modes-of-being as designating fixed ontological categories.

---

[3]Recent work in formal semantics, such as dynamic logic (Goldblatt 1992; van Benthem 1988) or Gärdenfors's work on the dynamics of belief (1988), is starting to generate theoretical frameworks rich enough to accommodate the kinds of concerns Dewey addressed in his logical theory. These results were of course available to neither Dewey nor Russell in the 1930s and 1940s, and it would take us far afield to address them here. The present discussion will recount Dewey's treatment of propositions with minimal attention to these current developments.

The basic idea depicted in figure 2 is that, in any given instance within a given inquiry, the inquirer is performing certain actions, whereby qualities of things are subsequently registered. By virtue of the attunements and habits one embodies, these qualities in turn indicate the presence or absence of certain kinds of things in the given situation. The habits one has developed with respect to certain familiar kinds of things in turn suggest further operations which might be performed if current actions fail to resolve things. This cyclical interplay between actions performed and anticipations of results of future actions goes on until the dynamics of the situation stabilize. Over the course of this process, to the extent that a disengaged, reflective attitude is implemented (figure 3), propositionally formulated information of several different sorts may accrue, gain or lose relevance, and otherwise preempt the automatic dictates of mere habit.

The different sorts of propositions Dewey discusses are described briefly in the following list:

(1) A **particular** proposition attributes a *quality* to some ostensive thing in a given situation. "That is twinkling." "Its position is now *abcxyz*."

(2) A **singular** proposition classifies something in a given situation as being of a certain *kind*. "That is a planet." "It is now in retrograde motion."

(3) A **contingent-conditional** proposition states a conditional link among singular things of various kinds in a given situation. "If that moves, it is a planet." "If that comet does not go away, these crops will wither."

(4) A **generic** proposition states that a relationship holds among kinds instantiated in a given situation. "All planets are stars." "Comets are ominous." "Most stars are fixed."

(5) A **contingent-disjunctive** proposition differentiates a kind into a disjunction of subkinds, with an eye toward developing some working taxonomy of kinds in a given situation. "Stars either wander or are fixed."

(6) A **universal-hypothetical** proposition states a relationship *in principle* among *modes* of being. "All celestial motion is perfectly circular."

(7) A **universal-disjunctive** proposition exhaustively partitions a mode into constituent modes, but as a matter of principle. "All changes are of four sorts: locomotive, quantitative, qualitative, or substantial."

Meanwhile, a *judgment*, which is not a type of "proposition" in Dewey's logic, is an assertion attributing a mode-of-being or mode-of-action to a determinate situation. This is a possibly after-the-fact assertion of the result of transforming the given situation (as a dynamic field of current experience) from being unbalanced, incoherent, and unacceptable to being balanced, coherent, and acceptable.

The examples given in (1)–(7) are not Dewey's and have to be taken with a grain of salt. Dewey stresses that it is misleading to try to specify a proposition simply by means of a *sentence* alone. That is, any given sentence may be used to express not just any number of propositions but different *sorts* of propositions as well. If nothing else, terms like 'star' or 'omen' or 'motion' can stand for modes, kinds, and qualities, all three, depending on the context of use. But it is easy to imagine some particular context in which such uses are made definite. The point is simply to supply some examples in the context of a single inquiry, such as some phase of Ptolemaic cosmological inquiry.

For a more common example: to be able to recognize things of the kind *lemon*, you would have to be able to operate in the world in certain ways which happen to be typical ways of interacting with lemons; and those operations, if executed in the presence of and toward what is in fact a lemon, would yield certain qualitative data and not others. Visually, its color would include yellow hues; its size and shape would be such and so; its juice would taste sour; and so forth. These specifications need not be written out nor even be writable as linguistic "descriptions" so long as they come to be engrained in one's repertoire of possible experiences as a constrained set of operations with certain expected outcomes. In any case, in specific instances, we may obtain the information "this is a lemon" or "this is not a lemon."

This helps to pinpoint the difference between particular versus singular propositions: a particular proposition asserts that some ostensive thing has this or that quality (as the result of certain interactions with it), whereas a singular proposition asserts that some ostensive thing is of this or that kind (and therefore should afford evidence of a number of characteristic qualitative traits as results of manners of operation typical of that kind of thing). By saying that something is an instance of the kind *lemon*, one is committed to that thing being able to evidence a range of qualities characteristic of lemons (tastes, smells, colors, haptic textures, heft, and so forth). On the other hand, to say that something is exhibiting a yellow visual quality, independent of any other information, commits one to very little other than that it might be a lemon, a canary, a daffodil, or something which is typically yellow. This parallels the distinction between making a theoretical claim about an object (classifying it as one of a kind) versus stating evidence in support of or contrary to that claim (noting some of its qualities).

Contingent-conditional propositions are a special sort of if-then conditional between singular propositions. Dewey gives examples like "If this rain continues, the ball game will be canceled" or "If this drought continues, the harvest will be poor." The distinctive feature of these conditionals is that the respective antecedents and consequents are singular propositions concerning ostensible objects. Such propositions serve to systematize singular facts in a given context and to plot out spaces of possibilities on the basis of singular facts.

Generic propositions, on the other hand, are such as to state relations between kinds. Other examples would be propositions such as that "iron is a metal" or that "lemons are fruits" or that "tigers are animals," where all the general terms here are understood to denote kinds. Included here would be propositions involving various sorts of quantification: All *A*s are *B*s, Some *A*s are *B*s, Many *A*s are

Bs, Most As are Bs, Few As are Bs, No As are Bs, Exactly six As are Bs, The A is B, and so forth, where the different determiners reflect different sorts of relations between kinds. (See particularly Chapter 11 of *Logic* for a somewhat dense and lengthy discussion of such matters. This is clearly one of the more complicated parts of the book.)

Presumably something like 'tigers eat lemons' could express a generic proposition (most likely a false one), where the verb 'eat' would express a second-order relation holding between two kinds of things, 'tiger' and 'lemon', which we might write as *Eat* (*tiger*, *lemon*). Or such a sentence might be treated as synonymous with 'all tigers are lemon eaters', where the generic relation is quantificational, and the verb phrase 'eat lemons' essentially denotes a kind 'lemon eater': *All* (*tiger*, *lemon eater*). Or perhaps the verb 'eat' could express a first-order binary kind, where the given sentence expresses a generic classification of *its* two arguments, the implicit second-order relation again being quantificational (possibly "existential" in this case?): roughly, *Some* (*eat* (*tiger*, *lemon*)). Such considerations obviously raise a number of questions, but the basic definition of generic propositions should be relatively clear.

Contingent-disjunctive propositions are such as to resolve kinds into would-be exhaustive disjunctions of kinds. For example, "anything which is a metal is either tin or copper or lead or mercury or zinc or ..., and these are all the kinds of metals there are." That such a disjunction of a kind into subkinds is exhaustive will be contingent upon ongoing experience. It will in many instances be an intermediate goal of an inquiry to be able to resolve relevant kinds into exhaustive subkinds, to enumerate an exhaustive range of possible cases, since this would help (by subsequent elimination of alternatives) to refine one's abilities to articulate facts. For instance, if you have what you think is a complete taxonomy of all metals, and you think that sample X is a metal, then you are in a position to either classify it more specifically, or determine that it is not a metal after all, by testing it against the specifications of each of the different acknowledged kinds of metals. Or, if there is some reason to insist that it is a metal, but it does not fit specifications of any recognized kind of metal, you might conclude that your given taxonomy of metals is not exhaustive after all. This could of course have certain ripple effects in terms of one's having to reevaluate all sorts of previously given facts about metals.

Universal propositions, on the other hand, involve relationships between or among modes of being (rather than kinds or qualities). These are sharply distinguished from generic propositions involving quantification with 'all', which are classified as existential insofar as they involve specific kinds of things relevant in a given inquiry and hence specific to a given situation (qua universe of discourse). At the same time, universal propositions formulate constraints among modes of action which serve to determine the characteristics of given kinds of things. Recall that a given kind, like *tiger* or *lemon*, is distinguished by specifying certain characteristic actions and typical results of those actions. To say that a given thing is a lemon is to express a singular proposition. Or to say that all the lemons at a given grocery store are overripe is to express a generic proposition. But to formulate a system of constraints which distinguish the kind *lemon* from other kinds, independent of any particular situation, is to formulate a set of universal propositions characterizing the basic character of lemons (so far as one's past experience has discovered or otherwise determined this character). Such systems of constraints, when relevant, may be brought to bear in given situations as a way of determining possible courses of action and thereby directing courses of events.

Such propositions are presumed to hold across all situations (or universes of discourse), but not by virtue of their "logical form" (whatever that might mean, since we have not yet developed any kind of propositional "syntax" at this point). The idea of a proposition holding in every situation is not just a matter of formal validity, but rather these propositions are universal by virtue of their contents. They reflect the agent's best shot at formulating rules, laws, maxims, principles, constraints, etc., concerning how the world actually works.

Hypothetical propositions, in particular, have a simple if-then structure (a matter which Dewey does not elaborate sufficiently, and which will not be adequately discussed here either). For example, suppose you have gone to the grocery store for lemons because you plan to prepare some particular dish which requires some sort of souring agent. Then you would be acting in accordance with your maxim that "lemons are sour" (not to mention other principles such as that "lemons are food" and "food is obtained at grocery stores").

Universal-disjunctive propositions are useful in limiting or otherwise narrowing the range of possible courses of action, for the same reason that contingent-disjunctive propositions help to resolve classifications of things. If your recipe calls for a souring agent, and if you assume that "only lemons, limes, or various kinds of vinegar are viable souring agents," then that scopes out a range of possible purchases. That scope can be narrowed if one is able to eliminate one or more alternatives based on other considerations, such as that the souring agent should be citric rather than acetic.

Given these informal remarks, it is still not clear that items (1)–(7) above constitute a systematic taxonomy of propositions, much less a complete or adequate one. What is important at present is not whether it is complete or sufficient or redundant (etc.) but simply that it *is* systematic in an interesting way which goes beyond anything we can capture in a Russellian predicate calculus.

In particular, one of the more interesting aspects of this taxonomy is its way of separating out an existential/universal distinction and a specific/general distinction. The first five sorts of propositions listed are termed "existential" by Dewey insofar as their occurrence and applicability are specific to a given situation. For instance, a particular proposition says not just that some thing θ exhibits a quality Q but that θ exhibits Q in an immediately given situation s. Or a generic proposition says not just that anything of kind K_1 is of kind K_2, but that this is the case in an immediately given situation s—e.g., that all the green things here are books, not as a universal law of nature but as a general fact about my current surroundings. On the other hand, (6) and (7) are termed "universal," formulat-

TABLE 1 Dewey's taxonomy of propositional forms

| | EXISTENTIAL | | UNIVERSAL |
	MATERIAL	PROCEDURAL	
SPECIFIC	*particular*	*singular* *c-conditional*	
GENERAL		*generic* *c-disjunctive*	*hypothetical* *u-disjunctive*

ing constraints among modes of being, assumed to hold from one situation to the next.

Corresponding to the distinction between qualities and kinds, existential propositions are divided into two classes. Specifically, (1) *material-existential* propositions formulate information about qualities of things in a situation; and (2)–(5) *procedural-existential* propositions formulate information about kinds of things in a situation.[4] Keeping track of what qualities are registered and which kinds of things are instantiated in the situation make up the two classes of *facts* determined in the course of inquiry.

Orthogonal to this material/procedural distinction, Dewey distinguishes *specific*[5] and *general* propositions. Forms (1)–(3) are specific, while (4)–(7) are general. Further, the larger distinction between *existential* and *universal* propositions is orthogonal to both the *specific/general* distinction and the *material/procedural* distinction. For what it is worth then, his basic scheme for distinguishing different sorts of propositions is charted in table 1.[6]

---

[4]Dewey's sketchy, if not ambiguous, uses of the terms 'material' and 'procedural' are in fact somewhat hard to get a grip on (but see *Logic*, pp. 136 and 288–93, in particular). The present discussion reflects one simple and coherent way to interpret Dewey's uses of these terms, but I am not sure this reflects every use Dewey makes of them.

[5]This is not Dewey's term. Dewey does not actually use any one term to label the otherwise distinct category of "nongeneral" propositions.

[6]There are two blank spots in table 1. Why not fill them in? A judgment is not unlike a "specific/universal" claim, insofar as the subject is a particular individual and the predication involved is universal (in two senses discussed below). Can we make sense of the idea of a specific/universal *proposition*? One option might be to introduce a notion of "rigid designation" at this point, whereby universal

To sum up, *existential* propositions formulate "facts" in a given situation, pertaining to a given inquiry, serving ultimately to articulate various features of the *subject* of judgment. There are two sorts of existential propositions corresponding to two distinct classes of facts, namely, facts about the *qualities* things exhibit, and facts about the *kinds* of things there are in the current situation. On the other hand, *universal* propositions formulate systematic relations among prospective modes of being, serving ultimately to characterize the *predicate* of judgment.

We might note that judgments are "universal" in a related but

---

propositions might be formulated which refer nevertheless to specific individuals properly identified as universally-existent objects. Another line to take would be to characterize specific/universal propositions as tentatively considered "proposals" which eventually, in the course of inquiry, generate a judgment. The logical subject in this case is the current situation as a whole, which is in fact a singular individual. As for general/material propositions, why not have propositions that formulate general relations among qualities? The answer would obviously seem to be that we can; but the question then becomes one of giving a principled account of such propositions.

It should be clear that Dewey's theory of propositions requires a more refined theory of quantification than is characteristic of the predicate calculus, hence one will not see any upside-down *A*s and backwards *E*s in the present discussion of this taxonomy. At the same time, the distinctions charted in table 1 almost line up with well-known distinctions in first-order logic. A distinction between singular and general propositions, namely, between those which do not and those that do employ quantifiers, is a familiar one. And with regard to quantified propositions, there is the distinction between existential versus universal quantification. It might be useful then to contrast table 1 with a similar one distinguishing three sorts of propositions in a more traditional vein:

	EXISTENTIAL	UNIVERSAL
SINGULAR	$Pa, \neg Rab$ $Pa \wedge Rab, \ldots$	
GENERAL	$\exists x\, \psi(x)$	$\forall x\, \psi(x)$

Or perhaps singular propositions, in this more traditional vein, should be considered completely outside of the existential/universal distinction. Unlike table 1, the entries in this table are forms of *sentences* in a simple first-order language, corresponding to different sorts of propositions which such sentences express or by which they are interpreted.

different sense than are so-called universal propositions. A judgment is *about* a concrete situation which is immediately given and which otherwise will have been scoped out and classified by whatever exploratory and reflective means one will have brought to bear in that instance. In this sense, a judgment is singular, pertaining to a fixed "individual," with its subject matter limited in scope. But as well, a judgment is a claim that a specific course of action is appropriate with regard to that concrete situation as a whole. Built into the very notion of a judgment, as a supposed *end* of inquiry, is the idea of a natural compulsion to handle the situation correctly or rightly, i.e., to determine a course of action in such a way that the situation does not persist or recur as problematic. A judgment is meant to be a conclusive, once-and-for-all claim that the given situation requires a certain course of action. A judgment is inconclusive and therefore unacceptable if the proposed solution unravels and allows the problem to crop up again after supposing one had finished dealing with it. This "once-and-for-all" character of judgment therefore constitutes a kind of universality. In this sense, a judgment is not unlike a specific/universal proposition, corresponding to one of the blank spots in table 1. That is, in making a judgment, a claim is made that a specific course of action will in fact integrate or otherwise reconcile the given situation with "everything else"—with the "world at large" outside of the given situation and hence outside of present experience. The claim thus made is that the proposed solution is a solution not just temporarily or tentatively or conditionally with regard to this or that peculiarity of the given situation, but in a stable way, once and for all, so that further inquiry is no longer necessary. Of course, this describes an instinctive and natural compulsion constituting the drive to judge situations correctly, effectively, and conclusively, not that one always succeeds in realizing this ideal. Judgments are fallible, despite the natural and not-necessarily-cognitive intention that they be absolutely correct.

Further still, a properly made judgment concerning a given situation will be such as to confirm or modify if not establish a precedent for future conduct to the effect that *any* situation of the same type should warrant the very same course of action, as if one were making a universal claim about any future occurrence of situations of that type. In this regard, a judgment (that situation *s* calls for a course of action *A*) generates (but is not the same as) a universal proposition (that conditions *S* characteristic of situation *s* call for a course of action *A*). This is one way to formulate the idea that a judgment (as the end result of an inquiry) can be in some sense the establishment and support of a habit or rule, that is, of a general and dependable way of acting in the world under certain conditions (namely, in situations of a specific type). Perhaps not all judgments are like this; but many are, for example, judging when to cross a given street, or judging if a given television program is suitable for your children.

This characterization of the universality of judgment applies in particular to situations where the problems are ethical in nature. Our sense of morality can be characterized as a special case of an innate drive to judge correctly and deal effectively with problematic situations. If the solution to a problem has social ramifications to any degree, the problem is an ethical one. And the rational principles we bring to bear to determine our actions in such a situation are to be universally warranted in the two senses just described: as conclusively and properly dealing with the given situation, and as establishing or supporting a precedent for future actions in (all) similar situations.

In this regard, we could argue that some of the themes of a Kantian theory of morality (1785, 1788) are not incompatible with Dewey's account of judgment. We could argue indeed that a quasi-Kantian account of morality is something of a corollary in Dewey's theory of inquiry—not that the account follows the same lines of conceptual development and argumentation, but that all the basic ingredients of a Kantian moral theory are present. Just on the basis of what we have said so far as regards what a judgment is, every judgment (in Dewey's sense; i.e., every instance of determining the will, in Kant's sense), insofar as it is about a given situation, constitutes a claim about how to act in response to that situation, *but* as if one were making a universal claim about that situation, *and* as if one were establishing a rule of conduct with respect to similar situations. These aspects of judgment have already been established as *definitive* of what a judgment is. If one were to formulate a judgment (i.e., determine the will) without the aim of establishing a reliable and conclusive way of handling a given situation and situations similar to it, one would contradict the very conception of what a judgment is—hence the "a priori" character of this "moral law" (that every judgment is as if it were the precedent for a universal law) and its formulation as a "categorical imperative" (in recognition of the fallibility of judgment and the fact that we do not always do justice to this universal character of judgment). One would thereby violate what is in fact basic to the very constitution of experience itself, namely, an instinctive drive to conduct oneself in such a way that one's continued existence is guaranteed in a universally appropriate way.

One thing missing in this picture is the idea of freedom, which is central to any moral theory. The moral law is in some sense a product of the fact that we are free agents by virtue of our ability to choose how to act in the world by pure reason alone (Beck 1960, pp. 179–80). But we have seen in Section 5.1 how this same basic idea is manifested in Dewey's account of the nature of reflective inquiry. Our free-agency is evidenced by our ability to stop and think and to choose how to act on that basis alone, to put it simply. That there is such a thing as practical reason, i.e., purely reflective "determination of the will" (i.e., that judgments can be made by mere reason alone), is by no means ruled out in Dewey's picture of inquiry. But then this completes and preserves the essential ingredients of a Kantian moral theory. A sense of morality would not be typical of all inquiring agents, but rather it is a feature of the experience of agents who can reason, i.e., who can reflect on possible courses of action in a given situation and in *that* light appreciate the universal significance of the judgments they make.

This sense of morality, while being a feature of reflective rather than merely animal experience, would appear to be as basic as the instinct to survive; or rather we should say that it is a specific manifestation (in thinking agents) of the very same instinct. It is not that we must consciously contemplate any of these matters about the universality of judgment in making rational judgments; but we do feel the need to be correct and conclusive in making such judgments, as something built into the very nature of judgment. That feeling or drive underlying the use of reason in inquiry constitutes our moral sense.

In this respect, it would be erroneous to think of pragmatist ethics as a form of utilitarianism, or hedonism, or otherwise as a theory that identifies the good with the useful. An action, thought, habit, disposition, etc., is good just in case it serves to secure the well-being of the agent—*but* where we understand well-being not in terms of "pleasure" or "happiness" or subjective "satisfaction" (which are only unreliable measures of actual well-being) but rather in terms of universally appropriate survival. The subtler point here, which is too easily overlooked in Kant's writings as well, is that this theory of "the good" supplies not a decision procedure for making value judgments but rather a foundational account of our very sense of morality, including allowance for the fact that we are not always able to make an obviously right decision or otherwise deal handily with every moral dilemma. In the same sense that an affirm/deny (true/false?) distinction constitutes the yes/no character of propositions (in a theoretical sense), a good/bad distinction *is* the yes/no character of judgments (in a practical sense)—it is built into the very notion of "judgment," which is built into the very notion of "experience." In Dewey's case, then, we end up here with a definition of "the good" on the basis of a foundational theory of the nature of reflective experience. We don't have a theory of what is good, but we do have an account of what good is (Dewey 1922, pp. 210ff). It is appropriate to call this a *pragmatist* moral theory insofar as it produces a theory of the good out of a general theory of practice, rather than to produce a theory of practice on the basis of some prior notion of the good (e.g., in terms of utility or hedons). This perspective is not unlike Kant's Copernican Revolution in moral philosophy, as Beck (1960, p. 179) puts it, which we find preserved in its basic outline in Dewey's moral philosophy.[7]

5.3 Some Criticisms

Russell's criticisms of Dewey's *Logic*, insofar as they hinge on or otherwise pertain to Dewey's conception of propositions, do not directly address many, if any, of the details outlined above. Nevertheless, this section will address a number of points in Russell's

---

[7]We might pursue this comparison with Kant a bit further, though it is something of a digression at this point.

Note first that Dewey's distinction between the formulation of propositions and the making of judgments serves as an alternative to Kant's distinction between speculative or theoretical reason (in the *Critique of Pure Reason*) and practical reason (in the *Critique of Practical Reason*). Dewey's equivalent to an analysis of pure speculative reason would be a study of inquiry but with minimal regard for its teleological character—it would focus merely on the circular aspect of the corkscrew, as it were. Primary concerns there would be the functioning of habits in perception, and the interplay between perception and thought, with emphasis on how objects of perception supply and constitute the information that powers the processes of thought. Dewey's equivalent to an analysis of pure practical reason would be a broader study of the nature of judgment, focusing on the teleological character of inquiry but with particular emphasis on surveying the distinguishing characteristics of reflective inquiry and rational judgment. These two studies are facets of a single theory of inquiry, where their mutual relevance is obvious from the start.

More specifically, the general treatment of perception and thought outlined in this chapter, though different from Kant's picture of the various faculties of human experience, suggests a way to understand Kant's distinction between general and transcendental logic (1781, A50–64/B74–88; Strawson 1966, pp. 74–82).

Logic in a more or less Russellian vein would be identified nowadays as general logic, just as the latter was conceived of in an Aristotelean vein by Kant. So far as general logic is concerned, the basic forms of propositions (or what Kant would call judgments) are taken for granted as given, and their systematic properties are studied on these formal grounds alone. Their contents, and more specifically questions of how propositions might have or acquire contents to begin with, are put aside.

Transcendental logic, on the other hand, delves into the constitutive nature of propositions, particularly with regard to how it is they can be formulated in the first place. A central problem of transcendental logic is to understand the nature

arguments which bear on Dewey's distinction between propositions and judgments—to argue that Russell showed no cognizance of this distinction and, as a result, was not able to properly evaluate Dewey's conception of logic.

To fully appreciate Dewey's philosophy of logic, it is not possible to maintain an orientation to logic as nothing more nor less than a study of the predicate calculus, that is, the logic of Russell's *Principles of Mathematics* (1903). There is more to be considered beyond fitting the basic subject-predicate structure of linguistic expressions to a mathematical function-argument idiom. Anything in

---

of *satisfaction*, at least in one sense of that term, namely, to understand how it is or what it means to say (at all, much less validly) that an object of intuition falls under a given concept. For Dewey, this is largely a matter of the correspondence between processes of reflection (understanding?) and processes of perception (sensibility?). In his survey of the scope of what we can know, Kant appealed to a principle (taken from Hume) requiring empirical grounds for applications of concepts to objects and more generally for the formulation of information involving concepts at all. Strawson (1966, pp. 16, 145, 241–3) refers to this requirement as the principle of significance. A concept lacks epistemic significance without this requisite empirical grounding. This principle is essentially the source (or original version) of Peirce's pragmatic maxim, in which case Kant might just as well be counted as the first pragmatist.

Kant presented these matters in such a way that a proper account of propositions involves an account, or at least an acknowledgment, of the underlying unity of experience, whereby the simplest kinds of propositions—attributions of concepts to objects of intuition—are possible only by virtue of a synthesis of understanding and sensibility. It is not too much of a stretch to think of the *Critique of Pure Reason* as a treatise on the foundations of semantics insofar as it includes an extended investigation of the constitution of propositions, that is, of that unity of faculties by means of which contents of propositions are even possible. It is in that sense an exercise in logic, specifically transcendental logic, insofar as it is a study of the foundations (i.e., the "necessary conditions for the possibility") of general logic.

On the other hand, we do not want to sound *too* friendly to Kant here. One contrast between "American" pragmatism and Kant's "pragmatism" is that Peirce, Dewey, et al., accepted the principle of significance and a more or less aprioristic theory of experience (though of a naturalistic flavor), but rejected any form of subjectivism or idealism, transcendental or otherwise. For a short and explicit statement of this kind of nonsubjectivist relativism, see Mead's account of the "objective reality of perspectives" (1927). In other words, there is a distinction to

Dewey's logic which did not suggest or support this orientation to the subject was likely to draw Russell's fire.

When Russell turns to a discussion of Dewey's instrumentalism (Russell 1939, pp. 142ff), his focus is on how Dewey's picture of inquiry seems to have no place for "truth"—whereas inquiry "might, from other points of view, be defined as 'the attempt to discover truth.'" It *is* the case that Dewey did not make very much of the concept of truth as a working concept in logic, and Russell regarded this as a major flaw. But this only illustrates how Russell's attitudes about the concept of warranted assertibility arise from a misunderstanding of Dewey's concept of judgments, and in particular Dewey's manner of distinguishing judgments and propositions. It is hardly surprising that if you read Frege's definitions of propositions and judgments into Dewey's uses of these terms, the results are nonsensical. Russell's criticisms are such as to point out this nonsense, but as if to assume that Dewey (or any logician worth his or her salt) must conform to Fregean definitions of these terms.[8]

---

be made between aprioristic perspectivism and idealistic subjectivism (as briefly discussed at the very end of Chapter 3). Another contrast of course is that Peirce, Dewey, et al., were able to benefit from more sophisticated developments in physics and logic than was Kant. As a result of such contrasts, an American-pragmatist version of "transcendental logic" will look quite different from Kant's.

Dewey's account of "practical reason" will also differ from Kant's, but precisely because of the different ways the two depict the various facets of experience. Dewey's evolutionary philosophy of mind and the resulting account of "reason" is foreign to Kant's framework of faculties; though as we have seen, the two accounts allegedly support compatible theories of morality. One point to make about Dewey's theory of reflective judgment is that it is not presented initially as a theory of morality, though as a special case, it applies as much to moral theory as anything else. Dewey's theory of judgment applies as much to one's choosing what color to paint one's bathroom as to deciding whether or not to legalize abortion.

[8]See the early sections of Frege 1918:

> Without wishing to give a definition, I call a [proposition] something for which the question of truth arises. So I ascribe what is false to a [proposition] just as much as what is true. So I can say: the [proposition] is the sense of the sentence without wishing to say that the sense of every sentence is a [proposition].... We say a sentence expresses a [proposition].... [T]wo things must be distinguished in an indicative sentence: the content, which it

The basic idea underlying Dewey's conception of judgments is that inquiry is aimed not at admitting or recognizing or otherwise determining the truth value of some given proposition (insofar as that is not formally part of the definition of 'judgment') but rather at effecting coherent and effortless stability of some given situation—a manifold of experience which will typically involve the affirmation or denial of any number of propositions. This is not enough to insure "truth" in any robust sense of the term—almost anybody would agree, and Dewey was the first to say so—which only means that Dewey's conception of *judgment* (rather than truth as such) is different from Frege's.

---

has in common with the corresponding sentence-question, and the assertion. The former is the [proposition], or at least contains the [proposition]. So it is possible to express the [proposition] without laying it down as true. Both are so closely joined in an indicative sentence that it is easy to overlook the separability. Consequently we may distinguish:

   (1) the apprehension of a [proposition]—thinking;
   (2) the recognition of the truth of a [proposition]—judgment;
   (3) the manifestation of this judgment—assertion.

One also finds a number of years previously in Frege 1892:

   We have seen that the reference of a sentence may always be sought, whenever the reference of its components is involved; and that this is the case when and only when we are inquiring after the truth value.

   We are therefore driven into accepting the *truth value* of a sentence as constituting its reference. By the truth value of a sentence I understand the circumstance that it is true or false. There are no further truth values. For brevity I call the one the True, the other the False. Every declarative sentence concerned with the reference of its words is therefore to be regarded as a proper name, and its reference, if it has one, is either the True or the False. . . . [so] that in every judgment [Frege's footnote: "A judgment, for me, is not the mere comprehension of a [proposition], but the admission of its truth."], no matter how trivial, the step from the level of [propositions] to the level of reference (the objective) has already been taken.

The bracketed term 'proposition(s)' has been substituted for the term 'thought(s)' in these English translations. Developments in formal semantics and in the philosophy of language in the last forty or fifty years have tended to undermine this overly simplistic view of propositions and truth. Such advances lend support at least indirectly to the claim that Dewey was not totally off the mark by not adhering to a Fregean canon.

More generally, Dewey's conception of *logic* is different from Frege's. The methodological considerations Dewey attends to within a general theory of inquiry, which for Dewey constitute a central part of the subject matter of logic, are at best peripheral concerns for Frege and Russell. That inquiry is a dynamic process involving the manipulation of defeasible information, even if this were an acceptable account of inquiry, has little to do with the subject matter of logic, in their view.

At one point Russell considers Dewey's comparison of inquiry to a cooking process (Dewey 1938, e.g., p. 44), which of course comes across in Russell's hands as seeming somewhat ridiculous. Referring specifically to Dewey's uses of the terms 'subject matter', 'content', and 'object' as relevant to the same "existential material" in different stages of inquiry (see page 153 above), Russell suggests the following metaphor:

> The position *seems* to be that there is a certain activity called "inquiry," as recognizable as the activities of eating or drinking; like all activity, it is stimulated by discomfort, and the particular discomfort concerned is called "doubt," just as hunger is the discomfort that stimulates eating, and thirst is the discomfort that stimulates drinking. And as hunger may lead you to kill an animal, skin it, cook it, so that though you have been concerned with the same animal throughout, it is very different when it becomes food from what it was to begin with, so inquiry manipulates and alters its subject-matter until it becomes logically assimilable and intellectually appetizing. Then doubt is allayed, at least for a time. But the subject-matter of inquiry, like the wild boar of Valhalla, is perpetually reborn, and the operation of logical cooking has to be more delicately performed as the intellectual palate grows more refined. There is therefore no end to the process of inquiry, and no dish that can be called "absolute truth." (Russell 1939, p. 147)

This passage occurs as part of Russell's discussion of Dewey's apparent subjectivism and of Dewey's denial of any such thing as "immediate knowledge," the point being that such views lead to an unacceptable theory of truth. Except for the concept of truth, these matters have already been discussed at length in previous chapters. But this passage is interesting in the present context for what it reveals about Russell's views of Dewey's views about propositions. Russell simply misrepresents Dewey's account of the role of propositions in inquiry.

Russell's logical-cooking metaphor makes inquiry sound like a "cheat" of some sort, as if what counts is making the world over to fit current needs or whims at the expense of maintaining a detached and honest objectivity. Russell of course finds it unacceptable to think that inquiry can be justified if, rather than presenting a true *description* of some aspect of the world, it proceeds to *change* the world just in order to come to some sort of acceptable conclusion. But it is simplistic to think that the issues involved here come down to an exclusive distinction between describing the world and changing it.

This line of criticism is foreshadowed a few pages earlier, where Russell is not yet talking about inquiry in particular but, at least briefly, about different orientations to philosophy. At this point Russell is winding down his discussion of Dewey's supposed holism and moving into a discussion of his instrumentalism:

> The same conclusion [namely, that a holistic view of things is unac- ceptable] may be reached through consideration of language. Words are discrete and separable occurrences; if the world had as much unity as some philosophers contend, it would be impossible to use words to describe it. Perhaps it is impossible; but in that case there can be no excuse for writing books on philosophy. Dr. Dewey would reply that it is not the purpose of such books to *describe* the world but to *change* it. (Russell 1939, p. 142)

Russell perhaps derived this remark as much from a reading of Dewey's other works besides *Logic*—Dewey's *Reconstruction in Philosophy* (1920), in particular, comes to mind. In any case, driving a wedge between "describing" the world and "changing" it sounds directly contrary to anything Dewey would have proposed in any of his writings.

As outlined in Section 5.3, there are different sorts of propo- sitions in Dewey's scheme corresponding to different sorts of information having different functional roles in inquiry. It could therefore be misleading to talk too generally about *the* function of propositions in inquiry. But one of the definitive roles of existential propositions is to *describe* a given situation, to size it up, as part of the process of stabilizing it. One is then moved to ask why there must be an exclusive separation of the various processes of description and of change in inquiry, which Russell seems to presume is appropriate. In Dewey's view, the process of scoping out a situation has significance for no other reason but to aid in determining how to modify one's activities (and hence alter the situation). Conversely, Russell is ignoring the commonplace fact that even to be in a position to describe the world (or some part of it), one must be performing, and be prepared to continue to perform, various kinds of exploratory activities. In this regard, many of the changes we impose on a situation are a prerequisite to (and have significance only in service to) describing the situation. One of the key aspects of formulating a judgment, again, is to articulate its *subject*, which is essentially a matter of describing the situation (by formulating a system of factual propositions) which constitutes the subject matter of inquiry. So far as scientific inquiry is concerned, it is as if the point of Russell's cooking metaphor is to deny the validity of experimentation in service to theory construction (and vice versa). He surely does not mean any such thing, *yet* he balks at Dewey's generalization of the fact that any sort of inquiry will necessarily include certain exploratory activities in the world just to be able to subsequently describe it. Indeed, the alterations we impose on the world, by way of exploring it, are geared to the ongoing changes which are occurring there in any case. The world is *cooking itself*, whether or not we add our two cents' worth of inquiry.

But of course, Russell's cooking metaphor is only a tongue-in-cheek characterization of the dynamics of inquiry, and it is no surprise that Dewey's views are more sophisticated than that characterization would seem to entail. For Dewey, propositions formulate information about the changing features of a subject matter as it is subjected to ongoing inquiry. This will involve the immediate registration of qualitative information as the result of ongoing exploratory activities, tentative classifications of things in the given situation, speculations about future activities as well as about what sorts of consequences of those activities can be expected in the given situation, and so forth. The various sorts of propositions needed to formulate these different sorts of information and speculation are not reducible one to the other, and they are not properly treated by molding them to fit a first-order syntax. Whereas Russell is inclined to maintain a sparse ontology consisting of objects and relations in some fixed universe of discourse, Deweyan logic requires a richer ontology which also includes things like situations and modes of action—requiring an orientation to the subject which Russell finds foreign, if not incomprehensible.

Russell's lack of appreciation of Dewey's account of the dynamic character of inquiry (and hence of the subject matter of logic) is illustrated a number of pages later (Russell 1939, pp. 149–51), when he attempts to analyze a Deweyan account of what it might mean to say that a proposition is *true*. What I want to look at here is how Russell's own conception of *propositions* is unwittingly projected into his analysis of Dewey's view of inquiry. In the following passage, the humor in Russell's remarks should not obscure the fact that he is mishandling a number of issues.

> Beliefs, we are now supposing, may be tested by their consequences, and may be considered to possess "warranted assertibility" when their consequences are of certain kinds. The consequences to be considered relevant may be logical consequences only, or may be widened to embrace all kinds of effects; and between these two extremes any number of intermediate positions are possible. In the case of the car that won't go, you think it may be this, or it may be that, or it may be the other; if it is *this* and I do so-and-so, the car will go; I do so-and-so and the car does not go; therefore it was not *this*. But when I apply the same experimental procedure to the hypothesis that it was *that*, the car does go; therefore the belief that it was *that* has "warranted assertibility." So far, we have only the ordinary procedure of induction: "If p, then q; now q is true; therefore p is true." E.g., "If pigs have wings, then some winged animals are

good to eat; now some winged animals are good to eat; therefore pigs have wings." This form of inference is called "scientific method." (Russell 1939, p. 149)

This is the first of a series of paragraphs which clearly show that Russell was not careful to distinguish propositions and judgments in Dewey's sense of those terms. The terminology is not so important as understanding the conceptual distinction. Russell might have chosen to use some other terminology, except that he does not seem to have discerned the distinction Dewey was getting at in the first place. First of all, Russell allows that "warranted assertibility" may be attributed indiscriminately to "beliefs" and, in later paragraphs, to "hypotheses" and "sentences," none of which in Dewey's terms are said to be "judgments" in any definitive sense. The terms 'belief' and 'knowledge', in particular, are used in numerous ways in the philosophical literature to the point of almost irreparable confusion (Dewey 1938, pp. 7–9), which moved Dewey to avoid them and to talk instead in terms of "warranted assertion." And it is judgments and only judgments, in Dewey's scheme of things, which are said to be warrantably assertible or not. Hence Russell has skewed his analysis of Dewey's position to the point that, no matter what Russell means by warranted assertibility or belief, he is not addressing Dewey's views on these matters.

The remarks about induction, the fallacy of affirming the consequent, and scientific method are of course amusing. But scientific inquiry is, for Dewey, a significant source of illustrations and intuitions about inquiry and is otherwise not such a peripheral concern as these remarks might indicate. To counter any insinuation that Dewey's thinking about such matters was unsophisticated, it is interesting to compare these remarks by Russell with Dewey's discussion of induction and scientific generalization in Chapter 21 of *Logic*, particularly pp. 426ff where Dewey's delves into how generic and hypothetical-universal propositions are formulated in concrete inquiries. Of course, it goes without saying that the simple form of fallacious inference Russell refers to in jest as "scientific method" is not particularly scientific, nor is it appropriate to call it "induction."

It is, in any case, confusing that the entities—beliefs, etc.—which are said by Russell to be warrantably assertible or not are at the same time supposed to be analyzed as propositions. Dewey's carefully developed distinction between propositions (which are properly said to be confirmable or refutable) and judgments (which are properly said to be warrantably assertible or not) is simply overlooked by Russell. Yet this distinction between propositions and judgments, and the concept of propositions as *means* (i.e., as articulating *information*), is central to an understanding of Dewey's conception of the "instrumental" character of propositions. Looking more closely at Russell's example of fixing a stalled car will help to make this point clear.

Russell's cursory analysis of this example is not intended to be anything but cursory. Nevertheless it is not at all obvious that "actions," "beliefs," "hypotheses," and so forth can all be collapsed into "sentences" of the propositional calculus and still reflect Dewey's views. Yet such an erasure of important distinctions is just what Russell proceeds to do (presumably in the name of simplicity, clarity, distinctness, and the sentential calculus), the result being an analysis which is too coarse to handle the issues involved. After remarking that Dewey's theory of inquiry allows that problem solving can often be quite mindless in the sense of being devoid of "intellectual content," Russell proposes the following account of a car-fixing episode:

> We may, eliminating the intellectual element as far as possible, schematize our behavior as much as possible: we desire a certain change C (in our illustration, the change from rest to motion on the part of the car); in our past experience, various acts A_1, A_2, A_3, ... have been followed by this change; consequently there exists an impulse to perform some one of these acts, and, if it fails to be followed by C, some other of them, until at last, with luck, C takes place. Suppose the act A_n is followed by C; then A_n is appropriate to the situation. So far, everything that I have been describing could be done by an animal and is done by animals that are actuated by strong desires which they cannot immediately gratify. But when we come to human beings, with their linguistic proclivities, the matter becomes

somewhat different. The acts A_1, A_2, A_3, ... may all be sentences: "Perhaps it is this," "Perhaps it is that," "Perhaps it is the other."... Each of these sentences causes certain further acts, which, in turn, set up a chain of effects. One of the sentences causes a chain of effects which includes the desired change C. If this sentence is A_n, we say that A_n is "true" or has "warranted assertibility." (Russell 1939, pp. 149–50)

It is not clear why Russell would want to consider a case of "mindlessly" fixing a car, since to say that inquiry *can* be mindless and that some inquiries *must* be mindless does not mean that they all must be mindless. But it is not a serious problem to consider such an example, so long as we do not draw overly general conclusions from it. In particular, we should distinguish being mindlessly driven by habit from behaving like a "subhuman" animal. One can be driven by habit and still behave in a humanly intelligent manner, depending on the situation and the nature of one's habits. Many distinctively human things which human beings normally do can be done mindlessly or, in any case, without intellectualizing the process.

In any case, besides being a faulty characterization of "truth," Russell's sentential analysis of the stalled-car example sounds like the converse of his causal account of perception, amounting to a classical causal account of "volition." Actually, Russell is only attempting to weave a terminological knot here, to show that Dewey is committed to nonsense if he insists on using this terminology. But Russell could not have succeeded in this case because he did not take care to insure that the *meanings* of Dewey's terms were accurately stated and preserved. In particular, this paragraph clearly shows that Russell failed to appreciate Dewey's conception of the role of propositions in effecting judgment, even in the case of "mindless" inquiry, by suggesting that propositions might be warrantably assertible or not in their role as propositions. We can contrast Russell's car-fixing scenario with how such an inquiry might proceed according to a Deweyan scheme of things.

Assume you have enough experience with cars so that your behavior is not completely random when it comes to auto repair.

You are not a mechanic but simply have learned a few tricks and strategies which sometimes get your car to move again when it will not move. Unless you are intent on being inefficient, you will probably not just enumerate by means of some kind of inner sentential speech all the activities you have performed in past car-fixing episodes and proceed to try them out one by one until by brute force something works again in this particular case. Rather, the first thing you might do—purely as a matter of intelligent (though perhaps mindless) habit—is to scope out a few facts about the car before proceeding to do much of anything else, particularly by taking note of anything which is unusual and which might serve as a symptom of a familiar problem. Otherwise there is no call to act one way or the other. Even then, but especially if the details of the problem are not yet obvious, your initial actions will tend to be exploratory in order that you might gather more information about the problem. You will thereby begin to accrue information (or mis-information) which will serve to guide your subsequent problem-solving activities. Such information is defeasible in the sense that its stability, as to its being confirmed or refuted, is not guaranteed in the course of your ongoing activities. Dewey's taxonomy of propositions (outlined in Section 5.2) is supposed to be a summary of the different sorts of information one might have recourse to in such a situation. For instance, if you hear hissing noises coming from under the hood and subsequently see steam escaping from the radiator after opening the hood, you might classify the problem, purely out of habit, as another one of those "boiling-over" episodes, in which case a certain course of action is in order, such as finding water or coolant to put into the radiator. Assuming this is done and the car starts up again, you then drive the car, assuming the problem is fixed so long as the car continues to move. This continued moving of the car (and only so long as it continues to move) contingently *warrants* the judgment that the problem is solved by your putting coolant into the radiator. The judgment is not necessarily made all of a sudden and once and for all, but it is simply further and further warranted the farther and farther the car moves, to the point that the whole episode might recede into insignificance as you go about your usual business. But if the car soon stops moving again due to overheating, the warrantability of that judgment is undermined, and the inquiry continues. You might later find that there is a leak in the radiator so that merely replenishing the coolant mixture will get the car moving again for a short time but will not really solve the problem. You proceed then to have the radiator fixed and (to end the story) are warranted in judging that such an action *will* solve the problem so long as the car moves normally and does not boil over.

Not every inquiry is exactly like the one in this story, so we should be wary of generalizing its features improperly. The point of the story is to illustrate the distinction between propositions versus judgments by expanding Russell's example appropriately. The various pieces of information about hissing noises, about escaping steam, about having just put new water into the radiator, about the car's current state of motion, and so forth, are all propositions which describe details of the situation at hand. The speculation (appraisal, possible judgment) that replenishing the water will fix the problem is derived from the fact (a proposition) that replenishing the water is even a possibility. At one point in the story, the *proposition* that the radiator lacked water was confirmed by several pieces of data (hissing noises, escaping steam, etc.), but the *judgment* that the action of replenishing the water would solve the problem of the car's immobility was ultimately not warranted. Otherwise, Russell is making what is essentially a category mistake to say that the proposition is warranted or not. Propositions can suggest actions which are warranted or not, so that the judgment that the given situation calls for this or that action is warrantably assertible or not; but it is the actions which are warranted or not, and judgments which are warrantably assertible or not, not propositions.

Propositions are said to be "tools" or "instruments" of inquiry in just the sense that, by articulating factual and hypothetical details of a situation, they are able to suggest alternative courses of action to take in that situation in order to effect some sort of stable solution to the problem at hand. More than just "describing facts" and thereby being true or false, propositions (as pieces of information relevant to the given situation) are also evaluated in terms of how they facilitate management of ongoing behaviors toward instituting warranted judgment.

It should be obvious, then, that Russell's conception of propositions, as evidenced in the Schilpp volume and elsewhere, does not accommodate Dewey's theory of propositions and judgments. Russell's discussion implicitly assumes a comparatively simple theory of propositions which ignores or otherwise skews most of the details of Dewey's picture of inquiry, and the results sound odd. But the only conclusion we can justifiably draw from this is that it is a problem for Russell's analysis, not for Dewey's views. In spite of everything Russell had to say, Dewey's views have yet to be evaluated.

Dewey's reply to Russell in the Schilpp volume in regard to their different conceptions of propositions is not unsubstantial, though it may appear to be somewhat oblique if one does not first appreciate how irrelevant Russell's criticisms are. Russell's way of presenting the issues is simply not compatible with Dewey's way of thinking. Rather than try to untangle Russell's strange account of his views, it is as if Dewey attempted to start over and redirect the discussion in his own terms.

With regard to the issue of distinguishing propositions and judgments, Dewey makes basically two points in his reply in the Schilpp volume (1939a, pp. 572–4). His first point is simply a reminder that in *Logic* (1938, pp. 287–8 and elsewhere) he was careful to make a distinction between the *validity* or *invalidity* of propositions in a given inquiry and the *truth* or *falsity* of propositions (period). This distinction rests on a conception of propositions as *means*:

> The view most current at the present time is probably that which regards propositions as the unitary material of logical theory. Propositions upon this view have their defining property in the property of formal truth-falsity. According to the position here taken, propositions are to be differentiated and identified on the ground of the

function of their contents as *means*, procedural and material, further distinctions of forms of propositions being instituted on the ground of the special ways in which their respective characteristic subject-matters function as means.... [A]t this point it is pertinent to note that, since means as such are neither true nor false, truth-falsity is *not* a property of propositions. Means are either effective or ineffective; pertinent or irrelevant; wasteful or economical, the criterion for the difference being found in the consequences with which they are connected as means. On this basis, special propositions are *valid* (strong, effective) or *invalid* (weak, inadequate); loose or rigorous, etc.

Validity-invalidity is thus to be distinguished not only from truth-falsity but from formal correctness. Any given proposition is such that it promotes or retards the institution of final resolution. It cannot be logically adjudged, therefore, *merely* on the basis of its formal relations to other propositions. The syllogism "All satellites are made of green cheese; the moon is a satellite; therefore, it is made of green cheese" is formally correct. The propositions involved are, however, *invalid*, not just because they are "materially false," but because instead of promoting inquiry they would, if taken and used, retard and mislead it. (Dewey 1938, pp. 287–8)

The terms 'valid' and 'invalid' are used differently these days: in proof theory, these terms apply to arguments, proofs, or sequents rather than to propositions (whereas Dewey refers here to arguments as being "formally correct" or not); and not merely coincidentally, the term 'valid' is used in model theory to refer to sentences "true in every structure" (or something similar, depending on the given formal apparatus). For Dewey, validity has to do with reliable utility of propositions as information in inquiries. This is only a terminological difference, not a substantive problem, since Dewey was consistent in his use of these terms. The important point is that propositions are to be evaluated according to their usefulness to a given concrete inquiry—which is not to say that that makes sense with regard to a Fregean conception of propositions, but rather that Dewey is presenting a different conception of propositions.

But this is Dewey's second point, namely, that Russell uncon-

sciously assumes what amount to Fregean conceptions of propositions and judgments throughout his entire discussion of Dewey's
views. That is essentially the point of the following passage:

> The exclusive devotion of Mr. Russell to discourse is manifested in his
> assumption that *propositions* are the subject-matter of inquiry, a view
> assumed so unconsciously that it is taken for granted that Peirce and I
> likewise assume it. But according to our view—and according to that
> of any thoroughgoing empiricist—*things and events* are the material
> and objects of inquiry, and propositions are *means* in inquiry, so that
> as conclusions of a given inquiry they become means of carrying on
> further inquiries. Like other means they are modified and improved
> in the course of use. Given the beliefs (I) that propositions are from
> the start the objects of inquiry and (II) that all propositions have
> either truth or falsity as their inherent property, and (III) then read
> these two assumptions into theories—like Peirce's and mine—which
> deny both of them, and the product is just the doctrinal confusion
> that Russell finds in what we have said. (Dewey 1939a, p. 573)

That is to say, Russell assumes that the goal of inquiry is to determine the truth or falsity of various propositions, i.e., to formulate
Fregean judgments. One need not cite any other evidence for this in
Russell's statements beyond simply noting his propensity to revert
to talking about "sentences" rather than objects and events. And
this adversely affects his rendition of Dewey's views. He repeatedly
treats warranted assertibility as a peculiar concept of truth which
is apparently supposed to apply to propositions (sentences?) in the
final phase of inquiry. The general aim of Deweyan inquiry, according to Russell, is to determine that some number of propositions are
warrantably assertible, viz., "true" in some odd sense. It is in this
sense that the propositions themselves become in Russell's hands
the "subject matter" of inquiry. Russell finds all this to be incomprehensible, of course, because it is, and precisely because it distorts
important features of Dewey's conception of inquiry.

Perhaps it is a novel and complicated view, but for Dewey,
propositions are the *means* by which the subject matter of an inquiry
is described and subsequently made determinate; and though it is
not entirely meaningless to say that they may be true or false in

what they say about the world (Dewey 1941, p. 347–8), that is not what distinguishes them as *propositions*. What is more relevant to characterizing propositions is their "validity value" (to coin a phrase) as means to instituting warrantably assertible judgment. This involves not truth values but things like relevance, salience, coherence with other propositions, persistence in the face of ongoing inquiry (i.e., failing to be disconfirmed by ongoing experience), and so forth. These are existential factors which an inquirer has a direct handle on, whereas "truth" is a metaphysical idealization about which one too often can only speculate. (In Kantian terminology, truth is an Idea, and perfectly legitimate as such, whereas warranted assertibility is a feature of assertions which we can reliably gauge within the bounds of our experience.)

Russell responded to these remarks a year later in a chapter in *An Inquiry Into Meaning and Truth* (1940). This chapter is an extended discussion of Dewey's notion of warranted assertibility; and the first topic Russell takes up is in fact the notion of propositions, responding in particular to Dewey's claim that he (Russell) takes propositions to be the subject matter of inquiry. Russell begins his response with another attempt to summarize Dewey's position, but he echoes the same confusion of propositions and judgments which appeared in the Schilpp volume:

> Inquiry uses "assertions" as its tools, and assertions are "warranted" in so far as they produce the desired results. But in inquiry, as in any other practical operation, better tools may, from time to time, be invented, and the old ones are then discarded. Indeed, just as machines can enable us to make better machines, so the temporary results of an inquiry may be the very means which lead to better results. In this process there is no finality, and therefore no assertion is warranted for all time, but only at a given stage of inquiry. "Truth" as a static concept is therefore to be discarded. (Russell 1940, pp. 401–2)

He then quotes and proceeds to reply to the passage of Dewey's quoted on page 205 above. But before looking at this latter reply, consider three clauses in the passage just quoted which, for the record, signify that Russell still has not properly presented Dewey's distinction between propositions and judgments. The very first sentence states that "inquiry uses 'assertions' as its tools." Dewey would say rather that inquiry uses *propositions* as its tools, while he uses the term 'assertion' exclusively with regard to judgments.

Now of course propositions formulate facts (etc.) in a given situation, and in that sense they are declarative or assertive. One might say that this is just a terminological issue, that we could allow Russell his own choice of words, and that what he means by 'assertions' is what Dewey means by 'propositions'. But unfortunately the problem is not so straightforward. If we take this latter route, then the next clause, saying that "assertions are 'warranted' insofar as they produce the desired results," cannot be right. Propositions, for Dewey, are *not* said to be warranted, but rather assertions of judgments are. In other words, Russell is not free, at least in a critique of Dewey's views, to use the term 'assertion' in place of 'proposition', since the former term already plays a different technical role in Dewey's scheme of things, namely, as used in the phrase 'warranted assertion'.

So if this second clause were acceptable, then the first clause could not be. If 'assertion' is used in Dewey's sense, then it is wrong, or at least misleading, to say that assertions are used as tools in inquiry. Assertions are rather the *results* of inquiries, whereas *propositions* are tools for achieving such results.[9]

This explains why a third clause—"therefore no assertion is warranted for all time, but only at a given stage of inquiry"—is not right either. Dewey would say instead that no proposition is guaranteed to be *valid* for all time, but, if at all, then perhaps only at a given stage of the inquiry in which it is formulated. (That the information one uses should be valid is certainly desirable, but we are now ques-

---

[9]This pinpoints a major problem with the passage Dewey referred to toward the end of the quote on page 115 above: "In Dr. Dewey's view, a belief is 'warranted' if, as a tool, it is useful in some activity, i.e., if it is a cause of satisfaction of desire" (Russell 1940, p. 405; Dewey 1941, p. 346) Not only does this misrepresent the goal of inquiry (as being satisfaction of desires), but it then proceeds to confuse tools of inquiry (propositions) with the results of inquiry (warranted belief).

tioning to what extent such validity is *guaranteed*.) Judgments, on the other hand, are warranted (so far as the inquirer can discern) in the instance of terminating inquiry, being only provisionally suggested at earlier stages of inquiry. In that sense they can even be warranted "for all time" insofar as they can be the result of inquiries which terminate on irrevocably legitimate grounds—such as when you stop your car at a stop sign, look both ways, and judge whether you can proceed through the intersection. Once you pass through the intersection without incident—based largely on the defeasible proposition that no other vehicles or pedestrians were coming from either direction—the judgment that you should have moved into the intersection when you did is and will for evermore be warranted. Of course, not all judgments are like that.

One could also say that the propositions which led to your making that warranted judgment are valid for all time—not that there will never again be cars coming from either direction at that intersection—but that it will never be the case that there was any such traffic *in that particular situation* in which you came to your decision to move through the intersection. It is somewhat ironic, given the history of the discussion of propositions and truth, that by relativizing propositions to concrete situations in this way, it becomes plausible, if not useful, to talk about "eternal validity" (viz. context-relative monotonicity?). That no cars are approaching, period, is hardly always a valid proposition; but that no cars were approaching *in a given instance* is absolutely and unrevocably valid if valid at all.

Of course, this is plausible only from a detached perspective (such as that of the logician qua spectator, or of the reminiscent driver) which is different from (or at least not typical of) the perspective taken by the inquiring agent invested in the given situation. Failure to distinguish such differences of perspective can only lead to oversimplification and confusion. That is, what is seen to be valid from a spectator's perspective may not be seen (nor perhaps even see-able) as such from the inquiring agent's perspective—and vice versa—so that information available from the former perspective can be irrelevant to how the given inquiry actually should and does proceed. The validity of a given proposition in practice is something which is gauged only by its being tested and confirmed—by the agent, in the situation to which it is relevant. Failure to appreciate the difference in these two perspectives, the logician's and the inquiring agent's, can only lead to confusion in what is meant by key terms like 'fact', 'validity', 'warranted', and so forth.

A piece of information can serve as a valid fact for the inquiring agent, and yet be an obvious fiction or piece of misinformation from a spectator's perspective. This is not a matter of waffling on the definition of the term 'fact', but rather of acknowledging that, in a study of concrete inquiries of real inquiring agents, it should be defined not absolutely but "functionally," relative to an inquiry, in terms of what the agent is justifiably able to take as factual. Referring back to the discussion in Chapter 3, facts are existential— they are the features and elements of existence—and in that sense may not be true to reality (however one might presume to discern that); but this is only to say that we have two ideas paralleling the existence/reality distinction, namely, facticity (or factuality) versus truth, which should not be confused with each other. This admission does not justify taking just anything for a fact. It is essential to the *function* of facts in inquiry that the inquiring agent actually *take them* to be indicative of the way things are—this is why Dewey's calling them "facts" is not inconsistent with common usage of the term. For the logician to admit that they may not be true to reality is simply to note that information is defeasible and that even the best of inquiries are fallible. This notion of reliable but fallible factuality is at odds with Russell's looking for "stubborn facts" in the form of sense data, as we will discuss further below.

In any case, Russell goes on to deny that propositions for him are the subject matter of inquiry. He claims to be more concerned with "the relation between *events* and the propositions that they cause men to assert." But then Dewey did not say that Russell purposely conceived of propositions as the subject matter of inquiry, but only that this was unconscious or implicit in his treatment of basic propositions as elementary objects of knowledge. (This point is taken up again on pages 216ff.)

For Russell (1940, pp. 404–5), the aim of inquiry is to *know the truth*, which in more specific terms means that inquiry aims to determine the truth values of some number of propositions, that is, to formulate some number of Fregean judgments.

Russell accepts the idea that some propositions, namely, scientific hypotheses, can have instrumental value independent of being simply descriptively true or false—"but I regard all such hypotheses as a precarious superstructure built on a foundation of simpler and less dubious beliefs, and I do not find, in Dr. Dewey's works, what seems to me an adequate discussion of this foundation" (Russell 1940, p. 403). Russell does not find an adequate discussion of this view because of course Dewey's view is different in this regard. It is rather telling that Russell sees this "precarious" nature of scientific hypotheses as a somewhat peripheral matter so far as logic is concerned, whereas Dewey thinks it reveals something rather characteristic about propositions and sees it as a central concern of logic.

In offering his own view of the nature of scientific hypotheses, and having just denied that he takes propositions to be the subject matter of inquiry, it is slightly surprising that Russell then depicts inquiry as beginning, proceeding, and ending with the increasingly precise analysis of "assertions," being in this sense a modification of assertions in order to dispel their vagueness or undue complexity:

> I should say that inquiry begins, as a rule, with an assertion that is vague and complex, but replaces it, when it can, by a number of separate assertions each of which is less vague and less complex than the original assertion. A complex assertion may be analyzable into several, some true, some false; a vague assertion may be true or false, but it is often neither.... When Newton's theory of gravitation was replaced by Einstein's, a certain vagueness in Newton's concept of acceleration was removed, but almost all the assertions implied by Newton's theory remained true. I should say that this is an illustration of what always happens when an old theory gives way to a better one: the old assertions failed to be definitely true or false, both because they were vague, and because they were masquerading as one, some

of the many being true and some false. But I do not see how to state the improvement except in terms of the two ideals of precision and truth. (Russell 1940, pp. 403–4)

But this indicates why Dewey would say that for Russell propositions are the "subject matter" of inquiry, even if Russell would not describe his view in quite those terms. Russell is talking here about the dynamics of inquiry as an increasingly refined analysis of propositions, aimed at culling the false ones from the true ones. There is in Russell's account only an implicit reference to experimentation and verification of assertions—they are simply just true or false—whereas inquiry is pictured as the concern of the analytical theorist intent on rendering theories more and more precise. Dewey devotes a good bit of attention to explaining the importance of clarification and disambiguation in inquiry. But this cannot be all there is to inquiry. This is precisely Dewey's point in calling attention to Russell's overemphasis on "discourse" and the formal analysis of sentences: one also has to consider the capacities of propositions to select and direct ongoing activities. Their "validity" depends as much on the observed consequences of such activities as it does on the analytical precision and mutual coherence of the propositions themselves; and a formal treatment of propositions should accommodate, if not explain, this particular function of propositions as much as anything else. This is simply a matter of generalizing fundamental principles of scientific methodology in all of its aspects, not just in regard to abstract analyses of theories.

It is somewhat ironic, then, that Russell attempts to contrast his own views with Dewey's by claiming to be the hard-nosed empiricist while Dewey is *merely* the rationalist. In fact, Russell discusses two closely related litmus tests in terms of which he thinks he can distinguish his own views from Dewey's (in addition to the description-versus-alteration criterion introduced in the Schilpp volume and discussed earlier in this section). Russell claims at one point that Dewey is primarily concerned with "theories and hypotheses," while he himself is more concerned with "assertions about particular matters of fact" (as if one could not be equally concerned with each of these but as they play different roles in different contexts of inquiry).

> I hold [moreover] that, for any empirical theory of knowledge, the fundamental assertions must be concerned with particular matters of fact, i.e., with single events which only happen once. Unless there is *something* to be learnt from a single event, no hypothesis can ever be either confirmed or confuted; but what is to be learnt from a single event must itself be incapable of being confirmed or confuted by subsequent experience. (Russell 1940, pp. 408–9)

This distinction—between stressing hypothesis and stressing fact—is echoed later in his chapter on Dewey in *A History of Western Philosophy* (1945, pp. 824–6).

Russell makes a similar distinction (1940, p. 154) when he claims that "the Hegelians and the instrumentalists . . . deny the distinction between data and inference altogether. They maintain that in all our knowledge there is an inferential element, . . . and that the test of truth is coherence rather than conformity with 'fact'. . . . I think that, if taken as a whole truth, it renders the part played by perception in knowledge inexplicable." In other words, Russell wants to say that there are such things as "stubborn facts," in the form of primitive data (corresponding to absolutely valid propositions in the sense discussed earlier?), whereas "the instrumentalists" purportedly do not, given their alleged claim that "knowledge obtained from perception is always an interpretation based upon accepted theories, and may need subsequent correction if these theories turn out to be unsuitable."

> If I say, for example, "Look, there is an eclipse of the moon," I use my knowledge of astronomy to interpret what I see. No words exist, according to the instrumentalist, which do not embody theories or hypotheses, and the crude fact of perception is therefore for ever ineffable.
>
> I think this view underestimates the powers of analysis. It is undeniable that our every-day interpretations of perceptive experiences, and even all our every-day words, embody theories. But it is not impossible to whittle away the element of interpretation, or to invent an artificial language involving a minimum of theory. By

these methods we can approach asymptotically to the pure datum. . . .
The essential characteristic of a datum is that it is not inferred. . . .
I shall henceforth assume that there are data, in the sense of
propositions for which the evidence is not wholly derived from their
logical relation to other propositions. I shall not assume that the
actual data which we can obtain are ever completely certain, nor yet
that a proposition which is a datum cannot be also a consequence of
other accepted propositions. This latter case occurs whenever we see
a predicted eclipse. But when a proposition concerning a particular
matter of fact is inferred, there must always be among the premises
other matters of fact from which some general law is obtained by
induction. It is therefore impossible that all our knowledge of matters
of fact be inferred.

The question of how to obtain from perceptual experience propositions which are premises for empirical knowledge is difficult and
complicated, but fundamental for any empirical theory of knowledge.
(Russell 1940, pp. 154–6)

According to Russell, instrumentalism holds that all knowledge is
theory laden, including basic perceptual data (as a simple kind of
knowledge). So the instrumentalist focuses solely on theory and
hypothesis, to the exclusion of primitive, theory-free data.

Though these particular remarks neither mention Dewey nor
occur in the chapter on warranted assertibility, Dewey takes them
to be directed at his own views, because it was Dewey who was
most closely associated with "instrumentalism" around the turn of
the century (though the meaning of the term took on an independent life of its own in subsequent developments in the philosophy
of science), and Russell never did cease to read Hegelian themes
into Dewey's views and so most likely considered himself to be
addressing Dewey's views in this instance as well.

It is as if Russell assumes there are only two choices: a coherence theory of truth, or else his "logical datumism." In claiming that
Dewey is concerned with hypotheses and theories while he is concerned with facts, or that Dewey admits no distinction between data
and inference while he does, Russell is taking the datumist position
while Dewey is portrayed as a proponent of a coherence theory.

These distinctions—hypothesis versus fact, and inference versus the acquisition of data—will be discussed in the next section, particularly with regard to how they bear on Dewey's distinction between propositions and judgments.

5.4 Dewey's Later Reply

Dewey's response (1941) to Russell's chapter on warranted assertibility in *An Inquiry into Meaning and Truth* (1940) was considerably more focused than his shotgun response to the many contributors to the Schilpp volume. In this later reply to Russell, he dealt specifically with the topic of propositions and with the notions of warranted assertibility and truth. The following sections address Dewey's response in regard to the two litmus tests Russell suggested as grounds for distinguishing their respective views, which were introduced at the end of the previous section.

5.4.1 Hypothesis and Fact

Dewey (1941, pp. 332–3) responds first to Russell's statement that Dewey is primarily concerned with theories and hypotheses while Russell himself is more concerned with assertions about particular matters of fact. It should be noted that the language of "hypotheses," "theories," and "data" is geared to a discussion of scientific inquiry and, unless read metaphorically, does not supply the most general perspective one can take in a theory of inquiry. But Dewey's theory of inquiry should certainly apply to the special case of scientific inquiry, and he should be able to talk in just those terms if necessary.

Dewey begins by saying that, though he is not "mainly concerned" with either hypotheses or facts alone, hypotheses do have an essential role to play in the process of achieving *warranted* judgment. *Any* judgment, if warranted, will involve the formulation and confirmation of hypotheses. That is to say, every judgment worth its salt will be made on the basis of one's having tested and confirmed various hypotheses about the subject matter of the given inquiry.

Notice that this does not say that every *proposition* is hypothetical, but rather that every (scientific) inquiry, and hence every *judgment,* involves the formulation and confirmation of hypotheses. This could easily sound like nonsense if one did not take care to maintain Dewey's distinction between propositions and judgments. As the discussion in previous sections has tried to show, Dewey was concerned with the reciprocal roles of both hypothesis formation and fact-finding in inquiry. Formulating and refining hypotheses is necessary as part of the process of reaching warranted judgment; but then, so is being clear about particular matters of fact, both prior to and subsequent to altering the dynamics of a given situation. Both hypotheses and facts—formulated propositionally— have their respective roles to play in inquiry, particularly as they serve to articulate (defeasible) features of the given situation. If certain hypotheses, suggested by prior facts, are further confirmed by subsequent results of actions performed in accordance with the given hypotheses, and if this success remains stable in the course of ongoing testing of those hypotheses, then one is *warranted* in asserting that those hypotheses are applicable to and descriptive of the given situation. (Otherwise new hypotheses have to be considered, and given facts need to be reviewed.)

It is incorrect to say, then, that Dewey refuses "to admit facts." The operationalistic character of Dewey's views suggests a different conception of "facts" from what Russell would accept. But rather than say that Dewey refuses to admit facts, all Russell can rightly say is that Dewey does not admit facts as Russell conceives of them.

That Russell fails to assess their differences in this way is further evidence, by the way, that he did not discern the distinction in Dewey's views between the existential and the real, as discussed in Chapter 3. Insofar as Dewey is interested in logic and not metaphysics, he talks about facts as elements of existence, not as elements of reality (as if that made any sense), and not as primitive and absolutely unquestionable ("stubborn") elements of knowledge.

So while Dewey is clearly concerned with both facts and hypotheses in his characterization of inquiry, he posits neither simply as primitively given. As discussed in Section 5.3, he divides facts into two sorts, qualitative and classificatory. Qualitative facts constitute what may be termed the *data* of inquiry. Classificatory facts are themselves divided into various sorts, whether singular or generic. Qualitative facts regarding singular objects serve as evidence for singular facts, i.e., for classifying those objects as being of this or that kind. Generic facts, on the other hand, concern general features of a given situation. To say that facts, as propositions, are formulations of *information* is, among other things, to admit their defeasibility. This does not mean they are "hypothetical," at least not in Dewey's sense of the term. All propositions are in principle defeasible—this is just another way to express the idea of the fallibility of inquiry. But then there are different sorts of propositions, some which are factual and others which are hypothetical. Propositions are taken as *factual* only if they have been appropriately validated, i.e., operationally tested in experience, and continue to resist disconfirmation. Hypotheses, on the other hand, currently lack adequate validation, though they formulate possibilities inferred from given facts and standing principles and ought to be operationally testable.

The process of validating propositions does not serve to guarantee the truth of those propositions, though the question of truth is a standing question for the inquirer that is constantly, if only implicitly, being asked and addressed with respect to virtually any given fact or hypothesis. Dewey is concerned with how information is reliably validated not because this provides a method for guaranteeing truth but in order to explain how it is that information can function as *factual* whether or not truth remains an elusive ideal. What the inquiring agent justifiably takes to be factual in a given inquiry may or may not be what the spectator-logician would take to be factual in that instance; but what is important in a theory of inquiry is to understand how information justifiably gains and maintains the status of factuality for the inquirer and what functions it serves by virtue of attaining that status.

5.4.2 Atomic Propositions

Dewey next considers, over the course of several paragraphs (1941, pp. 333–5), what he thinks is wrong with Russell's view of propositions, particularly with regard to why Russell would think there is such a thing as atomic-propositional knowledge.[10] There are several things to note so far as this claim pertains to Dewey's and Russell's different conceptions of propositions. One upshot of the following discussion will be that Russell is "mainly concerned" with facts, as he says, only in the sense that he takes for granted some basis of "less dubious" beliefs which ground one's theory construction in facts. Some of these basic beliefs are just true—they have to be—or else the whole business of science, as Russell conceives of it, is built on sand. Without recourse to such data, he would be left with nothing but a coherence criterion of truth. So he is compelled to postulate the existence of indubitable "data," revealing what are supposed to be basic facts which ground our knowledge of what is true.

Dewey reacts to this by arguing that Russell's various examples of elementary matters of fact are not elementary in the sense which Russell requires. A simple proposition "known in virtue of its immediate direct presence," such as 'redness-here', can hardly be said to be self-contained or to have an independent self-evident meaning in Russell's absolute sense. It has no meaning at all, argues Dewey, except in contrast with 'redness-there', or 'nonredness-here'. And such contrasts seems to presuppose and directly involve at least an elementary theory of space-time as well as some kind of theory of color.

This is suggestive of one aspect of Quine's web metaphor which still holds even if we follow the suggestion in Chapter 3 and turn that metaphor inside out. The totality of our knowledge is depicted by Quine as a "man-made fabric which impinges on experience only along the edges" but such that any sentence, even one at "the edge" (such as 'redness-here'), derives its meaning and truth as much from its logical interconnections with the other sentences in the system as

---

[10]This issue arose in an exchange between Dewey and Russell in the 1910s (Dewey 1916b; Russell 1914, 1919). This earlier debate is discussed in Hook 1979, for one reference. We are focusing here on how they dealt with this issue in 1940.

a whole (such as those making up theories of space-time and color) as from the effects of "experience." Whether this "fabric" impinges on experience along the edges or centrally is not so important now as the fact that it is an interconnected fabric.

This line of thought also echoes arguments against Carnap's primitive "protocol sentences," which led eventually to the consideration (by some logical positivists, particularly Neurath, Hempel, and Carnap himself) of a coherence theory of truth—the idea being that science aims at constructing a system of sentences, none of which is sacrosanct and all of which are evaluated on the basis of their coherence and utility within the system as a whole.

This is not to say that Dewey is committed either to the holism of Quine's "Two Dogmas" or to a logical-positivistic coherence theory—his view of logic is as different from theirs as it is from Russell's—though he shares their reservations against putting too much epistemological weight on the notion of atomic propositions.[11]

Dewey questions the idea of basing the "ultimacy and purity" of basic propositions on the claim that such propositions concern perceptual experiences, as if their atomicity is guaranteed by virtue of their representing immediate sensible experiences (*sensa*). Such representations of immediate experience are supposed to guarantee the truth of such propositions by virtue of the immediacy of the experience; yet, as Dewey points out,[12] Russell elsewhere contradicts this by supposing "a considerable process in the brain" whereby the "causation" of the proposition by the sensory experience "is by no means direct" (Dewey 1941, pp. 334–5).

Moreover, despite this reference to perception as a complicated

---

[11]See Dewey 1941 (p. 336n): "Instrumentalists do *not* believe that "knowledge is an organic whole"; in fact, the idea is meaningless upon their view. They do *not* believe the test of truth is coherence; [but rather] in the operational sense . . . they hold a correspondence view." See Section 6.1 below for further discussion of this last claim.

[12]This brings us back to the discussion in Chapter 3 of Russell's and Dewey's different theories of perception.

causal process, Russell effectively ignores the "bodily *motor* element" involved in any kind of perception. That is, he ignores the active, dynamic nature of perception, preferring to think of it as an instantaneous event which instigates causal processes eventuating in the cognizance of propositions in the visual centers of the brain. This sounds much like Locke, and Dewey indeed responds with the remark that Russell's view constitutes "the most adequate foundation yet provided for complete skepticism."

Atomic propositions are supposed to count as elementary pieces of *knowledge*, according to Russell, such that "all complex propositions depend for their status *as knowledge*" upon them. But it is problematic that Russell merely legislates their existence, supplying only some classical hand waving about the causal nature of perception as a justification for their existence. When laid bare, the real thrust of his argument is nothing more than that a coherence criterion of truth by itself is inadequate, hence there must be something else that grounds claims to knowledge. Russell's legislating a solution ad hoc, in the form of atomic propositions, is merely a reflection of the fact that all he can really guarantee by virtue of a syntactic conception of propositions, despite abhorring the prospect of having to settle for it, is a coherence criterion. This tends to speak against his view of propositions.

In opposing Russell on this matter, Dewey does not deny the occurrence of immediate sensible experiences. But (1) he does deny the absolute simplicity of such experiences as well as the atomicity of propositions concerning such experiences. And (2) he denies that such propositions formulate or constitute elementary bits of "knowledge." That is just a simplistic and otherwise bad way of talking about knowledge. Each of these points will be considered in turn.

Even the simplest of utterances like "redness-here" can have as complicated a content as you like, depending on its context of use. It might serve to report a primitive datum in a given inquiry, such as when one attempts to make sense of a given painting or some other visual scene; or it might be the outcome of a complex inquiry where the subject matter (pointed to with the word 'here') is *judged* to be red, such as when you are groping in a darkened room for a bank of color-coded electrical switches and then have to visually probe each switch at length to determine its color.

Dewey equally appreciated the inadequacy of a coherence criterion by itself, but he proceeded to develop a richer view of logic, embedding it within a general theory of inquiry, rather than proposing stopgap remedies for an impoverished epistemology. Establishing an abstractly coherent subject matter is important to, but is by no means sufficient for, the success of a given inquiry. Equally important is the process of measuring the actual consequences of actions suggested by one's hypotheses against expected consequences of those actions. Recall that there are several categories in Dewey's taxonomy of propositions, and propositions about "qualities" of things are propositions about immediate features of things. Qualities in Dewey's logic include what Russell refers to as immediate sensible experiences. Russell is therefore mistaken when he states (quoted on page 212 above) that "[n]o words exist, according to the instrumentalist, which do not embody theories or hypotheses, and the crude fact of perception is therefore for ever ineffable." In Dewey's framework, words whose role in a given instance is to denote *qualities* have precisely this theory-free function in inquiry.

At the same time, (*a*) qualities occur in immediate experience only as the results of certain ongoing actions being performed then and there in that situation (involving bodily motor activities, complex electrochemical processes in the brain and nervous system, energy transfers in the environment and within the organism/environment system, and so forth), so that their possible significance in a given situation can be determined only with reference to the complex of specific operations by which they are produced and in terms of which they are eventually explained and "learnt from," as Russell would say. And (*b*) propositions formulating such information, though they function simply to register qualitative features of this or that thing in a given phase of inquiry, are not necessarily atomic. Trivially, the registration of the information expressed by 'redness-and-squareness-here' can be both immediate, sensible, unitary, and yet "compound" insofar as it might be resolvable into 'redness-here' and 'squareness-here'. More importantly, the *operational* complexity involved in the formulation of such propositions confutes any claim to their absolute simplicity. Their *functional* simplicity in a given inquiry rests on their being regarded as having what we might refer to as zero significance in and by themselves: they simply register what is immediately given, whereas any significance to be drawn from them is determined with respect to, and formulated by, other sorts of propositions (particularly existential-procedural propositions dealing with classifications of things according to some working repertoire of kinds, as discussed in Section 5.3; see Dewey 1938, p. 290).

So when Russell emphasizes "single events which only happen once" as being what basic propositions are about (see the quote on page 212 above), he is not appealing to anything which Dewey does not appropriately emphasize. The fact that single events can never be repeated is precisely what is meant by saying that the events themselves are *not* "stubborn"—they happen and then they are gone. One can only continue to gather ever-new evidence which, with reference to some set of explanatory hypotheses, is perhaps consistent with the record of old evidence. "There is *something* to be learnt from single events" after all; though nothing is learned from basic propositions in themselves except in conjunction with other information, particularly with regard to prior and subsequent consequences of ongoing actions which, as suggested by some set of hypotheses, seem appropriate for the situation. One does not undo old evidence by gathering new and contrary evidence, but one *can* confirm or confute what is *learned from* old evidence by gathering overwhelmingly contrary new evidence which recommends a different regard for the old evidence—in which case one cannot count for certain on the "stubbornness" of what is learned from single events.

This helps to explain why Dewey rejects Russell's claim that basic propositions, once apprehended, constitute elementary bits of knowledge. According to this claim, to grasp a basic proposition, e.g., a perceptual datum such as "redness-here," is to directly grasp and know an elementary fact or a self-evident truth about the world. This is a stopgap measure designed to solidify some kind of foundation of knowledge. But no account is given as to how to tell the difference between apprehending a true basic proposition (and thus knowing a fact) and apprehending what only seems to be a true basic proposition (and thus only seeming to know a fact but actually being mistaken). This constitutes not a theory of knowledge but simply an assertion that we have knowledge (where presumably we have some folk-psychological understanding of what that might mean). Of course, Russell's orientation here is such as to assert that sometimes we are wrong about the world, but often enough we are right about things; and logic, meanwhile, is a study of formal features of propositional systems, where the focus is on how facts can be inferred from given facts. When it comes right down to it, the question of how facts are given in the first place is simply not part of this formal enterprise. Which is to say, Russell offers no theory of knowledge which does not beg the question. But this tends to undermine his referring to apprehensions of basic propositions as instances of knowledge. If it is not possible to say anything more, i.e., if this only begs the question (as if to implicitly appeal to some sort of folk epistemology), then one has not said anything particularly substantial. One has simply glossed over an epistemological problem in order to simplify logical theory.

The real problem here, so far as Dewey is concerned, is that Russell's logical machinery is too simple and coarse-grained in the first place to handle the issues involved, or else he would not be forced to posit solutions ad hoc and to otherwise avoid so many fundamental epistemological issues. Russell is compelled to posit atomic propositions with definite and nondefeasible truth values ("stubborn facts") (and to call "perception" of such facts knowledge) only because he has not developed the necessary theoretical apparatus for dealing with the issues involved. In particular, Russell lacks the distinction between propositions and judgments which allows Dewey to work epistemological issues into his logic in a constructive, non-question-begging way. Russell also assumes a rather simple theory of properties and relations which does not afford the expressiveness and conceptual depth of Dewey's theory of qualities, kinds, and modes of action. One of the main themes of this chapter has been that Russell failed to see such distinctions at work in Dewey's writings. As for atomic propositions, Russell's thinking must have been simply that either one must admit them, or else one is stuck with mere rationalism and a coherence theory of truth. He thus mistook Dewey's denial of atomic propositions, by disjunctive elimination, to be an assertion of a coherence theory of truth and a commitment to rationalism.

Dewey claims rather that it is only in terms of judgments (not propositions) that one can start to talk about "knowledge" as such. Dewey prefers to speak primarily in terms of knowing rather than knowledge, where knowing is a kind of doing, a kind of conduct (activity, or process), and as such is understood to be the product of successful inquiry. In this regard, there is no rhyme or reason to positing "atomic knowledge" or "atomic judgments" (which is *not* to say, on the other hand, that consequences of established judgments cannot *function* as primitive "givens" in subsequent inquiries).

It has to be granted, of course, that Dewey's theory of knowledge, despite its many practical aspects, does not comport well with folk epistemology at every turn. One of the features of Dewey's epistemology which is bothersome to Russell and others is that "knowing" in this account appears to be subject to revision—to the extent that different inquiries can change the way one conducts oneself in the world. If we were to ignore the details of Dewey's theory and apply this claim to what counts as knowledge in Russell's framework, then we would be in a position of having to allow that the "facts" cannot change without our having to change what we know, as if to have to deny or "un-know" what we previously knew. But this is not acceptable. We can revise our beliefs, and perhaps we can forget what we once knew; but if we do know something, then we *unreservedly* know it. Knowledge, like truth, admits neither degrees nor revision.

There are several points to be made as a response to this line of thought. The first point concerns what it means, in Dewey's view, to say that knowledge should be characterized as something which can change. This is not simply the observation that we can discover ourselves to have been wrong and so reevaluate what we know. That is one way to take the point, but it requires some attention to distinguishing *knowing* from tested but potentially mistaken *believing*. It *is* in such terms that we can talk about unwarranting a previously warranted assertion. But the term 'knowledge' used in this sense would have to suffer the same fate as terms like 'reality' and 'truth'—to be understood as metaphysical ideals which we do not always have a good experiential handle on.

But another way to see the point about the changeability of knowledge is that we can take different perspectives on things, in different situations, and "know" them in different ways. This is, for instance, at the root of Dewey's manner of reconciling commonsense knowledge with scientific knowledge (of the very same things)—namely, neither is more or less right than the other, but either is more or less appropriate to the perspective it assumes. We "revise" knowledge in this sense by changing our perspective, not necessarily by falsifying previous beliefs. This applies to what are taken to be "the facts" as much as to any respective hypothetical apparatus involved. The facts in the one case are simply not facts in the other (which is not to say they are now false but simply that they are no longer part of the situation).

Here is a mundane example. When you sit at one end of the table, the salt is to the left of the pepper, while from the other end of the table, it is the other way around. Which of the two facts is true and which is false? Do the truth values of the respective "basic propositions" change when you move to the other end of the table? Or do these simple perceptual facts not correspond to basic propositions? If not, what counts as a basic proposition? Why would "whiteness there" count as a basic proposition while "this is to the left of that" not? These are problems for Russell. Dewey meanwhile introduced a theory of facts, propositions, and truth within the context of a theory of inquiry which does not lead to these sorts of puzzles. Elements of perspectivity are as much a part of the contents of the propositions under consideration as are the respective sense data.

Another point in response to the claim about the nonchangeability of knowledge echoes Dewey's claim about warranted assertibility (as the only practical handle we have on what in folk epistemology is termed knowledge) applying not to propositions but to judgments. Namely, propositions, in Dewey's view, are not properly said to be "known." Grasping basic propositions does not constitute a kind of basic knowledge, because the grasping of *any* kind of proposition whatsoever is not to be characterized as "knowing." In other words, Dewey is not asserting a coherence theory, as Russell claims, but asserting rather that Russell has made a category mistake by treating propositions, atomic or otherwise, as the objects of knowledge.

It is this faulty treatment of propositions as objects of knowledge (that is, treating knowledge as a "propositional" attitude) which lies behind Dewey's saying that Russell takes propositions to be the subject matter of inquiry (see pages 206ff above). Knowledge, in Dewey's view, is the product of successful inquiry, where

(1) Objects of knowledge are the subject matters of inquiries.

But if

(2) Propositions are the objects of knowledge,

it follows from (1) that

(3) Propositions are the subject matters of inquiries.

Insofar as Russell denies (3) (1940, p. 402), he either has to give up (1) or (2). But he accepts (1) (Russell 1940, p. 403, with some basically irrelevant reservations about whether subject matters should be treated as "events" as opposed to "things"), in which case (2) has to be rejected.

Dewey does not deny either the existence of matters of fact or the important function of data in inquiry. Surveying the facts of the matter is an essential feature of any inquiry. But Dewey denies that a designation such as "fact of the matter" is absolute, and he denies that propositions are said to be "known" rather than simply registered and duly considered. The first point is a reflection of the principle that it does make sense to talk about propositions as being simple and basic, but only functionally and tentatively so, relative to ongoing contingencies of given inquiries. Secondly, one does not "know" facts; rather one infers and observationally confirms facts, employing such information in conjunction with various hypotheses and their implications, to develop a working knowledge of the given subject matter. This essentially reiterates the thesis that Dewey was formulating an information-theoretic conception of propositions.

Dewey's opposition to the idea of atomic propositions is, as a positive point, an observation about the *function* of information in inquiry. Information formulated propositionally in a given inquiry I_1 does not in that light function as knowledge. But as illustrated in the examples in Section 4.3, and according to Dewey's three-way distinction among objects, subject matters, and contents (Dewey 1938, pp. 118–19; and Section 3.2 above), this is not to deny that, relative to other inquiries $I_2, I_3, \ldots$, some sort of knowledge (knowing, judgments) will have been involved in perceiving or otherwise individuating the objects which the information in I_1 is about. One begins to get a picture here of inquiries embedded within inquiries, where judgments resulting from embedd*ed* inquiries are the basis for, but are not simply equal to, information in an embedd*ing* inquiry. Such information will be determined rather by the qualitative consequences of those judgments insofar as they affect one's conduct in the larger inquiry, because the domain of experience of which this conduct is a part is somehow problematic. At the same time, harking back to issues considered in Chapter 2, it is pertinent here that the "boundedness" of situations is governed in one respect by what are taken as *data* in that inquiry. The *functional* simplicity of data does not guarantee any kind of atomicity, but the fact is that at some point in any given inquiry certain things are tentatively taken just as they are given as determining the "simplest terms" of that inquiry, probably because they are not problematic in themselves, so that one can proceed without delving further into them. There is perhaps nothing *in principle* to oppose delving into everything without limit, so that the concept of atomic knowledge is suspect, but there is nothing in principle to compel limitless delving either. What *in fact* opposes such limitless delving are the contingencies of given inquiries. One delves only as far as is needed to solve given problems. One therefore need not appeal to the idea of atoms of knowledge in order to ground a theory of knowledge, but rather the idea that data can be *functionally simple* is enough to achieve that end.

5.4.3 Inference and Acquisition of Data

Dewey (1941, pp. 335–40) devotes roughly half a dozen pages to answering Russell's charge that he "den[ies] the distinction between data and inference" (see Russell 1940, p. 154; and page 212 above).

Dewey begins his response by considering the remarks cited above on page 212, where Russell attributes to "instrumentalists" the idea that "in all knowledge there is an inferential element." Dewey asserts that this can be read in two ways, one of which is acceptable and the other not. Inquiry is a process which leads to knowledge, and inference plays an important role in this process. Inference is essential to establishing what is known in particular cases, but it does not thereby occur in and of itself as a constituent of what is known.

Inference is an integral part of inquiry, where its function is to facilitate articulation of the subject matter of the given inquiry in which it operates—to interpret current observations as well as to explore possibilities relative to currently accepted principles formulating a working knowledge of how the world works. Whatever is inferred in particular instances must in turn be checked against ongoing experience; that is, its predictable observable consequences must be compared with actual data. If what is inferred is already consistent with all prior data, it is essential that the test data be *new*, calling therefore for *further* observation. New observational information may support further inference, and new data are on the other hand interpreted and otherwise given any significance by virtue of their capacity to confirm or refute given hypotheses. The cooperative interplay of these two *complimentary* aspects of inquiry continues for as long as the inquiry goes on.

If we fix a given inquiry in some stage of development and consider the data and hypotheses involved in that instance, it may very well be difficult to trace which way the multiple dependencies go. There will no doubt seem to be an intractably complex, if not hopelessly circular, relationship between the two. But inquiry is a dynamic and progressive affair, where new observations and new inferences are being made in a controlled manner dictated by old observations and old inferences. Viewed "endwise," as if projected onto a simple 2-D framework of fixed data versus fixed hypotheses, the whole thing will look circular—as in figures 2 and 3 (pages 161ff). Analogies can be misleading, but as outlined in Section 5.1, an image which better captures Dewey's views is that the process of inquiry follows a pattern more like that of a corkscrew, eventually to converge, if successful, to a stably coherent system of theory and observation. The analogy with a corkscrew can actually do some work for us in the present context.

By ignoring the progressive (teleological) component of inquiry, Russell is compelled to posit some way of breaking into a "circle" of dependencies among data and hypotheses. He assigns this function to perception:

> It is surely obvious that every perceptive experience, if I choose to notice it, affords me either new knowledge which I could not previously have inferred, or, at least, as in the case of eclipses, greater certainty than I could have previously obtained by means of inference. (Russell 1940, p. 154)

Inference alone is not enough to break into or out of the circle, but only winds around inside of it.

But in Dewey's view, these dependencies are not entirely circular. There is no need to *break into* a "spiral" of dependencies among data and hypotheses, insofar as inquiry progressively breaks new ground (or should we say "cork") as a normal matter of course, by turning up new observations and inferring new hypotheses. Inference can produce new results which observation alone would hardly if ever have uncovered, *and* vice versa. (See Dewey 1911/1933, pp. 139–40, for a discussion of what is referred to as the "spiral movement" of inquiry. The focus in that discussion is on the accumulation of knowledge as a reciprocal interaction between concepts and meanings that are taken for granted in a given inquiry and those that are worked out and articulated in the course of that inquiry. The "hermeneutic circle" is thereby recast as a "hermeneutic helix.")

As an aside, some of the puzzles familiar in ethics and formal decision theory can be viewed as artifacts of the same kind of metatheoretic collapse of perspective. In such cases, various dilemmas are presented in such a way that circumstances are fixed, both as to available "data" and in terms of options available to alter those circumstances. The problem moral theorists pose for themselves is to find some set of basic principles and rules of inference which, in some general way not geared exclusively to this or that particular dilemma, will explain how to *analyze* one's way out of such dilemmas in one fell swoop. Now certainly there are real situations where one's only recourse is to use one's head to determine a solution, as if one had only one shot at solving a do-or-die, truth-or-consequences problem. But it would be misleading to assert that this is paradigmatic of moral problem solving. It is more likely that circumstances and options are not always fixed. That is, moral problems, like problems in general, are the sorts of things which can be anticipated or otherwise held at bay in such a way that possible solutions can be explored and tested before circumstances come to such a brittle state. If, in the real world, mere analysis is not enough to solve an apparent dilemma, one may be able to exploit ongoing observations to try to uncover new facts bearing on the case, and one may be able to put some effort into reevaluating one's analytical preconceptions. One can try to augment given circumstances by finding new and useful information and new and more effective ways to think about the information one is given, even if this does not yet put one in a position to finally solve the problem. Moral theory could probably benefit from acknowledging and trying to effectively accommodate this dynamic aspect of problem solving. The fact that puzzles can be designed where purely formal techniques are not sufficient to save the day only confirms the point that pure analysis, without recourse to open-ended processes of exploring circumstances, is not generally sufficient to solve problems. This dynamic orientation to moral problem solving is developed by Dewey in "Logical Conditions of a Scientific Treatment of Morality" (1903a), in *Human Nature and Conduct* (1922), and in *Theory of Valuation* (1939b), among other places. See also *How We Think* (1911/1933), pp. 115-16, for a brief discussion of the value of treating overt activity as experimental, so far as that is possible, in any kind of problem solving that permits some kind of reflective thought, including moral and other kinds of practical problem solving.

But to return to Dewey's response to Russell: to claim that the processes of observation and inference are interdependent is not to claim that their products (data and hypotheses) cannot be properly distinguished. This is at least part of what Russell *is* claiming when he attributes to instrumentalists the "repl[y] that any statement of the new knowledge obtained from perception is always an interpretation based upon accepted theories, and may need subsequent correction if these theories turn out to be unsuitable." This means, Russell claims, that data, for instrumentalists, are hypothetical.

Dewey rejects this suggested reply on two grounds. For one thing, it verges on contradiction (1) by acknowledging no method for reevaluating and correcting theories, at least not as a concern for logic, and yet (2) asserting that theories can be both "accepted" and "unsuitable." This is perhaps just an oversight due to Russell's hasty formulation of the position, or possibly Russell intends to attribute this contradiction to instrumentalists. Dewey rejects it as a statement of his own views, in any case.

Secondly, there is a subtler problem in Russell's alleged reply when he refers to the "new knowledge obtained from perception." This returns us to the problem of Russell's holding that data directly present "cases of knowledge"—a position which only serves to collapse a number of distinctions which Dewey is trying to draw, such as between data and hypotheses and between propositions and judgments.

> For Mr. Russell holds, if I understand him, that propositions about these data are in some cases instances of knowledge, and indeed that such cases provide, as basic propositions, the models upon which a theory of truth should be formed. In my view, they are not cases of *knowledge*, although propositional formulation of them is a *necessary* (but not sufficient) condition of knowledge. (Dewey 1941, p. 338)

For Dewey, both data and hypotheses are "formulated propositionally" in the course of a given inquiry. That does not mean that both are hypothetical. Hypotheses are hypothetical, while data are observational; and both are fallible. And the fact that they are formulated propositionally means that, in that regard, they do *not* count as cases of knowledge. A case of knowledge is formulated, not propositionally, but as a judgment, i.e., as a conclusive end product of some inquiry. Propositions, in contrast, play an intermediate role in inquiry. As "means" or "instrumentalities," propositions (either observational or hypothetical) are better thought of as *information* serving a process which should lead eventually to the making of a successful judgment.

By collapsing these distinctions, one loses any grip one might have had on the progressive nature of inquiry, effectively erasing any distinction between intermediate and final stages of inquiry. The outcome is troublesome, as Russell notes, since the resulting picture of inquiry will now appear circular. He attributes this problem to Dewey, when in fact it is a product of projecting Dewey's writings in a bad light.

In fact, the claim that Dewey does not properly distinguish data and hypotheses is almost certainly based on Russell's not distinguishing the concept of 'hypothetical proposition' from that of 'defeasible proposition'. The interdependence of processes of observation and inference serves to test not only the products of inference, but to progressively evaluate and reevaluate given data as well. In this sense, both hypotheses and data are understood to be defeasible. But to say that data are defeasible is not to say they are hypothetical, nor is it to say that the datum/hypothesis distinction is collapsed.

To connect this to the central theme of this chapter, the mistake of not distinguishing hypothetical from defeasible propositions is a result of not having appreciated Dewey's distinction between propositions and judgments. That is, in his treatment of data and hypotheses, Dewey was working out details of his theory of propositions, where different kinds of propositions are distinguished as to the sources of the information they formulate (such as by observation or by inference), as to the status of their validation (such as having been tested and confirmed or disconfirmed, or being not yet adequately tested), and so forth. Generally speaking, there will be substantial amounts of information (whether singular or generic) which is not hypothetical but rather factual, because it has been adequately tested and validated and because it continues to be relevant and to resist disconfirmation. Meanwhile, *all* propositions in any given stage of a given inquiry, whether factual or hypothetical, are defeasible insofar as the entire inquiry as it stands may or may not be proceeding appropriately, which is a matter of *judgment* concerning the inquiry as a whole. One may consider almost any familiar example of actual scientific inquiry to see that this is the case. With regard to Ptolemaic astronomy back in the fifteenth century, there will be all sorts of facts and hypotheses which will have been undermined within the next couple of centuries as a result of that particular way of doing astronomy being deemed inappropriate and being superseded by astronomers' taking a different perspective on the whole subject matter (see Dewey 1938, pp. 425–6). All of those Ptolemaic facts will no longer be accepted as facts, not because they were reevaluated and deemed merely hypothetical (whatever that might mean) but because a Ptolemaic perspective on things will have "defeated" itself.

Russell's motivation for claiming to be the hard-nosed empiricist, in contrast to Dewey's allegedly overemphasizing "theory and hypothesis," becomes more apparent when we realize that Russell basically turned a blind eye to Dewey's discussions of many of these distinctions and consequently did not acknowledge the experimentalist principles at work in Dewey's views. But then it is only more surprising to see Russell making statements (see the more extensive quote on page 212 above) such as that

> [the instrumentalist] view underestimates the powers of analysis. It is undeniable that our every-day interpretations of perceptive experiences, and even all our every-day words, embody theories. But it is not impossible to whittle away the element of interpretation, or to invent an artificial language involving a minimum of theory. By these methods we can approach asymptotically to the pure datum.... The essential characteristic of a datum is that it is not inferred.... I shall henceforth assume that there are data, in the sense of propositions for which the evidence is not wholly derived from their logical relation to other propositions. (Russell 1940, p. 154)

Russell wants to say here that, presumably within a given inquiry or perhaps in some absolute sense, we can virtually eliminate all theory and hypothesis to come to discern pure data as pure data. By devising the right sort of representational system (something like the language of first-order logic) with a minimal amount of interpretation or theory packed into it, one will be in a better position to distinguish data from what is only inferred. What this seems to say is that by being more and more like mathematicians, we move into a better position to recognize empirical data, in the sense that among all true propositions, "the pure datum" is what is pointed to when one traces backwards through one's inferences to what stands on its own as primitively given, as if "analysis" could eliminate all but the data.

One hardly wants to deny the value of mathematics in the sciences, but Russell's characterization of data as what is true but not inferred is difficult to get a handle on in any practical sense. The fact is that there is no need to whittle away anything to get at data, but rather to note the concrete operational foundations of the distinction between data and hypotheses. Data are given, immediately and up front, by virtue of one's actually performing concrete operations in the world. Analysis can predict what *types* of data to expect under certain types of circumstances, but "pure data" are immediately given as here-and-now results of concrete actions in the world.

To say that data are not inferred is otherwise ambiguous if not slightly uninformative. We do not want to say that data cannot be *predicted* or *retrodicted* from some given set of facts and working hypotheses. As Russell puts it, we should not assume "that the actual data which we can obtain are ever completely certain, nor yet that a proposition which is a datum cannot be also a consequence of other accepted propositions. This latter case occurs whenever we see a predicted eclipse." But then one wonders what he was thinking Dewey must have meant if not precisely this when talking about the interdependencies of data and hypotheses in given inquiries. This is not quite to say that data are inferred, since such "analysis" does not get outside of talking about *types* of data. Without underestimating the power of analysis, we can say that actual data are gotten only by concrete observations. Analysis cannot and need not be expected to usurp this function. Neither Russell nor Dewey would believe otherwise. But it is odd that Russell simply posits data as absolutely given, where analysis is somehow able to point, by elimination, to which propositions these are. As a hard-nosed empiricist, why not appeal to something like processes of observation rather than processes of analysis as the way to get at "the pure datum"? This is of course what Russell eventually does in the passage under discussion, but as if this were somehow missing in Dewey's allegedly rationalist views:

> But when a proposition concerning a particular matter of fact is inferred, there must always be among the premises other matters of fact from which some general law is obtained by induction. It is therefore impossible that all our knowledge of matters of fact be inferred.
>
> The question of how to obtain from perceptual experience propo-

sitions which are premises for empirical knowledge is difficult and complicated, but fundamental for any empirical theory of knowledge. (Russell 1940, p. 156)

Russell unfortunately does not acknowledge Dewey's extensive investigations and discussions, in *Logic* and elsewhere, of the "difficult and complicated" nature of scientific method and of how such considerations are relevant to logical theory. One tends to get the impression from Russell's remarks that Dewey oversimplified matters and failed to appreciate what he was up against (for another example of this, see Russell's remarks quoted on page 197 above concerning induction and scientific method). But it is more likely that Russell was unable or unwilling to see that Dewey was already way ahead of where Russell thought he was in directly facing up to these difficulties and complications. His unusual taxonomy of propositions, his different types of attributes (qualities, kinds, and modes of being), his distinction between propositions and judgments, not to mention his detailed and innovative treatment of mathematics, induction, and numerous other topics not discussed here nor addressed in Russell's review, were all part of an attempt to delve into some of these complications.

Russell's picture of inquiry, as we have seen, is by comparison rather anemic. He often proceeds as if inquiry were merely "analytical," as if mathematical inquiry were paradigmatic of inquiry in general. But this *over*estimates the powers of analysis, as if one had a reliable measure on what the facts are because of their correspondence to syntactico-deductive features of sentential representations. Russell's appeal to "an artificial language involving a minimum of theory" as the ultimate tool of analysis, and hence of inquiry, is precisely the sort of thing to which Dewey was referring when he said that Russell was invested too much in "discourse" and in taking propositions to be the subject matter of inquiry, not saying enough about what besides "analysis" is involved in the process of solving concrete problems.

6

Conclusion

One goal of this book has been to show that Dewey's theory of logic is considerably more sophisticated than Russell would have us believe. Dewey's logical theory has been thought to be obscure, naive, and irrelevant, when in fact it is complex, subtle, and quite relevant to current investigations of language, information, and intelligence.

Several topics which receive a good deal of attention in the Dewey/Russell debate but which have not been adequately addressed here are Dewey's conceptions of warranted assertibility and truth, his conceptions of knowing and knowledge, and the theory of intelligence these conceptions support. These topics are in some sense the most significant topics of the debate. The preceding chapters have, on the other hand, discussed some technically fundamental concepts and issues which were slighted by Russell but which need to be squared away before jumping ahead to deal with these more significant topics.

In this closing chapter I will briefly discuss these larger topics, to help anchor any loose references to these notions in the preceding chapters, and to outline points to be addressed if the Dewey/Russell debate were to be analyzed further.

6.1 Warranted Assertibility and Truth

It would virtually double the size of the present book to adequately address Russell's criticisms of Dewey's concept of warranted assertibility. But the bottom line is that Russell mistook Dewey's notion of warranted assertibility for a theory of truth, so that many of his arguments were based on, motivated by, or otherwise addressed to points and principles irrelevant to Dewey's actual views.

Without going to great lengths to address these criticisms directly, I will discuss two points here as a way of briefly explaining Dewey's theory of truth. The first point to be made is that, while Dewey's views are operationalistic in character, his logical theory can accommodate a metaphysically robust notion of truth. Secondly, I will discuss what Dewey meant when he claimed that "[his] *type* of theory is the only one entitled to be called a correspondence theory of truth" (1941, p. 344).

1. *Dewey's operationalism*. The concept of warranted assertibility is in a sense a feature of Dewey's later thinking. In his earlier work, he sometimes talked about truth (that is, he used the word 'truth') as he would later talk about warranted assertibility.[1] This no doubt influenced Russell's review of *Logic*, in that Russell was acquainted with some of Dewey's work dating back to 1903 if not earlier. One way to understand this particular line of development in Dewey's thinking is that, in his earlier work, he was advocating a fairly radical theory of truth with certain verificationist (but ultimately non-Millean) features. This would be the result in large part of the influence of James's *Principles of Psychology* (1890) on Dewey's thinking around the turn of the century. It eventually became apparent that this view of truth was not going to be able to accommodate broader analytical and metaphysical uses of the term, yet it was clear to Dewey that he was developing a theory of *something* which is relevant not just to epistemology but to logic, whether or not it is appropriate to call it "truth." The resulting refinement and shift of terminology, from 'truth' to 'warranted assertibility', was accomplished by the time Dewey wrote *Logic*. He had let go of the term 'truth', but held on to logic.

---

[1] See, for instance, the last several paragraphs of Chapter 6 of Dewey 1920. And Tiles 1988, particularly Chapters 5 and 6, though not specifically a historical account of Dewey's views, gives a good sense of the gradual development of Dewey's notions of truth and warranted assertibility.

As has been argued in the preceding chapter, Russell's mistake of conflating the notions of warranted assertibility and truth reflects a failure to grasp Dewey's distinction between propositions and judgments. This was a result of an unwillingness to accept the operationalistic and otherwise epistemological flavor of Dewey's logical theory. In Dewey's view, it is judgments, not propositions, which are warrantably assertible or not; and judgments are essentially rooted in concrete actions in the world insofar as the consequences of such actions serve to decide their warrantability.

> I hope it suffices to point out that the question of truth-falsity is *not*, on my view, a matter of [success or failure of] the effects of *believing*, for my whole theory is determined by the attempt to state what conditions and operations of inquiry *warrant* a "believing," or justify its assertion as true; that propositions, as such, are so far from being cases of believings that they are means of attaining a warranted believing, their worth as means being determined by their pertinency and efficacy in "satisfying" the conditions that are rigorously set by the problem they are employed to resolve.... [A]ccording to my view, understanding and misunderstanding, conception and misconception, taking and mis-taking, are matters of propositions, which are not final or complete in themselves but are used as means to an end—the resolution of a problem; while it is to this resolution, as *conclusion* of inquiry, that the adjectives "true" and "false" apply.... [Moreover] I believe most decidedly that the distinction between "true" and "false" is to be found in the relation which *propositions*, as means of inquiry, "have to relevant occurrences.".... [T]he relevant occurrences on my theory are those existential consequences which, in virtue of the operations existentially performed, satisfy (meet, fulfill) conditions set by occurrences that constitute a problem. (Dewey 1941, pp. 347–8)

This notion of warranting a judgment by concretely acting in accordance with its dictates (i.e., by "applying" it in the world), to see how it actually stands up, does not by itself supply a theory of truth, nor did Dewey claim that it did. What he did claim was that logic should address epistemological issues dealing with what *justifies* or *warrants* assertions of judgments (as true), and that warranted assertibility, rather than truth itself, should be a basic consideration in a theory of inference. Truth and falsity, insofar as anything is to be said about these notions, pertain to the conclusion, not the intermediate details, of inquiries. The truth or falsity of a given judgment is characterized in terms of relations and correspondences among expectations and actual results of actions formulated in the course of the respective inquiry, but, strictly speaking, it is the assertion of the judgment which is true or not, not the information involved in ascertaining the judgment—it is something of a "category mistake" to say otherwise.

There are of course several different yes/no distinctions besides the true/false distinction (e.g., affirm/deny, confirm/refute, accept/reject, include/exclude) which Dewey discussed at length in *Logic*, some of which apply to propositions rather than to judgments. By conflating propositions and judgments, one is compelled to collapse several such considerations into one alleged distinction, which leads fairly quickly to nonsense, as Russell's discussions of these matters show. We should instead put these other binary modalities in proper perspective as different but not irrelevant concerns, in an attempt to understand what Dewey meant by the truth or falsity of an assertion of a judgment.

One thing which recommends the notion of warranted assertibility as a working concept in logic is that the warranted assertibility of judgments is tangibly certifiable by means of one's concrete actions in the world, whereas the *truth* of one's assertions remains at bottom a metaphysical ideal. In an information-based logical theory, the concept of truth is therefore not always entirely relevant except as an abstract consideration. All the basic elements of Dewey's logical theory—all the elements assumed to have a role in the formulation of propositions and so (derivatively) in the determination of judgments—are given an operationalistic treatment. In affirming that object a is of kind K, one must be in a position to actively confirm that a satisfies qualitative specifications characteristic of things of kind K, either directly or else by inference from other directly confirmable facts. A given inquiry will tend toward a conclusion, a judgment, only as the active confirmations and refutations of such information in that inquiry tend to be successful, coherent, and show prospects for ongoing stability. On the other hand, we can think of the *truth* of an assertion of a judgment as being what an ideal inquirer would come up with if given unlimited resources, ingenuity, efficiency, tenacity, energy, time, and any other ideal abilities and capacities which could serve the needs of inquiry.

This operationalistic but idealized notion of truth is perfectly meaningful and robust.[2] Truth is characterized here in terms of the methods and would-be results of explorations and verifications of ideal inquirers, which is not to say that Dewey endorses "merely" a verificationist view of truth. On the contrary, this conception of truth does not entail that the efforts of actual finite agents cannot often yield exactly the same results which such an ideal inquirer would come up with (sometimes our assertions are true and we can know it—mathematical inquiry is often like this, for example), *but* it provides no general way of determining when this is or is not the case. Warranted assertibility is of course a different matter.

2. *Dewey's correspondence theory of truth.* We have seen in the previous chapter that Russell conflated the ideas of truth and factuality. For Russell, a proposition is factual if and only if it is true. From a folk-epistemological perspective, this is largely innocuous, as if to reflect a kind of redundancy in the English language. We do want to be able to talk about facts independently of talking about sentences which may or may not express facts, but there is assumed to be a tight relationship between truth and factuality: a sentence is true just in case it expresses a fact. Some facts are not purely formal but constitute concrete material features or aspects of the world. The world is the totality of all facts; and facts are what make propositions true or false. These logical-positivistic slogans are not unproblematic, but this is essentially the core of a correspondence theory of truth as commonly conceived.

Given that this is Russell's view, it is somewhat surprising,

---

[2]Except for a lack of a distinction between propositions and judgments, this is essentially Putnam's notion of "idealized justifiability" (1983, pp. xvii–xviii).

then, to read that Dewey claimed that his own theory of truth is a correspondence theory. But a careful reading shows that it is precisely because of the chronically enigmatic character of a simple sentence/fact conception of correspondence that Dewey aimed first to refine and ultimately reconstruct the notion of correspondence, and only then would he be willing and able to make such a claim. If Russell's assessments are any indication, there are several novelties in Dewey's view which will at first appear to be beside the point if not to go against the spirit of the usual account of sentence/fact correspondence. For better or worse, these novelties should be seen as features of a project of refining the discussion in order to iron out problems inherent in articulating what is basically a vague but commonsense view of truth.

Some of the complexity of Dewey's logical theory as a whole is due to the fact that there is more to consider than simply comparing sentences against facts. His focus on inquiry and experience, his reformulation of the very notion of facts in information-theoretic terms, his relatively complicated taxonomy of propositions (as distinct, moreover, from judgments), and so forth, are all part of an attempt to explain (1) what it means to say that a statement about how things are may or may not correspond to how things actually are, when at the same time, (2) it is not possible to step back and treat this correspondence as if it were a matter of comparing the statement against reality. It is not as if we have some statement-independent handle on bare reality so that we can hold it up to compare against our statements, since it is statements themselves and the processes that go into their making which are one's handle on reality.

> How can anybody look at *both* an object (event) and a proposition about it so as to determine whether the two "correspond"? And if one can look directly at the event *in propria persona*, why have a duplicate proposition (idea, or percept, according to some theories) about it unless, perhaps, as a convenience in communication with others? (Dewey 1941, p. 352)

There is something wrong with the idea of detachment by means of which assertions and the realities they involve are treated respectively like measuring device and measured object. The metaphor of correspondence as measurement is a good one—Dewey ends up using just such a metaphor. But while a "spectator" sense of detachment is not complete nonsense from an armchair perspective, it is neither descriptive nor explanatory nor perhaps even relevant to how agents actually handle information and come to grips with real situations.

For one thing, there is a kind of explanatory regress involved if one concludes that logic (or more specifically, semantics) can or ought to deal with some special means (such as a formal language) for presenting facts in their bare essence, against which linguistic assertions can then be compared. The problem simply emerges again in the case of the allegedly privileged "language of facts." The following two paragraphs, though a bit long, are worth quoting insofar as they present in relatively short order Dewey's argument against this simple view of correspondence:

> I would point out what seems to be a certain indeterminateness in [Russell's] view of the relation between events and propositions, and the consequent need of introducing a distinction: *viz.*, the distinction between the problem of the relation of events and propositions *in general*, and the problem of the relation of a *particular* proposition to the *particular* event to which it purports to refer. I can understand that Mr. Russell holds that certain propositions, of a specified kind, are such direct effects of certain events, and of nothing else, that they "must be true." But this view does not, as I see the matter, answer the question of how we know that *in a given case* this direct relationship actually exists. It does not seem to me that this theory gets beyond specifying the kind of case *in general* in which the relation between an event, as causal antecedent, and a proposition, as effect, is such as to confer upon instances of the latter the property of being true. But I cannot see that we get anywhere until we have means of telling *which* propositions in particular *are* instances of the kind in question. (Dewey 1941, pp. 342–3)

Dewey is not saying here that we should in fact have criteria that enable us to tell which atomic propositions are true. He is saying that our definition of truth should be such as to be applicable to specific propositions, not just *types* of propositions. In particular, in that kind of framework, we should be able to say more than simply that some propositions are true and some not. We should be able to give some sort of principled account of what that difference amounts to. Otherwise, Russell's conception of correspondence does not give any meaning to the notion of truth, but only points to it as a problematic notion.

> In the case ... of *redness-here*, Mr. Russell asserts, as I understand him, that it is true when it is caused by a simple, atomic event. But how do we know in a given case whether it is so caused? Or if he holds that it *must* be true because it *is* caused by such an event, which is then its sufficient verifier, I am compelled to ask how such is known to be the case.... The event *to be* known is that which operates, on his view, as cause of the proposition while it is also its verifier; although the proposition is the sole means of knowing the event! Such a view, like any strictly epistemological view, seems to me to assume a mysterious and unverifiable doctrine of pre-established harmony. How an event can be (i) what-is-to-be-known, and hence by description is unknown, and (ii) what is capable of being *known* only through the medium of a proposition, which, in turn (iii) in order to be a case of knowledge or be true, must correspond to the to-be-known, is to me *the* epistemological miracle. For the doctrine states that a proposition is true when it conforms to that which is not known save through itself. (Dewey 1941, p. 343)

While rejecting a spectator theory of detachment and comparison which Russell's concept of correspondence presupposes, we have the fact nevertheless that agents are concretely and dynamically embedded in the world. Hence, as integral parts of the world, they have direct access to it. Though certain aspects of Dewey's views may seem to entail a commitment to some form of idealism, his focusing on this concrete embeddedness explicitly denies such a commitment. He embraces rather a form of operationalism. One's measure of reality is not *simply* a matter of correspondence between statements of fact and facts stated (though this is obviously an important concern), but it is more fundamentally a matter of the correspondence between expected consequences and actual consequences of continuing activities aimed at maintaining some kind of stable career as a sentient being (see pages 170ff above).

> [M]y own view takes correspondence in the operational sense it [commonly bears]; the meaning, namely, of *answering*, as a key answers to conditions imposed by a lock, or as two correspondents "answer" each other; or, in general, as a reply is an adequate answer to a question or a criticism—as, in short, a *solution* answers the requirements of a *problem.* On this view, both partners in "correspondence" are open and above board, instead of one of them being forever out of experience and the other in it by way of a "percept" or whatever. Wondering at how something in experience could be asserted to correspond to something by definition outside experience, which it is, upon the basis of epistemological doctrine, the sole means of "knowing," is what originally made me suspicious of the whole epistemological industry.
>
> In the sense of correspondence as operational and behavioral (the meaning which has definite parallels in ordinary experience), I hold that my *type* of theory is the only one entitled to be called a correspondence theory of truth. (Dewey 1941, pp. 343–4)

This more basic kind of correspondence, between expectations and actual achievements, earns its fundamental status in part because the various "correspondents" are equally and directly accessible to inquiring agents (whether or not they are users of languages).[3]

---

[3] At least in this one regard, this compares well with Wittgenstein's verificationist theory of propositions:

> I should like to say: for any question there is always a corresponding *method* of finding. Or you might say, a question *denotes* a method of searching. . . . To understand the sense of a proposition means to know how the issue of its truth or falsity is to be decided. . . . You cannot compare a picture with reality, unless you can set it against it as a yardstick. You must be able to fit the proposition on to reality. . . . The method of taking measurements, e.g., spatial measurements, is related to a particular measurement in precisely the same way as the sense of a proposition is to its truth or falsity. . . . How a proposition is verified is what it says. . . . The verification is not *one* token [sign, criterion] of the truth, but it is *the* sense of the proposition. (Einstein: How a magnitude is measured is what it is.) (Wittgenstein 1930, pp. 77–8, 200)

Wittgenstein's proposition is, in effect, an expectation of a certain event together with a procedure that will generate either that event or another one that

And it *is* fundamental in the sense that other relevant notions of correspondence—such as between sentences and facts—are to be derived from or otherwise explained in terms of it.

In this latter regard, Dewey need not reject a Tarskian account of truth in a language *L*, but he would nevertheless point out that more can be said about how an account of correspondences between sentences and facts can be extrapolated from an account of "correspondences in the operational sense" as he describes it. This operational anchoring of languages would give Tarski's account of truth predicates a noncircular intuitive grounding, which it simply lacks. As for truth in the stronger epistemological sense in which Russell and Dewey discussed it, a given language *L* need not be some privileged language of facts (i.e., facts need not be described as if from a detached perspective) so long as its terms, as a matter of principle, have some kind of concrete operational connection with the real world.

6.2   Dewey's Logic and Formal Semantics

In the preceding chapters, it has been assumed that readers are not familiar with the basic details of Dewey's work. In addressing Russell's various criticisms, Dewey's views have therefore been presented and explained from scratch. But if one were to analyze the debate further, and in particular if one were to defend Dewey's treatment of truth and warranted assertibility, it would be preferable to be able at the outset to work more from a position of strength.

One way to move into such a position would be to try to formalize Dewey's ideas, insofar as they might have anything to contribute

---

will refute that expectation. In this sense we may endorse a realist picture according to which we compare propositions with reality or with experience; and there is no mystery in this comparison, since what we contrast are two elements in the same space (like the meterstick and what it measures): the expected event and the outcome of the process. To compare the claim that the clock will strike in five minutes with reality is simply to compare the expectation that I will hear a certain type of sound under given circumstances with the actual sound I hear once I bring about those circumstances. The mystery of the comparison between a claim and experience is solved by placing experience within the claim. (Coffa 1991, pp. 360–1)

to formal semantics. There are at least a couple of areas of interest in the philosophy of language that are ripe for Deweyan-flavored ideas.

For instance, one might try to build on some recent developments in the philosophy of language which are geared to accommodating demonstratives (for example, Weinstein 1974; Kaplan 1978, 1989b). The idea of operationally anchored languages, if worked appropriately into a theory of semantics, could yield a principled treatment of demonstratives in the sense that one would be in a position to make explicit theoretical sense of concrete actions in the world which constitute "demonstrations" and other occurrences of direct reference.

In particular, a situation, as a concrete instance of disequilibrium or imbalance in the ongoing activities of some given organism/environment system, is defined as being present "here and now" as a "this" to or for that agent. In this regard, situations are thoroughly indexical in nature. As an immediately occurrent field of unitary experience, a situation is a focus of directed activities. Situations are not given arbitrarily nor are they specifiable a priori, but they are concrete instances of experience determined by contingent circumstances and fortunes of an organism/environment system aiming to maintain its systemic integrity. Though not strictly describable as "possible worlds," partial or otherwise, in any currently acceptable sense of the term, situations nevertheless should be viewed as contexts of concrete experience to which meanings and informational contents of utterances may be referred.

But the primary innovation involved in formalizing Dewey's logic, besides allowing a treatment of demonstratives, would be to incorporate an operation-based conception of properties and relations (including Dewey's treatment of qualities, kinds, and modes-of-being in the context of his distinction between propositions and judgments). That is, "predicate symbols" (in a now traditional sense of the phrase) would be interpreted not extensionally but with respect to specifications regarding operations of verification. This idea can be traced directly to Peirce's "pragmatic maxim" (first stated in Peirce 1878), which in Dewey's hands would become the cornerstone of a theory of semantics.

In short, Dewey endorses an operation-based theory of *meaning*. This is not to say that logic should be psychologistically empirical, and this is hardly a version of Bridgman's "operationism," nor is it an endorsement of a verificationist theory of truth. It is rather a proposal that interpretations of grammars be specified at bottom in terms of actions and consequences, not in terms of individuals and sets of individuals. It is not that Dewey was not developing a formalizable theory of semantics by not following Frege or Tarski, but that he was proposing a different choice of semantical primitives. The notions of "individuals" and "objects," for instance, would be derived notions.

An important goal of such a project would be to show how to reconcile a Tarskian treatment of truth with an appropriate formalization of these ideas. This may not be a trivial exercise, but it ought to be a manageable one. One would certainly be in a better position at that point to address issues of truth and warranted assertibility.

Presumably this would constitute not a radical alternative to classical semantics, but a refinement of it. Recent developments in formal semantics and in the philosophy of language tend to vindicate Dewey's hesitance to treat logic as just a formal study of syntax, regardless of whether or not he understood things in exactly the way that logic is currently understood. Dewey's views are still rather radical, proposing that we treat logic as a more concrete science than many mathematical logic texts would seem to recommend. But we do not have to conclude that Dewey's views are incompatible with the development of logic over the last fifty years. It is just that he would have the latter be put in some kind of broader perspective.

Consider, for instance, the epistemological turn, toward the end of Kaplan 1989a, where an instrumentalist view of language is recommended:

> There is another, possibly more fundamental, use of the notion [of a historical chain of acquisition by which a name is passed from user to user ...]: to tilt our perspective on the *epistemology* of

language away from the subjectivist views of Frege and Russell and towards a more communitarian outlook. The notion that a referent can be carried by a name from early past to present suggests that the language itself carries meanings, and thus that we can *acquire* meanings through the instrument of language. This frees us from the constraints of subjectivistic semantics and provides the opportunity for an *instrumental* use of language to broaden the realm of what can be expressed and to broaden the horizons of thought itself.

On my view, our connection with a linguistic community in which names and other meaning-bearing elements are passed down to us enables us to entertain thoughts *through the language* that would not otherwise be accessible to us. Call this the *Instrumental Thesis.* . . .

Contrary to Russell, I think we succeed in thinking about things in the world not only through the mental residue of that which we ourselves experience, but also vicariously, through the symbolic resources that come to us through our language. It is the latter—*vocabulary power*—that gives us our apprehensive advantage over the nonlinguistic animals. My dog, being color-blind, cannot entertain the thought that I am wearing a red shirt. But my color-blind colleague can entertain even the thought that Aristotle wore a red shirt. (Kaplan 1989a, pp. 603–4)[4]

This is hardly an endorsement of Dewey's logical theory, nor does it evidence the richness of Dewey's views. But it is an encouraging sign that theoretical seeds planted by the American pragmatists in the first half of this century are able to take root in the philosophy of language.

In the opening chapters of *Logic*, particularly in Chapter 3, Dewey presented an unusually broad conception of language. He included as a language virtually any medium of social interaction. And logical theory was born "when some one began to reflect upon language, upon *logos*, in its syntactical structure and its wealth of meaning contents" (*Logic*, pp. 57–8). Subsequently, as an effect of the early "hypostatization of *Logos*," logic has come to be thought of as a study of linguistic or propositional form independent of content.

---

[4]Similar sentiments are touched on more than once in Kripke 1972.

There is nothing particularly wrong with a study of "pure form," i.e., where abstract form is the subject matter of inquiry. This is definitive of mathematics, and mathematics is good. But beyond such formal concerns, a proper study of actual languages used as means for coordinating shared activities in the real world must accommodate the fact that communicative utterances are typically designed to transform experience. Logic ought to be able to deal with this transforming aspect of natural linguistic behavior and, more generally, be grounded in a theory of changing experience. Dewey's logic attempts to do that, particularly by focusing on inquiries as transformations of situations.

It is significant that Dewey characterized logic not primarily as a study of language, nor even of propositions or propositional forms, but as a study of *inquiry*. Dewey's point that language is what eventually gave rise to the invention of logic is not that language is necessarily the sole and proper subject matter of logic but that the existence of language, as a contingent evolutionary fact, is ultimately what makes inquiry into inquiry possible. The invention and use of symbols allows us to at least partially distance ourselves from our own activities, which, as facets of inquiry, may themselves serve as subject matters of inquiry (*Logic*, pp. 56–8); but we cannot afford to lose sight of the fact that logic, in Dewey's view, is concerned primarily with dissecting and analyzing the concrete experiential nature of inquiry.

A study of inquiry includes a study of the various roles that propositions play in the kind of transformation of experience which leads to effecting judgments. It is not enough to study formal-syntactic properties of linguistic expressions, natural or artificial, and call that logic. At the same time, as relatively complex inquirers, linguistic expressions may be among the more reliable handles that we have on our own experience, and the study of their syntactic properties is an important part of logic.

Of course, not all inquiries are couched in verbal garb: certainly not when one quickly scans a terrain visually to determine the direction of one's next step, nor when one determines how to get a sandwich from plate to mouth, nor when one drives a car from point A to point B, and so on and so forth. But those inquiries which *are* characteristically verbal should also measure up to the general pattern of inquiry as predicted by logical theory. In this regard, while logic is not just a study of purely formal and overt properties of verbal expressions, verbal utterances are nevertheless a primary source of analyzable evidence of many actual inquiries.

This suggests that linguistic expressions, while not themselves the primary object of concern in logic, are, nevertheless, when properly produced, overt evidence of relatively more complex biological and sociological realities which *are* the subject matter under investigation. Any serious theoretical work concerning these realities characteristic of human nature and intelligent agency will be tied to predictions about such expressions (or something equally tangible) if there is to be any measure of the validity of that theoretical work. In this sense, verbal utterances are to logic what scatter diagrams (for instance) are to nuclear physics. And the theory of syntax is to such utterances what geometry is to scatter diagrams. In the latter case, any theoretical work concerning subatomic realities is generally tied to predictions about such scatter diagrams (or something equally tangible), but of course physicists hardly believe that such lines of bubbles are all there is to subatomic reality or that the geometry of those lines is all there is to physical theory. Those lines, when properly produced, are rather macroscopic evidence of hypothetically understood microscopic realities.

From Dewey's perspective, then, a theory of propositions is incomplete if it tries to consider their formal features, or the formal features of their linguistic representations, independently of their function in inquiry. Essentially involved in the subject matter embodied in some actual inquiry, the role of propositions is to articulate and otherwise help transform this subject matter. It is only in such terms that one can understand formal characteristics of propositions.

So how do we resolve this inquiry-theoretic orientation with modern logic? We cannot adequately answer that question here. But we can say something. Some distinctions which are now standard in logic, such as between syntax and semantics, or between model theory and proof theory, were only just beginning to be worked out in the 1930s and 1940s. Russell, in particular, viewed logic basically as a formal theory of linguistic syntax, which he did not clearly distinguish from formal semantics (evidenced, for instance, in his tendency, not uncommon at the time, to refer interchangeably to sentences, statements, judgments, assertions, and propositions). Otherwise he hardly offered a coherent development of what we would now call a theory of semantics, making only some hedged remarks about how the structure of the world is mirrored in the structure of language (see Russell 1940, pp. 22, 437). Few people today would openly endorse Russell's views in detail, but something like the position he outlined lies behind the development (via Carnap, Tarski, et al.) of what we now know as model theory.

As we have seen, Russell applied a mathematics-oriented conception of logic too broadly as a general guide to ontology, in the sense that he was attempting to draw unjustifiably broad metaphysical conclusions from the merely formal dictates of mathematical exposition. He needed a fixed set of data as premises—*the facts*— because that is the supposed ground upon which first-order formal "discourse" is built. This is not unlike someone insisting that there are indeed point masses in the world because Newtonian models of some physical systems take them for granted.

The predicate calculus is, in this same sense, an abstract *model*.[5] It is an artificial language whose design was inspired primarily by the needs of mathematical exposition and which, like an artificial model in any other science, cannot be reliably extrapolated beyond its expressed limitations. Russell's all too common mistake was to not realize that he was working simply with a model of a language, not some privileged "language of facts."

In building up this taxonomy of propositions the way he did, Dewey was motivated to explain not just the needs of mathematics but also the workings of natural languages. Deweyan logic can

---

[5]See Barwise and Etchemendy 1989 for a development of this view.

easily accommodate the idea that the simple and familiar language of first-order logic is a theoretical model of a natural language.

As such, this model is not a very good model, in the sense that it handles only a limited range of features of natural language well, and it handles many others quite badly if at all. In this regard it is hardly more successful in linguistic theory than Bohr's model of the hydrogen atom is in physics or a simple Copernican model of the solar system is in astronomy. It does, on the other hand, manage to capture those features of natural language that it does capture—so well as to have inspired a complete retooling of mathematics in the last hundred years (which was, of course, Frege's initial aim) and to have supplied for philosophy an ideal language which could function as a standard means of clear and coherent expression and argumentation. Its use in linguistics and computer science is equally impressive.

This claim that the language of first-order logic is only an abstract model of something which is otherwise a natural phenomenon (namely, natural language) is perhaps a bit contentious. Some may prefer to see this formal language not so much as a model but as a "level" of linguistic analysis—as if it were to supply an account of a level of "logical form" at the root of any analysis of natural language expressions. In this view, translations between English (say) and a first-order language are supposed to evidence how this level of logical form is apparent on a surface level of analysis.

In contrast, the view recommended here would be that linguistics, much like any other empirical science, relies on building, analyzing, testing, and revising models of naturally occurring phenomena, which in the present case will be aspects of natural languages and their use. Different sciences have different model-building methodologies, depending on the nature of their subject matters. In the case of linguistics, this is sometimes thought to consist in providing a syntax and a semantics for a language fragment, or a grammar characterizing the formation of expressions plus a manner of interpreting those expressions, which can then be used to make predictions about actual linguistic behaviors. This should yield what is supposed to be a grammatically closed model of a substantial piece of a natural language. Translations between actual natural languages and such a model, rather than reflecting a connection between "deep" and "surface" syntactic structures, will constitute what is essentially a comparison between a model of a real language and the real language itself, or more precisely, between hypothesis and fact.

6.3 Knowledge, Intelligence, and Intentionality

We might contrast Dewey's and Russell's views in general terms as follows. By focusing on the confirmation and refutation of propositions, and by de-emphasizing the notions of truth and falsity, Dewey took an epistemological approach to semantics. On the other hand, Russell's view, if not purely mathematical, was metaphysical. Without making this difference in orientations clear, they were unwittingly playing the semantics game according to different rules. It is not clear that metaphysics and epistemology have to be so much at odds, but in the case of Dewey's epistemology and Russell's metaphysics, they certainly were.

Russell held "that 'truth' is the fundamental concept, and that 'knowledge' must be defined in terms of 'truth', not vice versa." Logic is supposed to be prior to and otherwise independent of epistemology, requiring a nonepistemological definition of 'truth' and 'falsity'. Indeed logic in Russell's view was to independently "afford a basis" for certain epistemological and metaphysical doctrines (1940, pp. 22–3).

In contrast, Dewey preferred not to have to tailor his epistemology and metaphysics to fit an independent and prior study of language in the abstract. He viewed logic as a larger study addressing issues in epistemology and the philosophy of mind as well as issues in the philosophy of language.

For Dewey, logic could not be prior to epistemology because (1) logic encompasses semantics and (2) semantics is unavoidably epistemological in that it is based on an information-theoretic treatment of objects and facts and possibilities, couched not necessarily in psychological terms but nevertheless in terms of agents' activities in the real extralinguistic world. In this regard, Dewey's focusing on inquiry meant that logic would have to be about something other than purely formal features of language, making it more than just a mathematical discipline.

It does not follow trivially from what I have just said, but Dewey's view of the relationship between epistemology and logic is not unlike Kant's view of transcendental and general logic (see page 190, footnote 7, above). One can go a long way in understanding features of formal (general) logic independently of its epistemological (transcendental) foundations; but a theory of logic is not complete—it is hardly more than a technical canon—if it does not also include an investigation into its sources and functions in human experience. One cannot even say what propositions are and hence what logic is without addressing these foundational concerns. For Dewey, neither epistemology nor logic is prior to *or* independent of the other, in contrast with Russell's attributing to Dewey an epistemology-first, verificationist position directly opposed to his own logic-first position.

1. *Knowledge and Intelligence.* So what relation specifically does a theory of knowledge have to logic viewed as the theory of inquiry? It is not feasible to give more than a brief sketch here of Dewey's notions of knowledge and intelligence, though parts of the preceding chapters call for at least a brief discussion. There are basically two things to note about Dewey's concept of knowledge in the context of discussing Dewey's and Russell's different conceptions of logic.

The first point is that, outside of the final chapter of Dewey's *Logic* (where he discusses how his theory of knowledge relates to existing alternative theories), most of this book did not overtly include more than a passing treatment of knowledge as such. He worked instead in terms of the notion of warranted assertibility. As he explicitly pointed out in the opening pages of the book, he focused on this latter notion insofar as closely related notions of knowledge or belief were ambiguous, vague, laden with undesirable connotations, or otherwise too restricted in their meaning to be able to accommodate the ideas emerging in the course of developing a theory of inquiry (Dewey 1938, pp. 7–9).

But secondly, enough of the Dewey/Russell debate hinges on these notions that they should eventually be addressed. While not responding specifically to Russell, Dewey's response (1939a) to his supporters and critics in the Schilpp volume includes some passages worth discussing (pp. 520–1), especially since they contain a kind of summary of Dewey's views on these matters. These passages explain several finer distinctions central to Dewey's views which Russell often overlooked—a distinction between knowing and knowledge, one between knowledge and intelligence, and one between intelligence and habit—all of which were cast in terms of the notion of inquiry and one way or another involve the principle of continuity. The first two of these three distinctions are mentioned in the following passage.

> At various places in my writings I have said that, from the standpoint of empirical naturalism, the denotative reference of "mind" and "intelligence" is to funding of meanings and significances, a funding which is both a product of past inquiries or knowings and the means of enriching and controlling the subject-matters of subsequent experiences. The function of enrichment and control is exercised by incorporation of what was gained in past experience in attitudes and habits which, in their interaction with the environment, create the clearer, better ordered, "fuller" or richer materials of later experience—a process capable of indefinite continuance. Dr. Ratner [1939] is quite right in indicating that the word "intelligence" represents what is essential in my view much better than does the word *knowledge*, while it avoids that confusing of knowing—inquiry—and attained knowledge which has led some of my critics astray in their accounts of my position. (Dewey 1939a, pp. 520–1)

So Dewey admits a certain degree of ambiguity in his uses over the years of the term 'knowledge', and he subsequently recommends a three-way distinction among knowing, knowledge, and intelligence:

> At present, after reading criticisms of the kind of *instrumentalism* that is attributed to me, it is clear that I should, from the start, have systematically distinguished between knowledge as the outcome of

special inquiries (undertaken because of the presence of problems) and *intelligence* as the product and expression of cumulative funding of the meanings reached in these special cases. Nevertheless, there are in my earlier writings many indications of the distinction and of the rôle it plays, as well as references to the principle of organic habit as the physical agency by which the transition from one to the other is effected. (Dewey 1939a, p. 521)

Particular *knowings* as inquiries, i.e., as specific instances of the applications of one's dispositions, aptitudes, and habits to solving given problems, are distinguished here from *knowledge*, constituting the stable outcomes of specific inquiries (in the form of judgments), both of which are distinguished from *intelligence*, which is the result of the development and accumulation (learning, habituation, standardization, routinization) of capabilities to act (inquire) in specific ways. Knowledge is the result of successful inquiry, whereas knowing consists in using one's intelligence in given inquiries. Intelligence is stabilized knowledge, such as it is, which can be utilized in other inquiries, given the principle of continuity and given the fact that judgments are not merely abstract decisions but constitute a kind of conduct (assertion)—see pp. 115ff above for a discussion of this point. Knowing is to intelligence roughly what asserting is to being disposed to assert. Particular existential judgments constitute knowledge to the extent that the conduct they recommend in given circumstances (the predicates they attribute to given subjects) are worth assimilating into one's store of habits, dispositions, or capabilities.

> I cite [the following passage from *Democracy and Education* 1916a]: "The function of knowledge is to make one experience freely available in other experiences. The word 'freely' marks the difference between the function of knowledge and of habit," while [other works] show that the difference is not ultimately one between habit and intelligence but between routine habits and intelligent ones.... (Dewey 1939a, p. 521)

This latter passage makes the further point that intelligence is more than just a store of habits and context-sensitive dispositions. Intelligence is habitual, but not all habit is intelligent. Experience guided by intelligent habit, rather than merely routine habit, is experience characterized by resourcefulness, inventiveness, ingenuity, tenacity, efficiency, and any such "pragmatist virtue" designed to anticipate not only the regularities and constancies of experience but also the inevitable uncertainties and indeterminacies.

One is struck if not overwhelmed by the complexity of the issues involved in Dewey's theory of knowledge, in contrast, for instance, with treatments (pro and con) of knowledge as "justified true belief." This latter characterization of knowledge is plausible on the surface, at least in capturing intuitions underlying ordinary uses of the term 'knowledge', but it requires that we address methodological ("justified"), ontological ("true"), and psychological ("belief") issues which are too often not adequately addressed. For instance, Gettier's counterexamples (1963), designed to undermine such a characterization, exploit the fact that, in the absence of addressing such issues, there is no guarantee of any proper relation among the reasons that X is true and the reasons that belief in X occurs and is justified. (Different kinds or grades of knowledge might be distinguished by different relations between these three sets of reasons: they might be *the same*, or they might be *logically equivalent*, or one set might *entail* the others, and so forth.) Gettier's examples at least serve as a warning against compartmentalizing various philosophical disciplines (e.g., epistemology versus logic) to the point that such relations cannot be properly discussed. But more specifically, they cut to the heart of the view "that 'truth' is the fundamental concept, and that 'knowledge' must be defined in terms of 'truth', not vice versa." It is not at all clear that we can understand the concept of truth prior to or otherwise independently of developing a theory of knowledge.

2. Intentionality and Mentality. In the preceding quotes, Dewey refers to "mind" and "intelligence" not necessarily interchangeably but nevertheless as closely related concerns. Dewey's naturalistic conception of mind has already been discussed to some extent, in view of which it is important to understand (*a*) that Dewey was interested in giving a constructive, naturalistic account of what mind *is*, and (*b*) that he attempted to construct such an account on the basis of his concept of inquiry (see Sections 3.4, 4.1, and 5.1 above for discussions of these points). Particular instances of mentality—particular instances of agents' *being mental*—occur as intermediate phases or aspects of inquiry. Not every inquiry employs mental modes of experience, but mental modes of experience are to be understood in terms of their function in inquiry.

Dewey's notion of inquiry supports a notion of intentionality that is not entirely disjoint from existentialist or phenomenological views, particularly views of Heidegger, Sartre, and Merleau-Ponty. Reacting against a simple sense-data empiricism as well as a Cartesian-rationalist psychology in their respective attempts to explain what intentionality is, existential phenomenologists (following Husserl) agreed on several general points with which Dewey will have sympathized (which we may comfortably admit without agreeing that Dewey was subject to some kind of "unconscious Hegelian metaphysic"). For instance, they all viewed perception as a primary and basic concern in a theory of mentality; they all viewed the social character of human nature as an equally important part of the story; and they all appealed in varying degrees to some fundamental notion of referential "directedness" as a basic element of an account of intentionality. For instance, Heidegger used his own term, *Verhalten* (comportment), to express a foundational, non-mentalistic notion of directedness, as a feature not of consciousness as such but of our most fundamental nature (Dasein) (Dreyfus 1991, pp. 51, 57–8, 62, 68, etc.). Sartre posits a fundamental "prereflective cogito" as a primary sort of consciousness that is "intentional and directive, pointing to a transcendent object other than itself" (Sartre 1956, pp. x–xi). And Merleau-Ponty (1962, pp. 135–47, 152–3; 1964, p. 4) discussed "a sort of prospective activity in the organism" as being prior to self-awareness or intentional activity.

Dewey's notion of inquiry supplies a foundational notion of directedness if we think of inquiries as instances of life forces being directed *away from* an instance of instability, imbalance, dissolution, *toward* an object insofar as the latter is the result of a stabilization process, i.e., the resolution of the given problem. This directedness in and of itself does not constitute mentality or consciousness; but once we have this basic notion of directedness, we can begin to ask what it means to say that such directedness might be mental. We have already discussed Dewey's answer to this question at some length (in Section 5.1, especially), but we can recount two substantial parts of that answer. The first is that mentality is not a black-or-white feature of inquiry—inquiries can be more or less mental in character. Secondly, to nevertheless explain the distinction between mental and nonmental inquiry, the claim is that nonmental inquiry is largely routine, mechanistic, and a matter of immediate re-action to problems on the basis of whatever habits and dispositions have been learned or otherwise engineered into the constitution of the given agent. Inquiry takes on a mental character when such reactions are capable of being delayed, planned, and rehearsed prior to or otherwise independently of their actual execution. An inquiry is mental to the extent that it involves rehearsal of possible courses of action in service to finding a best course of action to follow in a given situation, without having to resort merely to trial and error and without having to actually suffer the consequences of every feasible action.

One can appreciate, in this regard, Dewey's emphasis (e.g., in Chapter 3 of *Logic*) on how the invention of languages—as media of discourse by means of meaningful symbols—facilitated the evolutionary development of mentality, that is, of an enhanced capacity in language users to internalize and rehearse problem-solving activities by working with systems of symbols to represent and manipulate information. Propositions, as symbolic formulations of different kinds of concrete information, are to be understood in terms of the role they play in such instances of "directedness" of the given agent's life energies. Any habits which might be developed in this regard, i.e., in the skilled use of languages to solve problems, would constitute an essential aspect of intelligence (though it would go too far to say that all mental inquiry is intelligent inquiry).

This kind of evolutionary approach to the philosophy of mind was worked out in some detail between 1910 and 1930 or so by George Herbert Mead (1934, 1956, 1964), who was Dewey's colleague at the University of Chicago. Dewey's views are similar to Mead's, though tending to be focused in other directions. Dewey and Mead were colleagues for much of their professional careers, not just at Chicago, and apparently were in close contact in the course of working out many of these ideas. A naturalistic philosophy of mind entails the view that at some point there was no mind on this planet, and that later, by natural evolutionary processes, there was. How did that happen? We should be able to give a plausible explanation, starting at an elementary level of biological organization. Mead and Dewey particularly emphasized the social nature of the evolutionary origins and constitution of human mentality. We will not go into great detail here (see Burke 1994 for a more extended discussion), but their account of the evolutionary emergence of mentality and self-consciousness is based on the claim that we mental beings are more fundamentally social beings. Social factors are not just incidental or derivative but rather are crucial to the natural emergence of mentality.

What would such an account look like? Both Mead and Dewey shared the fundamental conviction that all meaning and thought is grounded in the orchestration of concrete actions and their consequences. Such reference to operational abilities of individuals is fundamental to a pragmatist philosophy of mind, particularly with regard to understanding the constitution and function of habits in experience. This latter fact is the biological version of Peirce's "pragmatic maxim." But an evolutionary account of concepts and cognitive reflection as natural phenomena also requires a concrete, principled reference to social realities, not just to an individual's operational abilities. It is not that cognition is just a more complex version of life activities, nor is cognition just some manner of internalized behavior. Cognitive experience is a kind of life activity and is patterned after more basic life activities (it is exploratory, experimental, sequential, operational, directed away from breakdowns, takes place in an environment as much as in an organism, and so forth); but as such it is a new and unique kind of experience with a particular characteristic function. To understand this unique and definitive character of cognition, we cannot neglect the role of society, culture, and language in the evolution of human experience (Dewey 1926, pp. 258ff). Namely, cognitive activity (reflection, thought) is geared precisely to those aspects of the world that are social, cultural, and linguistic—in the sense that these latter features of the world, by affording a domain of representational activity, generate the capacity to *reflect*. The pattern of reflection is foreshadowed in the pattern of more basic life behaviors, but it is an entirely new kind of life behavior geared specifically to the use of language and more generally to membership and participation in a society. The basic idea is that social discourse, which was originally implemented as an essential part of group activities that were initially coordinated by means of gestures, was later adapted to public and then private analysis and planning of (other) concrete actions. According to this story, as gestures took on a kind of objectivity in their own right, they became symbols. They became objectified as representations of meanings and could be utilized as such to explore meanings; hence the emergence of language; and hence the emergence of reflective capabilities. Linguistic discourse emerged as a special kind of overt social activity aimed at delaying and planning other activities, and at possibly restructuring established behavioral patterns (i.e., habits) which constitute social institutions, traditions, customs, laws, and cultural norms. In a nutshell, this is the organic/social basis of the analysis of meanings and the progressive development of culture. An increasing sense in the individual of what Mead calls a "generalized other" as a particular bundle of habits (i.e., as a special kind of object) gave rise to individual reflection. Reflective thought is something like an inner discourse with this generalized other, the latter being more or less one's entire store of concepts and systematized meanings, as embodied in one's sense of what it means to be a member of the society or societies in which one participates. Subjective consciousness, then, is experience of oneself, in overt discourse and in thought, as one of a social and cultural kind.

This is only a rough outline; but if this story were to be told properly, it would explain the evolutionary/developmental linkage between the different kinds of experience depicted in figures 2 and 3 in Chapter 5.

Even in such broad terms, these generalizations about the nature of mind are clearly rather extraordinary. Mead and Dewey were not the only proponents of such a view. Vygotsky, for one, springs to mind. But with the advent of the computer metaphor, such an approach to the philosophy of mind, while probably never popular, has been entirely eclipsed and all but forgotten. Even before the advent of the computer metaphor, Russell certainly did not show any sign of an attempt to follow out these strands in Dewey's *Logic*.

But this evolutionary view of mind supplies a rather distinctive perspective on issues in the cognitive sciences, specifically those revolving around the project of trying to construct an artificial intentional agent. To bring matters into sharper focus, consider what is involved in building a robotic device which can explore, work in, and communicate the results of its ongoing activities in distant planetary environments or deep-sea floors or other domains not easily accessible to humans. Rather than be limited to current technological biases or current ways of conceptualizing this sort of engineering problem, let's think in the most ambitious terms of what we *want* this sort of machine to do. How do we build a super-deluxe autonomous machine which could work in remote environments without direct human manipulation, though it could communicate with us much as if it were another human agent?

More than just a "computer," we would want this machine to do a wide range of things: to explore its environment; to search out and recognize exploitable raw materials; to use and perhaps invent tools to do whatever it has to do; to report on and adapt to novel and hopefully useful things; to fix its own breakdowns as much as possible; to build and maintain a humanly inhabitable environment; and so on and so forth. It would probably have to be able to perceive its world much as humans would, not just in order to be able to communicate results and to take orders in human terms but to talk to humans about that world and to listen to and accommodate humans' concerns about it. And at such distances as the Moon or Mars are from the Earth, it has to be autonomous. That is, it has to be more than just a remote sensor or artificial appendage of some human operator (like mechanical arms in radioactive-materials laboratories or deep-sea roving cameras such as were used to explore the Titanic). We should be able to discuss things with it, and it should weigh our opinions heavily; but it also has to be able to make, and act on, its own decisions according to its own capabilities.

Dewey's logical theory, as it stands, cannot tell us how to build such a machine. But we can list a number of design principles which would, in his view, have to be treated as fundamental, not as goals to be achieved *later*, once other preliminaries are taken care of. An inquiry-based approach to building artificial intentional systems would, for instance, treat *stabilization* as a basic architectural feature. A canonical example of such processes would *not* be some sort of symbolic computational process but rather a process like maintaining balance in a gravitational field. The agent as such would not be a computer in a box but rather a kind of interactive contraption/environment system where the hardware and software involves environmental parameters as much as anything else. A computer metaphor would be secondary perhaps to a "shock-absorber" analogy, where we would think of intentional agents primarily as being inextricably bound up in a dynamic world, continually having to counteract destabilizing forces. This process of dealing with predicament after predicament would start to look more "intelligent" as the problem solving takes on a less immediate and impulsive character. In this regard, the notion of *representation* would not be so central as the notion rather of *internalization* of activities, attunements, and so forth. This may require some kind of socialization at the most basic levels of design, particularly if the architecture of intelligence is to be modeled on a human blueprint. Any emphasis to be put on symbolic computation would have to be based first on how the latter would help to constitute a capacity to rehearse actions and to anticipate their consequences. A more basic and centrally important process would be one of registering and comparing actual anticipations against actual achievements, and of adjusting one's actions accordingly. An ability to anticipate and *avoid* problems (such as learning how to adjust one's posture in the world before the imbalance is so extreme that corrective measures cannot take effect) would be as important as an ability to solve problems once they are given. Such a device would need to have the ability to apply results of given inquiries to new situations, as a way of developing and modifying habits and dispositions rather than being limited to some fixed repertoire of behavioral programs once and for all. This is perhaps a rather ambitious wish list of capabilities, but it seems, on Dewey's account, to be a more or less minimal list of what it takes to have a machine which is itself an intelligent agent. To try to build anything less may well be a waste of effort.

From the perspective of an engineer whose task it is to take a theory of intelligent agency and translate it into specifications for such a machine, Dewey's operationalist theory of intelligent agency would seem to be on the right track so far as it goes. There is virtually no way that the robotics engineer can foresee in any detail what domains of objects and properties the robot will encounter. Certainly there are lots of objects having properties and standing in relations up on the Moon—that is not in question here—but we are not able to scope out and otherwise specify beforehand the domains in which the robot is going to have to act. Yet this is what a Fregean/Russellian/Carnapian approach to logic assumes we can and must do. On the other hand, Dewey's operationalist theory of intelligent agency does not require that the robot know a great deal about specific Moon environments prior to gaining access to means and opportunities to explore such environments. We can specify what *types* of actions we want it to be able to execute up there— we can give it a certain basic level of general "intelligence" which promises to be useful and which is compatible with our own—and on that basis we would want to be able to turn it loose and allow it to build up its own "knowledge" of specific Moon environments in terms of the types of actions they afford.

No one is saying this is not a difficult project. But whereas it is clear that a Russellian metaphysics is sure to fail in such a case as a constructive, working theory of intelligent agency (e.g., Dreyfus 1972 is a not-very-glowing critique of a Russellian perspective on AI), it is not clear that a Deweyan epistemology will not work. This is certainly a proper challenge for a theory which claims to give a constructive, naturalistic account of mind and intelligence. Such an approach to AI and robotics is actually not so foreign to work found lately in the cognitive-science literature, as reviewed in Effken and Shaw 1992, for instance, and as evidenced to a degree in Brooks 1989, 1990, 1991a, 1991b, 1991c. One might want to claim generally that, whether or not Dewey's theory of knowledge is acceptable in every detail, his *type* of theory, namely, a naturalistic, operation-based theory geared to explaining problem solving in concrete contexts, is the only one which holds any promise for handling issues in the cognitive sciences which hinge on our knowing what knowledge is.

6.4 Appraising Russell's Review

Though many aspects of Deweyan logic have not been discussed here, and though many aspects of Russell's review of *Logic* remain unaddressed, this book has covered enough material so that it is possible to assess Russell's assessment of Dewey's views. The bottom line seems to be that the many absurdities emerging in Russell's analysis of Dewey's views reflect not so much on Dewey's credibility as a logician but rather on Russell's credibility as a critic of those views.

An emphasis on mathematics is characteristic of the tradition in logic based on Frege's and Russell's work. Formal logic as we know it today was invented to facilitate clear and concise exposition of mathematical concepts. If this puts any serious constraints on Dewey's more general orientation to logic as the theory of inquiry, it would pertain only to a treatment of expository aspects of a special case of inquiry, namely, mathematical inquiry, which Dewey's logical theory ought to be able to accommodate. And insofar as mathematical inquiry is often an important aspect of empirically grounded research efforts (that is, insofar as mathematics is not the subject matter of inquiry but nevertheless an important tool of inquiry), formal logic as we know it today supports an understanding of certain aspects of nonmathematical inquiry as well. But from Dewey's standpoint, more elaborate and more broadly conceived theories of information, experience, and action are called for if we are to really come to terms with what inquiry is, and hence what logic is, in a sufficiently general sense.

It is perhaps only after the limitations of Frege's logic have begun to be generally acknowledged, particularly as the result of its applications in the cognitive sciences over the last few decades, that it is possible to understand and properly evaluate Dewey's alternative approach to logical theory. As a contingent matter of sociopolitical fact, it has been difficult to appreciate what Dewey was doing without first carrying out Frege's project to see how far one could go with it.

It is regrettable that Dewey was not able to appreciate the significance of "symbolic logic" as it was beginning to emerge in the 1930s and 1940s. Much of the antagonism between Dewey and Russell might have been avoided, or at least toned down to more tolerable levels of intensity, if Dewey had not overstated his rejection of such developments as to their adequacy or their being appropriate to the study of logic. These developments have proven their value beyond a reasonable doubt, even if it turns out that Dewey was right that there is more to logic than such an orientation to the subject has so far allowed. Dewey was not helping his own cause by not showing any appreciation of the significance of the view he was criticizing.

One may say further in Russell's defense that he could hardly be expected to have fairly presented Dewey's views if Dewey himself was unable to work out the details of those views. His logical writings often seem obscure, not only because of their unusual emphasis on epistemological matters but also because, to some extent, many of the harder technical details seem to be put off indefinitely or never addressed. Dewey was not a mathematician, and the subject matters he was dealing with require a mathematician's talents. One should of course not confuse the fact that Dewey was not a mathematician with the claim that his work is not amenable to mathematical treatment. It is just that he did not take his work in that direction, which put him at odds with major currents in philosophy since the 1930s.

But whatever one says in Russell's defense, one should distinguish charging Dewey with being obscure from charging him with saying things one disagrees with, or which one does not understand, or which one would rather not hear. The fact of the matter is that Russell's very different orientation to logic blinded him to the rich if perhaps complicated scheme of things which Dewey *was* able to present. Dewey did not fully present all the details and consequences of his logical theory; but the primary reason Russell could not follow it so far as it went was because Dewey saw logic as a different and more complex subject matter than Russell was willing to allow.

It seems clear that such ideological differences served as barriers to Russell's giving Dewey an honest reading. To a larger extent than should have to be admitted, the early rejection of Dewey's logical theory was due not to any unusual obscurity on Dewey's part, but rather to the fact that he was not saying what logical theorists wanted to hear at the time. Dewey was of course not the first to fall victim to being out of step with the times. But it is all the more unfortunate that the prevailing negative regard for Dewey's views has been too much affected by accounts such as Russell's, which are superficial at best and often simply mistaken. Dewey's views may eventually require serious revision, if not rejection; but such judgments ought to be based on a fair and objective assessment of those views, which Russell was not able to provide.

Bibliography

Barwise, Jon. 1989. *The Situation in Logic*. Stanford: CSLI Publications.

Barwise, Jon, and John Etchemendy. 1989. Model-Theoretic Semantics. In *Foundations of Cognitive Science*, ed. Michael I. Posner, 207–243. Cambridge, MA: The MIT Press.

Barwise, Jon, and John Perry. 1981. Semantic Innocence and Uncompromising Situations. In *Midwest Studies in Philosophy VI: Foundations of Analytic Philosophy*, ed. Peter A. French, Theodore E. Uehling, Jr., and Howard K. Wettstein, 387–403. Minneapolis: University of Minnesota Press. Also in *The Philosophy of Language*, ed. A. P. Martinich (New York: Oxford University Press, 1985).

Barwise, Jon, and John Perry. 1983. *Situations and Attitudes*. Cambridge, MA: The MIT Press.

Beck, Lewis White. 1960. *A Commentary on Kant's Critique of Practical Reason*. Midway Reprint 1984. Chicago: The University of Chicago Press.

Bernstein, Richard J. (ed.). 1960. *On Experience, Nature, and Freedom: Representative Selections by John Dewey*. New York: Bobbs Merrill Company.

Boydston, Jo Ann (ed.). 1967–1972. *John Dewey: The Early Works, 1882–1898* (Vols. 1–5). Carbondale: Southern Illinois University Press. Cited elsewhere in this Bibliography as *Early Works*.

Boydston, Jo Ann (ed.). 1976–1980. *John Dewey: The Middle Works, 1899–1924* (Vols. 1–15). Carbondale: Southern Illinois University Press. Cited elsewhere in this Bibliography as *Middle Works*.

Boydston, Jo Ann (ed.). 1981–1990. *John Dewey: The Later Works,*

1925–1953 (Vols. 1–17). Carbondale: Southern Illinois University Press. Cited elsewhere in this Bibliography as *Later Works.*

Boydston, Jo Ann (ed.). 1991. *John Dewey: The Collected Works, 1882–1953: Index.* Carbondale: Southern Illinois University Press.

Bradley, Frances H. 1899. *Appearance and Reality,* Second Edition. New York: Macmillan.

Bridgman, Percy William. 1927. *The Logic of Modern Physics.* New York: Macmillan.

Brooks, Rodney A. 1989. A Robot that Walks: Emergent Behavior from a Carefully Evolved Network. *Neural Computation* 1/2:253–262.

Brooks, Rodney A. 1990. Elephants Don't Play Chess. *Robotics and Autonomous Systems* 6:3–15. Also in *Designing Autonomous Agents: Theory and Practice from Biology to Engineering and Back,* ed. Pattie Maes (Cambridge, MA: The MIT Press, 1990).

Brooks, Rodney A. 1991a. Intelligence without Reason. AI Memo 1293. MIT AI Lab, April. Also in *Computers and Thought,* Proceedings of the International Joint Conference on Artificial Intelligence, Sydney (Los Altos, CA: Morgan Kauffman, 1990, pp. 569–595).

Brooks, Rodney A. 1991b. Intelligence without Representation. *Artificial Intelligence* 47:139–159.

Brooks, Rodney A. 1991c. New Approaches to Robotics. *Science* 253:1227–1232.

Burke, Tom. 1990. Dewey on Defeasibility. In *Situation Theory and Its Applications,* Vol. 1, ed. Robin Cooper, Kuniaki Mukai, and John Perry, 233–268. Stanford: CSLI Publications. Reprinted in *John Dewey: Critical Assessments*, Vol. 4, ed. J. E. Tiles (New York: Routledge, 1992).

Burke, Tom. 1991a. *Ecological Psychology and Dewey's Theory of Perception.* Report No. CSLI-91-151. Stanford: CSLI Publications.

Burke, Tom. 1991b. Peirce on Truth and Partiality. In *Situation Theory and Its Applications,* Vol. 2, ed. Jon Barwise, Mark Gawron, Gordon Plotkin, and Syun Tutiya, 115–146. Stanford: CSLI Publications.

Burke, Tom. 1994. Dance Floor Blues and the Case for a Social AI. *Stanford Humanities Review* 4(1).

Carnap, Rudolf. 1950. Empiricism, Semantics, and Ontology. *Revue Internationale de Philosophie* 4:20–40.

Carnap, Rudolf. 1954. *Testability and Meaning* (2nd Printing). Yale University: Graduate Philosophy Club.

Carter, Dennis R., Marcy Wong, and Tracy E. Orr. 1991. Musculoskeletal Ontogeny, Phylogeny, and Functional Adaptation. *Journal of Biomechanics* 24, Suppl. 1:3–16.

Coffa, J. Alberto. 1991. *The Semantic Tradition from Kant to Carnap: To the Vienna Station.* Cambridge: Cambridge University Press.

Cohen, Morris R. 1940. Some Difficulties in Dewey's Anthropocentric Naturalism. *Philosophical Review* 49:196–228.

Cunningham, G. Watts. 1939. The New Logic and the Old. *Journal of Philosophy* 36(21):565–572. Reprinted in Morgenbesser 1977, pp. 549–56.

Dewey, Jane M. 1939. Biography of John Dewey. In *The Philosophy of John Dewey*, ed. Paul A. Schilpp, 3–45. New York: Tudor.

Dewey, John. 1890. Is Logic a Dualistic Science? *Open Court* 3:2040–2043. Reprinted in *Early Works* 3:75–82.

Dewey, John. 1891. The Present Position of Logical Theory. *Monist* 2:1–17. Reprinted in *Early Works* 3:125–141.

Dewey, John. 1893. The Superstition of Necessity. *Monist* 3:362–379. Reprinted in *Early Works* 4:19–36.

Dewey, John. 1896. The Reflex Arc Concept in Psychology. *Psychological Review* 3:357–370. Reprinted in *Early Works* 5:96–110.

Dewey, John. 1903a. Logical Conditions of a Scientific Treatment of Morality. In *Investigations Representing the Departments, Part II: Philosophy, Education.* University of Chicago Decennial Publications, first series, 3:115–39. Chicago: The University of Chicago Press. Reprinted in *Middle Works* 3:3–39.

Dewey, John (ed.). 1903b. *Studies in Logical Theory.* Chicago: The University of Chicago Press. Decennial Publications, University of Chicago, Second Series, Volume 11. Dewey's contributions reprinted in *Middle Works* 2:293–375.

Dewey, John. 1905a. The Postulate of Immediate Empricism. *Journal of Philosophy, Psychology, and Scientific Methods* 2:393–399. Reprinted in Dewey 1910, and in *Middle Works* 3:158–167.

Dewey, John. 1905b. The Realism of Pragmatism. *Journal of*

Philosophy, Psychology, and Scientific Methods 2:324–327. Reprinted in *Middle Works* 3:153–157.

Dewey, John. 1910. *The Influence of Darwin on Philosophy, and Other Essays in Contemporary Thought.* New York: Henry Holt and Company.

Dewey, John. 1911/1933. *How We Think.* Chicago: Henry Regnery. Reprinted in *Later Works* 8:105–354. Revised and expanded version of 1911 edition (Boston: D. C. Heath), reprinted in *Middle Works* 6:177–356.

Dewey, John. 1916a. *Democracy and Education.* New York: Macmillan Company. Reprinted as *Middle Works* 9.

Dewey, John. 1916b. *Essays in Experimental Logic.* Chicago: The University of Chicago Press. Essays reprinted separately in *Middle Works.*

Dewey, John. 1920. *Reconstruction in Philosophy.* New York: Henry Holt and Company. Reprinted in *Middle Works* 12:77–204, including a new introduction to 1948 reprint (Boston: Beacon Press), 256–277.

Dewey, John. 1922. *Human Nature and Conduct.* New York: Henry Holt and Company. Reprinted as *Middle Works* 14.

Dewey, John. 1926. *Experience and Nature.* Chicago: Open Court. Reprinted as *Later Works* 1.

Dewey, John. 1929. *The Quest for Certainty: A Study of the Relation of Knowledge and Action.* New York: Minton, Balch, and Company. Reprinted as *Later Works* 4.

Dewey, John. 1930. From Absolutism to Experimentalism. In *Contemporary American Philosophy*, ed. George P. Adams and William P. Montague, 13–27. New York: Macmillan. Reprinted in Bernstein 1960, pp. 3–18, and in *Later Works* 5:147–160.

Dewey, John. 1938. *Logic: The Theory of Inquiry.* New York: Henry Holt and Company. Reprinted as *Later Works* 12.

Dewey, John. 1939a. Experience, Knowledge, and Value: A Rejoinder. In *The Philosophy of John Dewey*, ed. Paul A. Schilpp, 517–608. New York: Tudor. Reprinted in *Later Works* 14:3–90.

Dewey, John. 1939b. Theory of Valuation. In *Foundations of the Unity of Science*, ed. Otto Neurath, Rudolf Carnap, and Charles Morris, 379–447. Chicago: The University of Chicago Press. Reprinted in *Later Works* 13:189–254.

Dewey, John. 1941. Propositions, Warranted Assertibility, and Truth. *Journal of Philosophy* 38(7):169–186. Reprinted in Morgenbesser 1977, pp. 265–282, and in *Later Works* 14:168–188.

Dewey, John. 1946. *Problems of Men.* New York: Philosophical Library. Essays reprinted separately in *Later Works.*

Dewey, John. 1949. Experience and Existence: A Comment. *Philosophy and Phenomenological Research* 9:709–713. Reprinted in *Later Works* 16:383–389.

Dewey, John, and Arthur F. Bentley. 1949. *Knowing and the Known.* Boston: Beacon Press. Reprinted in R. Handy and E. C. Harwood, *Useful Procedures of Inquiry*, 89–190 (Great Barrington, MA: Behavioral Research Council, 1973), and in *Later Works* 16:1–296.

Dreyfus, Hubert L. 1972. *What Computers Can't Do: A Critique of Artificial Reason.* New York: Harper and Row.

Dreyfus, Hubert L. 1991. *Being-in-the-World.* Cambridge, MA: The MIT Press.

Early Works. See Boydston 1967–1972.

Eddington, Arthur Stanley. 1928. *The Nature of the Physical World.* New York: Macmillan.

Effken, Judith A., and Robert E. Shaw. 1992. Ecological Perspectives on the New Artificial Intelligence: An Essay Review of *Intelligence as Adaptive Behavior: An Experiment in Computational Neuroethology*, by Randall D. Beer, and *Minimalist Mobile Robotics: A Colony-Style Architecture for an Artificial Creature*, by Jonathan H. Connell. *Ecological Psychology* 4(4):247–270.

Fodor, Jerry A., and Zeno W. Pylyshyn. 1981. How Direct is Visual Perception? Some Reflections on Gibson's 'Ecological Approach'. *Cognition* 9:139–196.

Frege, Gottlob. 1884. *The Foundations of Arithmetic.* Oxford: Oxford University Press (1950). Trans. John L. Austin.

Frege, Gottlob. 1892. On Sense and Meaning. *Zeitschrift für Philosophie und Philosophische Kritik* 100:25–50. English translation in Peter Geach and Max Black, eds., *Translations from the Philosophical Writings of Gottlob Frege*, 3rd Edition, pp. 56–78 (Oxford: Basil Blackwell, 1980).

Frege, Gottlob. 1918. The Thought: A Logical Inquiry. *Mind* 65:289–311

(1956). Translated into English by A. M. Quinton and Marcelle Quinton.

Gärdenfors, Peter. 1988. *Knowledge in Flux: Modeling the Dynamics of Epistemic States.* Cambridge, MA: The MIT Press.

Gettier, Edmund. 1963. Is Justified True Belief Knowledge. *Analysis* 23(6):121–123. Reprinted in *Human Knowledge*, ed. Paul K. Moser and Arnold vander Nat, pp. 263–265 (New York: Oxford University Press, 1987).

Gibson, James J. 1966. *The Senses Considered as Perceptual Systems.* Boston: Houghton Mifflin.

Gibson, James J. 1971. The Information Available in Pictures. *Leonardo* 4:27–35.

Gibson, James J. 1977. The Theory of Affordances. In *Perceiving, Acting, and Knowing*, ed. Robert E. Shaw and John Bransford. Hillsdale, NJ: Lawrence Erlbaum Associates.

Gibson, James J. 1979. *The Ecological Approach to Visual Perception.* Boston: Houghton Mifflin.

Gibson, James J. 1982. Notes on Affordances. In *Reasons for Realism: Selected Essays of James J. Gibson*, ed. Edward Reed and Rebecca Jones. Hillsdale, NJ: Lawrence Erlbaum Associates.

Ginsberg, Matthew L. (ed.). 1987. *Readings in Nonmonotonic Reasoning.* Los Altos, CA: Morgan Kaufmann Publishers.

Goldblatt, Robert. 1992. *Logics of Time and Computation,* Second Edition. CSLI Lecture Notes, No. 7. Stanford: CSLI Publications.

Goudge, Thomas A. 1973. Pragmatism's Contribution to an Evolutionary View of Mind. *Monist* 57(2):133–150.

Hempel, Carl G. 1952. *Fundamentals of Concept Formation in Empirical Science.* International Encyclopedia of Unified Science, No. 2(7). Chicago: The University of Chicago Press.

Hertz, Richard A. 1971. James and Moore: Two Perspectives on Truth. *Journal of the History of Philosophy* 9:213–221.

Hocking, William E. 1940. Dewey's Concepts of Experience and Nature. *Philosophical Review* 49:228–244.

Hook, Sidney. 1979. Introduction to Dewey's 1915 writings. In *Middle Works* 8:ix–xxxvi.

Hume, David. 1748. *An Enquiry Concerning Human Understanding.*

Lewis A. Selby-Bigge edition. Oxford: Oxford University Press, 1893.

James, William. 1890. *The Principles of Psychology*, in three volumes. The Works of William James, ed. Frederick H. Burkhardt, 1981. Cambridge, MA: Harvard University Press.

James, William. 1907. *Pragmatism: A New Name for Some Old Ways of Thinking*. New York: Longmans, Green, and Company. Reprinted in *Pragmatism and Other Essays* (New York: Washington Square Press, 1963).

James, William. 1909. *The Meaning of Truth: A Sequel to 'Pragmatism'*. New York: Longmans, Green, and Company.

Kant, Immanuel. 1781. *Critique of Pure Reason*. Trans. Norman Kemp Smith. New York: Macmillan (1929).

Kant, Immanuel. 1785. *Groundwork of the Metaphysic of Morals*. Trans. Herbert James Paton. New York: Harper and Row (1964).

Kant, Immanuel. 1788. *Critique of Practical Reason*. Trans. Lewis White Beck. New York: Macmillan (1993, 3rd Edition).

Kaplan, David. 1978. Dthat. In *Syntax and Semantics,* Vol. 9, ed. Peter Cole. New York: Academic Press. Reprinted in *The Philosophy of Language*, ed. A. P. Martinich (Oxford: Oxford University Press, 1985).

Kaplan, David. 1989a. Afterthoughts. In *Themes from Kaplan*, ed. Joseph Almog, John Perry, and Howard Wettstein, 565–614. New York: Oxford University Press.

Kaplan, David. 1989b. Demonstratives: An Essay on the Semantics, Logic, Metaphysics, and Epistemology of Demonstratives and Other Indexicals. In *Themes from Kaplan*, ed. Joseph Almog, John Perry, and Howard Wettstein, 481–563. New York: Oxford University Press.

Kaufmann, Felix. 1940. On Dewey's *Logic*. *Social Research* 7:243–246.

Kripke, Saul A. 1972. *Naming and Necessity*. Cambridge, MA: Harvard University Press.

Lamont, Corliss (ed.). 1959. *Dialogue on John Dewey*. New York: Horizon Press.

Langton, Chris G. 1990. Computation at the Edge of Chaos: Phase

Transitions and Emergent Computation. T-13 & Center for Nonlinear Studies, Los Alamos National Laboratory.

Later Works. See Boydston 1981–1990.

Lee, David N. 1980. The Optic Flow Field: The Foundation of Vision. *Philosophical Transactions of the Royal Society of London* 290:169–179.

Lewis, Clarence I. 1939. Meaning and Action. *Journal of Philosophy* 36(21):572–576. Reprinted in Morgenbesser 1977, pp. 556–560.

Mackay, Donald S. 1942. What Does Mr. Dewey Mean by an 'Indeterminate Situation'? *Journal of Philosophy* 39(6):141–148.

Marr, David. 1982. *Vision: A Computational Investigation into the Human Representation and Processing of Visual Information.* San Francisco: W. H. Freeman.

McCarthy, John, and Patrick J. Hayes. 1969. Some Philosophical Problems from the Standpoint of Artificial Intelligence. In *Machine Intelligence 4,* ed. Bernard Meltzer and D. Mitchie, 463–502. University of Edinburgh Press. Reprinted in *Readings in Nonmonotonic Reasoning,* ed. Matthew L. Ginsberg (Los Altos: Morgan Kaufmann Publishers, 1987).

McClelland, John L., and David E. Rumelhart. 1986. *Parallel Distributed Processing: Explorations in the Microstructure of Cognition,* Vol. 2. Cambridge, MA: The MIT Press.

McGilvary, Evander B. 1939. Professor Dewey: Logician–Ontologician. *Journal of Philosophy* 36(21):561–565. Reprinted in Morgenbesser 1977, pp. 545–549.

Mead, George Herbert. 1909. Social Consciousness and the Consciousness of Meaning. *Psychological Bulletin* 7:397–405. Reprinted in Mead 1964, pp. 123–133.

Mead, George Herbert. 1924–1925. The Genesis of the Self and Social Control. *International Journal of Ethics* 35:251–277. Reprinted in Mead 1932, pp. 176–195, and in Mead 1964, pp. 267–293.

Mead, George Herbert. 1927. The Objective Reality of Perspectives. In *Proceedings of the Sixth International Congress of Philosophy,* ed. Edgar Sheffield Brightman, 75–85. New York: Longmans, Green, and Company. Reprinted in Mead 1932, pp. 161–175, and in Mead 1964, pp. 306–319.

Mead, George Herbert. 1932. *The Philosophy of the Present,* ed. Arthur E. Murphy. La Salle: Open Court.

Mead, George Herbert. 1934. *Mind, Self, and Society,* ed. Charles W. Morris. Chicago: The University of Chicago Press.

Mead, George Herbert. 1938. The Process of Mind in Nature. In *The Philosophy of the Act,* ed. Charles W. Morris, Chap. 21, 357–442. Chicago: The University of Chicago Press. Reprinted in Mead 1956, pp. 85–111.

Mead, George Herbert. 1956. *On Social Psychology,* ed. A. Anselm. Chicago: The University of Chicago Press.

Mead, George Herbert. 1964. *Selected Writings,* ed. Andrew J. Reck. Chicago: The University of Chicago Press.

Merleau-Ponty, Maurice. 1962. *Phenomenology of Perception.* London: Routledge and Kegan Paul.

Merleau-Ponty, Maurice. 1964. *The Primacy of Perception.* Evanston: Northwestern University Press.

Middle Works. See Boydston 1976–1980.

Morgenbesser, Sydney (ed.). 1977. *Dewey and His Critics: Essays from the Journal of Philosophy.* New York: Journal of Philosophy.

Murphy, Arthur E. 1939. Dewey's Epistemology and Metaphysics. In *The Philosophy of John Dewey,* ed. Paul A. Schilpp, 195–225. New York: Tudor.

Nagel, Ernest. 1939. Some Leading Principles of Professor Dewey's Logical Theory. *Journal of Philosophy* 36(21):576–581. Reprinted in Morgenbesser 1977, pp. 560–565.

Nagel, Ernest. 1940. Dewey's Reconstruction of Logical Theory. In *The Philosopher of the Common Man,* ed. Sidney Ratner. New York: G. P. Putnam and Sons. Reprint, New York: Greenwood Press, 1968.

Peirce, Charles Sanders. 1877. The Fixation of Belief. *Popular Science Monthly* 12:1–15. Reprinted in Peirce 1931–1958, vol. 5, pp. 223–247.

Peirce, Charles Sanders. 1878. How to Make Our Ideas Clear. *Popular Science Monthly* 12:286–302. Reprinted in Peirce 1931–1958, vol. 5, pp. 248–271.

Peirce, Charles Sanders. 1931–1958. *Collected Papers of Charles Sanders Peirce.* Cambridge, MA: Harvard University Press. Vols.

1–6 ed. Charles Hartshorne and Paul Weiss; vols. 7–8 ed. Arthur W. Burks.

Perkins, Moreland. 1983. *Sensing the World*. Indianapolis: Hackett.

Perry, John. 1986. From Worlds to Situations. *Journal of Philosophy* 15:83–107. Also Report No. CSLI-87-73, CSLI Publications, Stanford.

Phillips, Denis C. 1971. John Dewey and the Organismic Archetype. In *Melbourne Studies in Education 1971*, ed. R. J. W. Selleck, 232–271. Melbourne: Melbourne University Press.

Phillips, Denis C. 1976. *Holistic Thought in Social Science*. Stanford: Stanford University Press.

Phillips, Denis C. 1984. Was William James Telling the Truth After All? *Monist* 67(3):419–434.

Piatt, Donald A. 1939. Dewey's Logical Theory. In *The Philosophy of John Dewey*, ed. Paul A. Schilpp, 105–134. New York: Tudor.

Poulus, Kathleen. 1986. Textual Commentary on Dewey's *Logic: The Theory of Inquiry*. In *Later Works* 12:533–549.

Putnam, Hilary. 1983. *Realism and Reason: Philosophical Papers,* Vol. 3. Cambridge: Cambridge University Press.

Putnam, Hilary. 1987. *The Many Faces of Realism*. La Salle: Open Court.

Pylyshyn, Zenon W. 1984. *Computation and Cognition*. Cambridge, MA: The MIT Press.

Quine, Willard van Orman. 1951. Two Dogmas of Empiricism. *Philosophical Review* 60:20–43. Reprinted in Quine 1953, pp. 20–46.

Quine, Willard van Orman. 1953. *From a Logical Point of View*. New York, NY: Harper & Row.

Ratner, Joseph. 1939. Dewey's Conception of Philosophy. In *The Philosophy of John Dewey*, ed. Paul A. Schilpp, 49–73. New York: Tudor.

Ratner, Sidney, Jules Altman, and James E. Wheeler (ed.). 1964. *John Dewey and Arthur F. Bentley: A Philosophical Correspondence, 1932–1951*. New Brunswick: Rutgers University Press.

Ross, Ralph. 1982. Introduction to Dewey's 1920 writings. In *Middle Works* 12:ix–xxx.

Rota, Gian-Carlo. 1985. The Barrier of Meaning. *Letters in*

Mathematical Physics 10:97–105. Reprinted in *Notices of the American Mathematical Society* 36(2):141–143 (1989).

Rumelhart, David E., and John L. McClelland. 1986. *Parallel Distributed Processing: Explorations in the Microstructure of Cognition,* Vol. 1. Cambridge, MA: The MIT Press.

Russell, Bertrand. 1903. *The Principles of Mathematics.* Cambridge: Cambridge University Press.

Russell, Bertrand. 1909. Pragmatism. *Edinburgh Review* 209(428):363–388. Reprinted in Russell 1910, chap. 4.

Russell, Bertrand. 1910. *Philosophical Essays.* New York: Longmans, Green, and Company. A revised edition, with a slightly different selection, appeared in 1966 (London: George Allen & Unwin).

Russell, Bertrand. 1914. *Our Knowledge of the External World as a Field for Scientific Method in Philosophy.* London: George Allen & Unwin.

Russell, Bertrand. 1919. Professor Dewey's *Essays in Experimental Logic. Journal of Philosophy* 16(1):5–26. Reprinted in Morgenbesser 1977, pp. 231–252.

Russell, Bertrand. 1939. Dewey's New *Logic.* In *The Philosophy of John Dewey,* ed. Paul A. Schilpp, 135–156. New York: Tudor.

Russell, Bertrand. 1940. *An Inquiry into Meaning and Truth.* New York: George Allen & Unwin.

Russell, Bertrand. 1945. John Dewey. In *A History of Western Philosophy,* 819–828. New York: Simon and Schuster.

Russell, Bertrand. 1959. *My Philosophical Development.* New York: Simon and Schuster.

Sartre, Jean-Paul. 1956. *Being and Nothingness: An Essay on Phenomenological Ontology.* New York: Philosophical Library.

Sleeper, Ralph W. 1986. *The Necessity of Pragmatism.* New Haven: Yale University Press.

Sleeper, Ralph W. 1988. Introduction to Dewey's 1939–1941 writings. In *Later Works* 14:ix–xxiv.

Strawson, P. F. 1966. *The Bounds of Sense: An Essay on Kant's Critique of Pure Reason.* London: Methuen.

Suchman, Lucy. 1987. *Plans and Situated Actions.* Cambridge: Cambridge University Press.

Tiles, James E. 1988. *Dewey.* New York: Routledge.

Turvey, Michael T., Robert E. Shaw, Edward S. Reed, and William M. Mace. 1981. Ecological Laws of Perceiving and Acting: In Reply to Fodor and Pylyshyn. *Cognition* 9:237–304. A reply to Fodor and Pylyshyn 1981.

van Benthem, Johan. 1988. *A Manual of Intensional Logic,* Second Edition. CSLI Lecture Notes, No. 1. Stanford: CSLI Publications.

van Heijenoort, Jean (ed.). 1967. *From Frege to Gödel: A Source Book in Mathematical Logic, 1879–1931.* Cambridge, MA: Harvard University Press.

Weinstein, Scott. 1974. Truth and Demonstratives. *Noûs* 8:179–184.

Wittgenstein, Ludwig. 1930. *Philosophical Remarks.* New York: Barnes and Noble (1975). Ed. R. Rhees and trans. R. Hargreaves and R. White.

Wong, Marcy, and Dennis R. Carter. 1990. A Theoretical Model of Endochondral Ossification and Bone Architectural Construction in Long Bone Ontogeny. *Anatomy and Embryology* 181:523–532.

Index